LACAN IN PUBLIC

LACAN IN PUBLIC

Psychoanalysis and the Science of Rhetoric

CHRISTIAN LUNDBERG

THE UNIVERSITY OF ALABAMA PRESS
Tuscaloosa

The University of Alabama Press
Tuscaloosa, Alabama 35487-0380
uapress.ua.edu

Hardcover edition published 2012.
Paperback edition published 2018.
eBook edition published 2012.

Typeface: Bembo and Stone Sans

Cover image: Copyright © Bluеximages | Dreamstime.com
Cover design: Todd Lape / Lape Designs

Paperback ISBN: 978-0-8173-5920-1

A previous edition of this book has been catalogued by the Library of Congress as follows:

Library of Congress Cataloging-in-Publication Data
Lundberg, Christian O. (Christian Oscar)
Lacan in public : psychoanalysis and the science of rhetoric / Christian Lundberg.
p. cm. — (Rhetoric, Culture, and Social Critique.)
Includes bibliographical references and index.
ISBN 978-0-8173-1778-2 (trade cloth : alk. paper) — ISBN 978-0-8173-8641-2 (e book) 1. Lacan, Jacques, 1901–1981—Criticism and interpretation. 2. Rhetoric. 3. Psychoanalysis and literature. 4. Psychoanalytic interpretation. 5. Structuralism (Literary analysis) 6. Criticism—History—20th century. I. Title.
P301.L86 2012
808.0092—dc23

2012015850

To Beth Lundberg, my exception to the universal predicate

Contents

Acknowledgments

This book is a product of the efforts of a number of people whose names do not appear on the title page but without whom it would not have been possible. I would like to thank my colleagues in the Department of Communication Studies at the University of North Carolina (UNC) at Chapel Hill for their support and feedback, including my fellow rhetoricians Carole Blair, Bill Balthrop, Eric King Watts, Cori Dauber, and Robbie Cox. I also owe debts of gratitude to Dennis Mumby, Julia Wood, Rich Cante, Ken Hillis, and the incomparable Della Pollock. I am profoundly grateful for an outstanding cohort of junior colleagues, including Renee Alexander-Craft, Sarah Dempsey, Michael Palm, Tony Perucci, and Kumarini Silva. Sarah Sharma, who began at UNC the same time that I did, deserves a special note of thanks for being an unparalleled interlocutor and friend. Finally, I would like to thank Lawrence Grossberg, who has been a generous mentor, a source of encouragement, and a model for responsible scholarly practice. I cannot express how deeply I value his counsel and friendship.

I am also very thankful for the outstanding collection of people with whom I had the opportunity to work as a graduate student in the Program in Rhetoric and Public Culture at Northwestern University. Robert Hariman, Bill Keith, and Keith Topper have been continuing sources of support. Dilip Gaonkar has been a model of rigor and intellectual creativity: most of what I know about rhetoric I owe to him. Angela Ray, David Zarefsky, Tom Goodnight, and Irv Rein each played a significant role in my development while at Northwestern. Alessia Ricciardi introduced me to many of the texts that I treat here. Finally, Daniel Fitzmier, Brett Ommen, Randy Iden, Randall Bush, and Tim Barouch served as tireless conversation partners around many of the issues that inform this book.

There are a number of people whose work made this book possible. Barbara Biesecker has been incredibly generous with her time and insight into the intersections of rhetoric and psychoanalysis, and I am humbled by her intellect and kindness. Joshua Gunn has been a source of continuing intellectual inspiration. Though we came to know each other as the result of an uninvited exchange, I have profited tremendously from his readings of Lacan, his friendship, and his scholarship. I would also like to thank Henry Krips, Diane Davis, and erik doxtader for their friendship, support, and for the ways that their work continues to inform my understanding of rhetoric. I would also like to thank John Lucaites, Dan Waterman, Jonathan Berry, and Alex Wolfe for their incisive editorial input. Finally, I would like to thank my parents, Steve and Cindy Lundberg and Rich and Vicki Homan. Lastly, but most significantly, I would like to thank Beth Lundberg for putting up with me in the process of writing this book. Without her care, support, tolerance, and sense of humor I would be a lesser person—in fact, I would be lost without her.

Portions of this manuscript have appeared in earlier publications. An earlier version of chapter 5 appeared in Barbara Biesecker and John Louis Lucaites's *Rhetoric, Materiality, and Politics.* Parts of the seventh chapter appeared in the *Quarterly Journal of Speech* and *Cultural Studies.*

Introduction

Lacan's Uncanny Rhetoric

This book is as much an argument for a conception of rhetoric as it is a reading of Jacques Lacan's interpretation of it. While I will argue that there are elements of Lacan's work that one cannot fully grasp without understanding his reliance on the rhetorical traditions, in the pages that follow I would also like to highlight the ways that Lacan's corpus engages in a significant reconfiguration of the traditions of rhetoric. The goal of Lacan's intervention into the rhetorical traditions is ambitious: he would like to take to task a vision of discourse situated within an increasingly complex but nevertheless fundamentally Aristotelian conception of rhetoric as the exchange of meanings between interlocutors in a given situation. This conception not only holds rhetorical action to be intelligible exclusively in the light of a given context but is ultimately reducible to the interplay of meaning, context, and propriety. As an alternative, Lacan calls rhetoric both to return to a focus on the formal properties of discourse and to theorize the constitutive function of the limit of rhetoric. I will not argue here that rhetoric should abandon its Aristotelian roots: instead, I would like to locate the Aristotelian tradition of rhetorical interpretation within a broader conception of rhetoric, arguing for attention to trope and investment as a means of locating and refiguring rhetoric's character.

In retheorizing rhetoric, Lacan engages pivotal figures (Aristotle, Cicero, and Quintilian) and topoi (the oratorical tradition, the power of trope, stasis theory, and questions of contingency and context) in the rhetorical traditions. But Lacan's commitment to rhetoric extends beyond mere citation: in declaring that "the psychoanalyst is a rhetor," Lacan refuses to separate the practices and fortunes of the two traditions.[1] This is why it is so surprising that rhetorical studies has not paid more attention to Lacan's work. Part of rhetorical studies' reticence to embrace Lacan likely stems from the substantial investment required to read his work: it is famously difficult, often bordering on the impenetrable. But it seems to me that there is more at play in rhetorical studies' lukewarm reception of Lacan's work than the difficulties involved in reading it: there is also something foreign about the way Lacan inflects rhetoric, rendering it in an accent that does not always sit well with the American traditions of rhetoric in composition and communication studies.

This foreign accent affords rhetorical studies an opportunity to reevaluate its received wisdom by encountering a vision of rhetoric that upsets and extends the practices of American rhetorical studies. A number of arguments that I forward on the basis of Lacan's theory of rhetoric upset hallowed maxims in rhetorical studies: articulating rhetoric and communication together fundamentally disfigures rhetoric; rhetoric is more science than art; rhetoric is not premised on the reciprocal exchange of meanings but on the impossibility of such an exchange; and finally, rhetoric never achieves adequation with the world. There is also an uncanny affinity to rhetoric's conventional wisdom in Lacan's work. For Lacan, one *cannot* understand discourse or the human condition without understanding them rhetorically. To account for human discourse, Lacan claims, one must attend to categories at the heart of the rhetorical traditions: to speech, addressivity, and the generative power of tropes. Lacan frequently reaffirms the rhetorical traditions almost to the letter, for example, in his reading of Aristotle's stasis, Quintilian's theory of trope, and of ancient oratory's pedagogical practices. Where he does not agree with the letter of the rhetorical traditions, Lacan invariably affirms their spirit.

Chapter 1 takes up the theme of "failed unicity," which forms the starting point for Lacan's theory of rhetoric. I argue that Lacan's theory of discourse ought not to be framed as a "structuralist poetics" but as a rhetorical theory of the circulation of tropes and affects in an economy of discourse. In situating this intervention, I engage a number of contemporary sites where the question of Lacan's relationship to rhetoric emerges, including the traditions of communication and composition studies, comparative literature, and political theory. In chapter 2, I focus on the theme of locating rhetoric. I begin by figuring the location of rhetoric in the contemporary rhetorical traditions, suggesting the Lacanian triad Real, Symbolic, and Imaginary as a schema for mapping the varied functions often conflated under the all-encompassing rubric of rhetoric. Next, I turn to a number of exemplary moments in Lacan's corpus where he explicitly engages the question of rhetoric, with the goal of laying the foundation for a systematic rhetorical theory drawn from his work. Chapter 2 concludes with a provocation that reflects on Lacan's injunction to "wring the neck of rhetoric."

Chapter 3 begins with Lacan's argument for disarticulating speech and communication, presenting a conception of rhetoric that centers on speech but that disavows an intrinsic connection between rhetoric and communication. Moving through treatments of Lacan's theories of meaning and the unconscious, this chapter is organized around a reading of Lacan's "Schema L," which reveals the way that a commitment to rhetoric as the intersubjective exchange of meanings occludes the symbolic charge in language. Chapter 3 concludes with a treatment of Lacan's call to understand rhetoric as a science, exploring the implications of his declaration that oratory was not simply an art but a science organized around an account of the formal properties of language.

Chapter 4 extends Lacan's call for a science of rhetoric by defining an economy of trope as the central object of a science of oratory. I begin by posing Lacan's conception of trope against the predominant characterizations of the formal properties of language in rhetorical studies, followed by an interpretation of the functions of metaphor and metonymy in Lacan's work from the dual perspectives of the formal properties of trope and the economy of affective investment that underwrites them. Finally, taking up the relationship between *tuché* and *automaton,* I argue for Lacan's conception of a rhetorical economy of discourse as opposed to a structuralist account of form, concluding with a provocation regarding rhetorical reading practices.

Chapter 5 introduces the character of Lacan's Real as the limit of rhetoric, focusing on the means by which rhetorical action negotiates this limit. I suggest Lacan's conception of enjoyment as a specific affective modality that lends durability to processes of signification. Specifically, I engage debates surrounding the "materiality of rhetoric" thesis to argue for enjoyment as a material practice in the context of immediation between the orders of discourse and that which is external to it. Chapter 5 concludes with a provocation on the materiality of rhetoric by posing the question of the relationship between theory and practice against the backdrop of failed unicity and specifically in the context of the impossibility of signification as reference.

If rhetoric is characterized by the work of trope and enjoyment as a mode of affective investment, it also requires an account of publics as privileged sites for the economic interchange between trope and enjoyment. In chapter 6, I take up the character of the public in Lacan's work, arguing that the public is the primary site at which Lacan conceives of the production of subjects and their discourses. Specifically, I argue that theorists of the public might profitably parse the processes through which publics are made into three distinct analytical categories on the basis of Lacan's work, distinguishing between the ontological, addressive, and identitarian functions of the public as a site of tropological and affective exchange. I conclude the chapter with a provocation on rhetorical praxis as a mode of consensus or identification, posing the dual problems of violence and stasis to consensually orient conception of public making.

In chapter 7 I take up two specific sites of tropological exchange. Reading two very different discourses—the imaginary economy of conservative American Christian evangelical publics and the demands of antiglobalization protestors—I hope to demonstrate the productivity of a conception of rhetoric that fully attends to its formal and affective charges in public life. Though these discursive fields undoubtedly admit other readings and might be fruitfully engaged employing other critical protocols, they lay out one possible trajectory for a scientific practice of rhetorical criticism that attends to the messy intersections of trope and persuasion in the economy of public discourses. In place of a provocation in chapter 7, I conclude the book with a brief postscript on recovering the prophetic, ornamental, and protreptic strands in the rhetorical traditions.

LACAN IN PUBLIC

I

On Failed Unicity

Rhetoric and Structuralist Poetics

The universe is a flower of rhetoric.

—Jacques Lacan, *On Feminine Sexuality, the Limits of Love and Knowledge: Encore.*

In a statement destined to become his theoretical calling card, in 1956 Jacques Lacan declared that "the unconscious . . . is structured like a language."[1] Nearly seventeen years later Lacan proffered his most explicit reflection on this claim: "the universe is a flower of rhetoric . . . that is what I am saying when I say that the unconscious is structured like a language."[2] Two accounts of rhetoric's flowering form the bookends of Lacan's career: the so-called Rome Discourse and one of Lacan's last published pieces, a section of his antepenultimate seminar *Time to Conclude.* The Rome Discourse, or "The Function and Field of Speech and Language in Psychoanalysis," was delivered to the Rome Congress of Romance Language Psychoanalysts in 1953. This lecture represents a pivotal moment in Lacan's career, both because it became the founding document for the Société Française de Psychoanalytique and because it comprised the first introduction of Lacan's thought to circles outside the psychoanalytic academy.[3] The Rome Discourse was revolutionary because of the role it afforded rhetoric: in it, Lacan heralds an analytic practice organized around "speech" and attention to the "ancient arts of rhetoric" as an antidote to the "arid scientism" of the theoretical humanities.[4] A quarter of a century later, in the closing days of his twenty-fifth seminar, *Time to Conclude,* Lacan declared that "the psychoanalyst is a rhetor." In the quarter of a century between these two statements Lacan composed a systematic theory of rhetoric grounded in public speech in the broadest sense of the terms: as a theory of how subjects are formed by, take on, and engage in discourse in the presence of others.

The claim that Lacan's psychoanalysis relies on a quintessentially rhetorical understanding of public speech upsets a commonly accepted vision of Lacan's work as a "structuralist poetics."[5] In locating rhetoric at the core of Lacan's thought, I argue that the metaphor of structuralist poetics that has prefigured the reception of his work ought to give way to a rhetorically tinctured account of discourse as an economy that constitutes subjects, speech, and the social world. To do so, I would like to argue for a rhetorical social ontology that figures the social as a crucially impactful but, nevertheless, epiphenomenal extension of tropological processes. For Lacan, the crucial questions for understanding the subject and its discourses lie at the intersection of a rhetorical social ontology and an ontology of rhetoric.

Ernesto Laclau has characterized Lacan's contribution to the poststructuralist moment as an articulation of an ontology of rhetoric and a rhetorical social ontology under the banner of "failed unicity." For Laclau, "failed unicity" means that there is no coherent totality underwriting the subject, sign, and the act of communication or of discourse that unites speaker, speech, and speech act in a coherent transhistorical whole.[6] What Laclau renders in the vernacular of poststructuralism, Lacan derived from everyday life. Even though subjects often act as if there is a "unifying unity" to human life, experience reveals no such thing: "It is always the unifying unity which is in the foreground. I have never understood this . . . life is something which goes, as we say in French, *à la dérive.* Life goes down the river, from time to time touching a bank, staying for a while here and there, without understanding anything—and it is the principle of analysis that nobody understands anything of what happens. The idea of the unifying unity of the human condition has always had on me the effect of a scandalous lie."[7] Failed unicity starts with the presumption—one now common in the theoretical humanities—that the nature of the subject, the social world, and discourse are not given in advance nor derivable from nature; instead, the subject, social world, and discourse are products of accident and contingency. Despite a failure in unicity, subjects think, speak, and act as if they inhabit a condition of unicity all the time. Life goes "down the river," foregrounding fantasies of a "unifying unity" that often contradict experience. Even though the illusion of unicity is a "scandalous lie," it effectively organizes the social world.

Paradoxically, these two facets of human life are intensely complementary. The failure of unicity necessitates imagined unicity to purchase the coherence of a subject's reality. Alternately, imagined unicities are the precondition for recognizing the failure of unicity, because unicity's failure only becomes apparent when the hard facts of the Real run up against our fantasies. Subjects and their discourses emerge at this nexus of failed and feigned unicity through rhetorical artifice, via the act of imagining and performing localized, contingent unicities in response to unicity's failure. Thus, Lacan's psychoanalysis "reads all speech" and, by extension, the discourses that constitute a subject "as a compromise formation."[8] Failures of unicity in speech, subject, and the sign are put to work as forces that call forth our investment in the supplements, fantasies, and imagined totalities that work to cover over failed unicity: instead of becoming fatal in the life of speech and the speaking subject, failures in unicity become the driving forces that animate human existence.

Thus, a provisional definition of rhetoric as a compromise formation: rhetoric is both *signifying in a condition of failed unicity* and a way of *feigning unicity in the context of failed unicity.* Failed unicity means, for example, that despite a subject's expectation that the social world should function as a coherent whole, this condition does not inhere in its experiences of the interhuman world. Similarly, despite the subject's presumption of an essential complementarity between language and the world, there is no automatic correspondence between signifiers, representations, and the objects to which they refer or between signifiers and that which they attempt to capture. Feigned unicity means that discourse is a contingently situated act of labor connecting signifiers and representations with their referents and providing the illusion of communion between subjects and their others. Feigned unicity between signs, representations, and their referents purchases the subject an ability to act as if words and representations effortlessly stand in for their referents. Feigned unicity also imagines a unified social field, despite the subject's experience of a fragmented social world. Failed unicity invites feigned unicity in the form of artificial practices that bind signifiers together, habitually repeat the presumption of the signifier's correspondence with the world external to it, and render signifiers communicable. Rhetorical artifice—tropes, modes of address, imaginary commitments, and the labor of investment—underwrites these practices, feigning unicity in the context of its failure. Rhetoric affords Lacan's psychoanalysis an account of the means by which feigned unicity underwrites the speaking subject, the idea of a shared communicative relationship and correspondence between discourse and the world. Simultaneously, Lacan's theory of rhetoric marks the fact that unicity fails because there is a world of things, forces, and relations that lie beyond the limits of rhetoric's ability to encode or capture them without remainder. If there is no ultimate point of unicity—if there is no transparent reciprocal intersubjective bond that unites subjects in communication and no natural correspondence between signs and the world—there are at least tropes and practices of investment that sustain subjects and their discourses.

Lacan figures trope as a process of signifying connection, disconnection, and investment that underwrites both the subject and its discourses. His understanding of trope is deceptively elegant: for Lacan, "trope" marks the idea that no connection in the life of the subject or its discourses is given in advance. Rather, such connections are the result of habituated accidental connections between signs, representations, and the world. Such connections have formal properties, but for Lacan, the formal properties of tropes are a function of the ways that ritually repeated connections elicit the investment of the subjects who employ them. Reading discourse as both a formal and affective economy, Lacan's psychoanalysis affords rhetoric a means for analyzing the cumulative effects of discursive labor in producing durable social formations. Thus, Lacan's turn to rhetoric hazards a response to the questions of structure, contingency, agency, and the allied constellation of terms occupying our contemporary theoretical context in the wake of poststructuralism. In reading signification and representation rhetorically—as products of both failed and feigned unicity—Lacan's rhetoric provides an account of the speaking subject's relationship to structure without determination; to contingency while still maintaining an account of the durability of the basic elements of social life; and to the problem of agency without asserting either that the human subject is a cog in a machine of discourse or that it is endowed with virtually deific agential capacities.

If rhetoric is understood to be both failed and feigned unicity, then a rhetorically inflected reading of Lacan's work provides a helpful critique of two alternatives for understanding discourse represented by the communicatively oriented tradition of rhetoric in composition and communication studies and by the structuralist Lacanian tradition in comparative literature, critical theory, and allied disciplines. Both traditions elide the dual and mutually dependent character of rhetoric as failed and feigned unicity demonstrated in Lacan's work. The American rhetorical tradition largely ignores the economically derived formal rhetorical functions of trope, which work to feign unicity, and the structuralist traditions largely ignore the rhetorical accent that Lacan places on the concept of trope as a compensatory function in the context of failed unicity. An implied tension between these two claims abates if one begins with a theory of rhetoric as both failed and feigned unicity. Rhetoric relies on a transcontextual logic of trope and signification that figures the means of its effectivity for the subject in specific contexts. But this transcontextual logic is the result of an encounter with the empirical world; it is neither an automatic nor a contextually agnostic iteration of structure because structuring functions are dependent on the affective labor and contingent situatedness of the subjects that inhabit them.

Lacan's theory of rhetoric confronts the rhetorical traditions in communication and composition studies with the necessity of attending to the economy of tropes as the transcontextual condition of possibility for rhetorical action. That this logic is transcontextual does not mean that it is a structure. Rather, it means that because there is no automatic relationship of correspondence between signifiers and the world, there are a limited number of ways that a speaking subject can both employ a signifier as a referent to the external world and differentiate it from other signifiers. This condition is so all encompassing that it figures the contents, modes of address, and social forms that underwrite rhetorical exchange. A theory of trope ought to gain primacy in rhetorical theory, because trope is always immanent within and constitutes the specific contexts where persuasion, identification, propriety, or any of the other readily available rhetorical means for understanding the function of discourse are operative. Lacan's conception of trope offers rhetoric the possibility of framing the ontological and discursive operations underwriting the varied contexts within which critics attend to rhetorical effect. Put more directly, Lacan's work identifies the overarching context of the specific contexts that the rhetorical traditions engage by providing a means of reading the general economy of discourse as the ground of specific, contextually bound discursive practices.[9]

Paradoxically, Lacan's commitment to a rhetorical conception of tropology also argues against identifying him with a strongly articulated structuralism. If rhetoric is inseparable from a condition of failed unicity, Lacan's conception of rhetoric critiques structuralist tendencies to reconstitute unicity in the form of a self-generating structure. Although the structuralist project rejected certain forms of unicity—the self-possessed subject, the idea of individual agency, and so on—a structure that automatically and unfailingly scripts reality reinstates unicity at the level of the structure itself. This tendency is manifest in the ideas that structure is defined by a set of transcontextual binary oppositions (as in the case of Levi-Strauss); that a discursive formation can exist independently of the contexts within which it is embodied; that structure can efficiently and unfailingly program or script social reality; or that reality is structure all the way down. Failing and feigned unicity imply that one must not only cast out the last vestiges of unicity in the idea of structure itself but one also must pay attention to the impossibility of separating the formal logic of signification from the empirical contexts within which discourse emerges. Although undoubtedly influenced by the structuralist tradition, and even identified by some as the high-water mark of this tradition, Lacan turns to rhetoric to understand the genesis and performance of the subject without reaffirming the automatic structuring function of language.[10] Instead, Lacan replaces "structure" with the metaphor of economy in a radical embrace of his maxim that "language is not the speaking being."[11] More to the point, one does not only find an account of structure in Lacan's work, one also finds a commitment to the materiality of speech, attention to the specificity of affects, an account of address, and, perhaps most significantly, a theory of the failures of structure in ordering the Real that works against a reduction of his thought to an unproblematic structuralism.

Lacan in Rhetorical Studies

Lacan's ruminations on rhetoric have not gone unnoticed by his readers, although the extent of his reliance on rhetoric is often overlooked. For example, Bruce Fink, who is deservedly regarded as one of Lacan's best readers, cites the rhetorically focused "Instance of the Letter in the Unconscious," which argues that "figures of speech are not 'mere manners of speaking,'" but "are at work in the rhetoric of the discourse that the analysand actually utters . . . *to the analyst, nothing is ever just a 'figure of speech.'*"[12] Fink claims that while "the analysand spontaneously employs well-known rhetorical figures to keep from saying certain things and to keep certain ideas from surfacing . . . [i]n his typical fashion, Lacan does not elaborate on this, neither here nor anywhere else, to the best of my knowledge."[13]

As I hope to show, Lacan's oeuvre contains a rich account of the regulatory function of trope in organizing speech. This realization has begun to take hold in the fields of composition and communication studies. Work on Lacan in communication studies extends as far back as 1977, when Lloyd Pettegrew introduced Lacan's work on transference to figure the place of metaphor in a theory of discourse.[14] Similarly, Michael Hyde took up Lacan's theory of the sign in 1980, arguing for a reading Lacan's structuralism in the context of the phenomenological and hermeneutic elements of his work.[15] These interventions sought to expand rhetorical studies's vocabulary for addressing "speech and language" by situating Lacan's account of signification against a number of experiential registers (transferential, phenomenological, and "hermeneutic").[16]

Work on Lacan in communication studies saw a fairly rapid expansion in the years after 1999, which marked the publication of Henry Krips's *Fetish: An Erotics of Culture.*[17] Krips's purpose in *Fetish* was to provide a theory of the fetish and the gaze informed by Marx's and Lacan's reading of Freud, detailing the ways that these concepts bridge the gap between the psyche and culture by attending to their production around specific objects, texts, and practices. For Krips, the central questions are both "how can a subjective psychoanalytic conception, like the gaze, account for the public, objective effects of images" and "how is it possible to bridge the gap between individual psychic responses and the communal effects of cultural artifacts?"[18] Asking similar questions of public politics, James P. McDaniel took up a reading of Lacan and Žižek to understand the roles of public address in American politics, specifically by attending to the role of fantasy and figure in democratic life.[19] Though neither Krips nor McDaniel focus on Lacan's account of the ontology and functions of rhetoric, both employ a rhetorically inflected understanding of psychoanalysis to engage political and cultural production.

Although also interested in sites of political production, Barbara Biesecker and Joshua Gunn have taken up the relationship between rhetoric and psychoanalysis in more direct terms. Gunn has argued for closer critical attention to Lacan's work in understanding the function of rhetoric in contemporary public culture. Gunn has done groundbreaking work in rehabilitating a conception of fantasy in rhetorical studies, with close attention to the understanding of the intersubjective bond in public life, in understanding the function of "voice," and the relationship between rhetoric and love by critiquing rhetorics of identification.[20] Biesecker's "Rhetorical Studies and the 'New' Psychoanalysis" begins with the "modest claim" that "rhetorical theorists and critics will be considerably enriched" by engaging Lacanian psychoanalysis in the process of "ideological critique."[21] Biesecker is "tempted" to make the stronger claim that "Jacques Lacan will have already been the great theorist of rhetoric for the twenty-first century" because his work "makes visible the limits of a number of contemporary theories of rhetoric that foreclose, disavow, or devalue the speaking beings' affective attachments . . . *and* gestures toward strategies for overcoming them."[22] Biesecker has taken up this task with deftness in both detailing the rhetorical production of the melancholic citizen-subject in the war on terror and in her treatments of national commemoration.[23] More recently, Biesecker has taken up the task of delineating an "evental rhetoric" defined by four qualities: "one, evental rhetoric is more than performative in Derrida's sense since it is full speech in the Lacanian sense; two, evental rhetoric takes the form of the exorbitant demand; three, evental rhetoric works by and through the logic of sublimation and not by and through the logic of representation or articulation; four, evental rhetoric does not abide the binary logics of the timely and untimely, the appropriate and inappropriate or the possible and impossible; it forces their displacement that, with Freud and Lacan, I would call the uncanny."[24] Biesecker's charge to think evental rhetoric has strong resonance with the reading of rhetoric that I will offer here, which is also premised on privileging the tropological charge in speech (which is the hallmark of Lacan's full speech), figuring speech as a demand, thinking beyond articulation and propriety. The question that occupies this book is whether evental rhetoric is an exceptional case in speech, or whether the event is always immanent in and the condition of possibility for speech.

Increasingly, composition studies have also taken up Lacan's work for theorizing rhetoric. Victor Vitanza has identified Lacan as one important contributor to a "critical sub/version" of rhetoric.[25] David Metzger's *The Lost Cause of Rhetoric: The Relation of Rhetoric and Geometry in Aristotle and Lacan* draws on a provocative homology between rhetoric and geometry as formal modes of knowing in the work of Aristotle and Lacan.[26] Susan Wells's *Sweet Reason: Rhetoric and the Discourses of Modernity* contains a rhetorically tinctured presentation of the role of language in Lacan's accounts of subject formation and agency.[27] James V. Catano's *Ragged Dicks: Masculinity, Steel, and the Rhetoric of the Self-Made Man* theorizes the relationship between Lacan's Symbolic order and the oedipal function. Thomas Rickert's *Acts of Enjoyment: Rhetoric, Žižek, and the Return of the Subject* takes up the processes and politics of writing pedagogy to situate a new pedagogy of writing as a mode of engaging ideology and enjoyment. Finally, Diane Davis has done insightful work that inspires the Lacanian thematics that I treat here, including critiques of understanding rhetoric simply in relation to persuasion and identification and of reducing rhetoric to the hermeneutic traditions of meaning making.[28]

Lacan and Rhetoric Beyond the Traditions of Rhetorical Studies

There are at least four major places where there has been sustained reflection on the place of rhetoric in Lacan's work beyond rhetorical studies. The first I address is the "structuralist poetic" approach, a school of thought primarily rooted in comparative literature.[29] Second, I treat Ernesto Laclau's work, which embodies a comparatively structuralist approach to articulation theory, highlighting the place of trope in Lacan's work as a means of engaging democratic politics. Third, I address Slavoj Žižek's critique of the reduction of Lacan's thought to a theory of discourse, which dissents from structuralism on the grounds of a commitment to materiality. Finally, I address Lacan's readers who argue that he ultimately replaced a focus on rhetoric with a focus on math (specifically on topology and set theory). Taking up these four diverse schools of thought, my overarching goal is to characterize the implications of locating Lacan's work within the tradition of structuralist poetics, arguing that many of the most incisive criticisms of the place of rhetoric in his work figure Lacan through structuralist poetics. Conversely, framing Lacan's work as a rhetorical theory of trope (as opposed to a structuralist poetics) redeems it from the debilitating implications of a too strongly articulated structuralism.

The reading of Lacan's work as a structuralist poetics is common: much of the debate surrounding rhetoric in Lacan has ultimately been about presenting Lacan as a pure structuralist and subsequently engaging him on the idiosyncratic use of metonymy and metaphor—treating him as a footnote to Roman Jakobson's formalist poetics.[30] Reading rhetoric as a foil to the structuralist impulse in Lacan's work upsets this account. The basis of this critique, grounded in Lacan's commitment to rhetoric, becomes clear in taking up the constituent terms of structuralist poetics. Structuralism argues that any phenomenon can be meaningfully engaged as a product of the structurally determined relations that precede and produce it. Conversely, as a practice of signifying in a condition of failed unicity, rhetoric names the fact that structures fail in efficiently structuring the world. While Lacan's work undoubtedly assimilates the structuralist insight that actors in the social world are figured by discourses that exceed and produce them, his work on the concepts of enjoyment and the labor of signification reveal a commitment to figuring the failure of structure in constituting the world without remainder. Next, poetics: those who read Lacan through structuralist poetics are primarily concerned with the effect of trope independent from speech as the medium that carries the trope. One of the strongest indicators of Lacan's commitment to rhetoric is that his work rarely engages the formal properties of discourse without noting the modes of relation and practices of investment that underwrite them. Consider this commitment from the perspective of the Aristotelian distinction between rhetoric and poetics: unlike rhetoric, poetics is primarily concerned with the question of mimesis—with the various ways that human discourse relies on imitation as the "method or process" of making actions or representations "imitate nature."[31] Poetics takes up the question of style to understand the ways that mimetic processes embody certain formal qualities, often in the form of language that draws attention to its character as tropologically inflected. As a result, a poetic account presumes a constitutive disconnection between the act of imitation and the imitated, driving Aristotle toward a treatment of poetics as an "art in itself."[32] Though focused on modes of discursive production, poetics takes the formal properties of mimesis as a primary site of concern. If poetics aims at the trope in itself, rhetoric aims at an understanding of tropes that refers them outward to the whole economy of discourse. Rhetoric's movement outward frames the formal properties of language as both a means of articulating the subject and relations between subjects with the world external to language. Substituting a rhetorical conception of trope for a poetic one frames the trope as the site of language's essential failure to seamlessly articulate the economy of discourse with the world of things, subsequently requiring an account of feigned unicity.[33] In the register of rhetoric the formal properties of the trope are productive, but the trope is also inextricably linked with the larger economy of socially situated practices of feigned unicity and, therefore, with the failures of discourse to inscribe the word onto the thing.

Lacan, Rhetoric, and Comparative Literature

The poetic approach to Lacan in comparative literature draws inspiration from places in Lacan's corpus where psychoanalysis is likened to literary criticism: "commenting on a text," wrote Lacan, "is like doing an analysis."[34] In the mid-eighties and late nineties comparative literature engaged this literary charge, focusing primarily on two issues: reading the relationship between metaphor and metonymy in Lacan's work in the context of debates over deconstruction, and reading the relationship between Lacan's theory of tropes and his conception of the subject.[35] Focusing primarily on metaphor's formal relation to metonymy and Lacan's theory of the subject, especially as manifest in individual literary texts, such treatments eschewed the opportunity to articulate a potentially broader conception of the production and circulation of everyday public discourses latent in a rhetorical conception of Lacan's work.

Some of Lacan's readers in comparative literature have extended their readings of his theory of trope to consider the broader orbit of culture but without necessary connection to the problem of the public, nor to the materiality of the addressed relation. By extension, the poetic approach to Lacan often draws inspiration from questions regarding the literary text as a privileged object of interpretation: What is the role of literature in Lacan's work? What are the literary conventions that mark Lacan's work? Given Lacan's theory of trope, how does a given trope or set of tropes in a text function for the reader?[36] How does transference explain the pleasures of the text for the reader, and how does it influence processes of meaning making?[37] How is subjectivity formed in response to the text?[38] And finally, given Lacan's tropologically configured unconscious, does the unconscious function as a "writing machine"?[39]

The poetic tradition of structures and machines has its roots in "screen theory," which set the agenda for Lacanian criticism beginning in the 1970s and extending through the early 1990s. Screen theory sought to develop a theory of spectatorship informed by Lacan's theories of the gaze, the mirror stage, and interpellation.[40] As an embodiment of the gaze, the screen "represents a point of identification, an ideological operation in which the spectator invests her/himself in the filmic image."[41] Christian Metz, one of the primary advocates of screen theory, argues that the screen represents the Lacanian mirror and therefore provides a mechanism for constituting the subject: even though the "spectator is absent from the screen," the subject is produced, via interpellation, by its presence in the film through the "look's caress."[42] Krips argues that this understanding of the gaze integrates Lacan's account of the imaginary functions of the mirror with Althusser's doctrine of interpellation and Roland Barthes's structuralist conception of signifiers determined by "their position within a network of oppositions and equivalences."[43] Similarly, Martin Hall succinctly characterizes screen theory as a "mixture of" doctrines of "sign systems, ideology and . . . the screen as Lacanian mirror" that "lent itself readily to the study of film" through an "appropriation of Lacan's mirror," which "allowed for a complex discussion of the pleasure available to the spectator . . . within the . . . imaginary plenitude of the darkened auditorium. This approach often referred to as 'screen theory' (after the British Journal of that name) . . . dominated the academic study of film throughout the 1970s and into the early 1980s."[44]

An identification with the screen has significant ideological implications. Laura Mulvey engages screen theory from a feminist perspective, arguing that the screen interpolates the spectator into a uniquely male perspective: "as the spectator identifies with the main male protagonist, he projects his look onto that of his . . . screen surrogate, so that the power of the male protagonist as he controls events coincides with the active power of the erotic look . . . giving a satisfying sense of omnipotence."[45] Although screen theory was productive, providing film a theory of the ideological labor film performs, it was beset by the same problems that mark any structuralist poetic reading of Lacan. A distinction between the poetics and the rhetoric of spectatorship as a cultural form is implicitly at stake here. McGowan argues, for example, that screen theory authorized a form of interpretation that framed spectatorship through the virtually automatic function of structure at the expense of attention to both the empirical specificity of viewership and to the function of the Real.[46] Similarly, Krips argues that screen theory falters because it does not fully theorize the misfirings and failures of structure in the experience of spectatorship.[47]

The distinction between rhetorical and poetic conceptions of Lacan's work may be a bit too clean to be taken seriously: culture and context play an important role in many "poetic" approaches to Lacan in comparative literature (for example in Gilbert Chaitin's *Rhetoric and Culture in Lacan*). Even screen theory, which represents the high-water mark of Lacanian formalism, engages culture, albeit with some limitations. But even in their most culturally sensitive moments, these traditions do not attend to the publically figured relationship between structure, situation, and failure in Lacan's work with the same vigor that a rhetorically tinctured conception does.

On Democratic Formalism, or Lacan and Rhetoric in the Work of Ernesto Laclau

Ernesto Laclau's work focuses on an understanding of democratic politics through an understanding of discourse, which he defines as "the primary terrain of the constitution of objectivity as such" and "not something that is essentially restricted to the areas of speech and writing, but any complex of elements in which *relations* play a constitutive role . . . [and] elements do not pre-exist the relational complex but are constituted through it."[48] Laclau's work comprises an influential strand in the critical cultural study of rhetoric, largely on the basis of *Hegemony and Socialist Strategy* (coauthored with Chantal Mouffe), which predates Laclau's later more robust turn to rhetoric.[49] As Michael Kaplan puts it, Laclau's later work "verges on becoming a theory of rhetoric," driven primarily by the tropological character of democratic demands.[50]

Laclau's *On Populist Reason* provides an elegant account of demand as the fundamental unit of the political and, by extension, of politics as a field of antagonism. Laclau's basic goal is to define populist reason, giving an account of populism as "special emphasis on a political logic which, as such, is a necessary ingredient of politics *tout court*" and "quite simply, [as] a way of constructing the political."[51] Demands serve a number of functions that derive from the split between the particular political aspirations that they embody and the more universal level of a struggle to define and engage the hegemonic order. For Laclau, demands make a claim on and figure the character of the hegemonic order, creating an implicit picture of how it functions and might change. Simultaneously, demands create possible lines of equivalential affinity between others also making demands on the hegemonic order. This is the place where a theory of the demand is most explicitly pegged to an understanding of trope: an equivalential affinity is premised on the metonymic connections between various democratic demands and on metaphoric condensation as a mode of articulating individual demands together as a more universal claim on the hegemonic order.

Thus, the demand is more fundamental, for example, than a theory of the "group," in that the operation of the demand inaugurates all "the various forms of articulation between a logic of difference and a logic of equivalence" that animate the social affinities that give groups their coherence.[52]

The logic of the demand is in turn the logic of equivalence, and equivalence is as important for how it animates a group identity as it is in positing claims on a hegemonic order. Here, as Kaplan argues, rhetoric "assumes a pivotal role . . . for Laclau, . . . [referring] to the contingent, discursive, and fundamentally tropological process that brings objective reality into existence by imposing on an array of heterogeneous elements the semblance of a structure within which they acquire identity/meaning. . . . [R]hetoric is distinguished from any sort of calculus capable of mandating relationships among elements; indeed, the necessity of establishing such a distinction underwrites the turn to the rhetorical idiom."[53] The question, which I take up in the seventh chapter, is the degree to which Laclau's emphasis on structuralism puts him at odds with a Lacanian reading of rhetoric.

Slavoj Žižek on Lacan and Rhetoric

Materialist readings of Lacanian psychoanalysis comprise the third site beyond rhetorical studies where the question of Lacan's understanding of rhetoric emerges. The materialist reading eschews an emphasis on rhetoric in Lacan's work for the sake of refuting the thesis that discourse shapes reality. In this account, Lacan's work is an antidote to the idea that discourse produces reality because it posits laws governing subjects and subjectivization and introduces the Real as a category independent of discursive production. For example, Slavoj Žižek invokes Lacan to recover a neo-Hegelian materialist sensibility, emphasizing that one cannot read Lacan through exclusive reference to discourse, much less rhetoric: "I find it a little bit too easy to [argue] that every denial of rhetoric is already in itself a rhetorical gesture—true, but the problem for me is that a thorough assertion of rhetoricity is no less inconsistent. . . . [T]he Freudian [question] here would be: 'Why are you arguing that rhetoricity is all-pervasive when rhetoricity is effectively all-pervasive, including your own argumentation?' . . . [I]n every instance of proper . . . reasoning there is always . . . argumentation that cannot be dismissed as an effect of rhetorical mechanisms."[54]

In "The Limits of a Semiotic Approach to Psychoanalysis" Žižek characterizes a "semiotic" or tropologically driven approach to Lacan's work as derivative of a misunderstanding of the idea that the unconscious is structured like a language: "Lacan's best known proposition is . . . [that] 'the unconscious is structured like a language,' which is usually understood as pointing toward a semiotic reinterpretation of psychoanalytical theory and practice. . . . Lacan's theory . . . is far from endorsing any such linguistic reductionism: his central effort is precisely to articulate the different modes of the Real kernel . . . which produces an irreducible obstacle to symbolization."[55] Žižek's goal is to critique a postmodernist penchant for discourse run amok. Thus, for Žižek, rhetoric ought to be understood as ornamentation or a secondary articulation of more foundational conceptual commitment. As Jeffery Nealon argues: "Žižek . . . doesn't really care about rhetoric. . . . [H]e goes so far as to speak against rhetoric in a kind of Platonic fashion. . . . Even his extensive use of examples, perhaps Žižek's most obvious mechanism for rhetorical persuasion, tends to get dismissed here as . . . frosting on the wedding cake. Rhetoric, then, seems to be something that's merely added to the rock of the Žižekian Real."[56]

The impulse to minimize the place of rhetoric in Lacan's work comes into sharpest relief around Žižek's treatment of the object relation. Focusing on Lacan's transition from "symptom to object," Žižek claims that Lacan "enables us to see [the] place outside the Symbolic as an emptiness opened by the hole in the Symbolic. The . . . object is always the presentification, the filling of the hole around which the symbolic command articulates itself, of the hole retroactively constituted by this command itself, and in no way by a prelinguistic fact."[57] Žižek figures the relation to objects as a materially centered process because the object relation does not rely only on discourse but also on the enjoyment entailed in it; thus Žižek focuses on the ways that the object relation is a result of the "hole" or lack in the Symbolic, as opposed to a function of the operations of discourse in isolation from their material and ontological preconditions. Though this critique provides a powerful antidote to the idea that the world is reducible to a formal understanding of the properties of language, implicitly reaffirming a limit to rhetoric, a rhetorically tinctured reconfiguration of Lacan's conception of trope locates language's formal charge at the core of psychoanalytic thought without sacrificing attention to the material world. Žižek is right to claim that the object relation is a significant element of the subject's relation to the material world that is not reducible to the role of discourse. But the object largely achieves this status as a result of the work of trope, which stems precisely from a failure or hole in the symbolic command as a form of feigned unicity in the context of failed symbolic unicity. The relationship to an object serves as both a kind of proxy for the failed relationship to reality of the sign and as a tropologically inflected mode of organizing the subject's relationship to itself and to affect that metaphorically stands in for and therefore sutures the hole in the symbolic command.

Thus, the labor of trope is the condition of possibility for the object serving as a metaphorical stand-in for an inaccessible other (as I discuss in chapter 3). Although Žižek would reclaim materiality of the object, the object only functions this way as a configuration of tropes organizing the subject's affects. Therefore, to dismiss the idea that discourse shapes reality in the name of a conception of the object is to miss the work of rhetoric in articulating objects as sites of feigned unicity in the context of failed unicity. Though the spirit of Žižek's critique is correct in complicating the automatic relationship between discourse and the production of reality in the name of the material and affective, the means by which he achieves this critique ignore the dual character of failed unicity (which is the site where objects and affects become necessary) as simultaneously a mode of feigning unicity (which requires the supplementary work of trope to produce objects as feigned proxy that covers over the failure of the symbolic command). Were Žižek to accept a framing of rhetoric that, instead of seeing it as an ornament or add on to a more fundamental conceptual or material process, embraced its ontological and material character, the concept of rhetoric would become a useful supplement to his understanding of the object as opposed to a specter invoking the worst tendencies of "postmodern" thought to reduce the construction of the material world to an epiphenomenon of discourse.

Math > Rhetoric?

Finally, I would like to briefly address an argument that Lacan largely abandoned a focus on rhetoric in his later career in favor of mathematized conceptions of set theory or topology. The most forceful version of this claim is found in the work Alain Badiou, who takes up Lacan's work on set theory to propose it as a model for ontology.[58] Borrowing from Bertrand Russell's paradox of the set of all sets—which holds that a set of all sets is impossible because it would not include itself as an element in the set of all sets—Badiou argues for a conception of failed unicity as the impossibility of a coherent totality, turning toward contingent mathematizable relations as the privileged locus of action.

Badiou's reading relies on a common periodization of Lacan's work, holding that while rhetoric was of interest to the early Lacan, his later work granted primacy to math. For example, Jean-Michel Rabate argues for a focus on "what could be called the literary turn in Lacan, or a moment halfway between the early 1950s with the stress on rhetorics, Hegelianism, and the Name-of-the-Father and the Lacan of the 1970s, with more and more mathemes, the algebra of the four discourses, leading to games with a topology still lacking the Borromean knot."[59] There is truth to the claim that as his career progressed Lacan increasingly thought ontology mathematically, as evidenced in the decline of tropological and rhetorical figures relative to mathematical articulations of ontology, beginning in the mid-sixties.[60]

But to argue for a complete displacement of rhetoric in Lacan's work, one would have to grapple with relatively late proclamations regarding rhetoric that I alluded to earlier; for example that the "universe is a flower of rhetoric" (*Seminar XX,* 1972) and that the "psychoanalyst is a rhetor" (*Seminar XXV,* 1977). Mathematization appealed to Lacan because it afforded him a vocabulary for understanding the subject as an effect of certain repeatable relations without implicitly reaffirming meaning and intersubjectivity as the primary loci for subjectivization. Thus, in accounting for the production of the subject as a formally determined effect of a set of relations that precede it, math offers Lacan a "desubjectivized" mode for talking about the production of the subject as an effect.[61]

The question in this "formulation" of the subject is the status of the mathematical representations in each of these schemas. Lacan is not claiming that the subject is a result of math; rather he is claiming that one can talk about the production of the subject as if it were mathematical. Thus, mathematical description is a metaphor that has the benefit of figuring the subject in desubjectivized terms, outside of the conventional vocabularies of intersubjectivity and social construction. Math affords Lacan an account of the figural economy that produces subjects, relates them to other subjects, and that authorizes the subject's discourses without installing a given in advance subjectivity or process of intersubjective exchange as the efficient cause of the subject. Thus, it is fruitful to read the turn to mathematization in Lacan's work as part and parcel of the project of framing the subject as an effect of tropological processes, albeit by means of a specific vocabulary of rhetorically saturated math tropes to emphasize the subject as an effect of relations that produce it without necessary reference to the a pre-given subject or intersubjectivity that mediates these processes.

The challenge, then, is to understand the ways that rhetorical processes are figured in Lacan's work. In foregrounding the metaphor of the mathematizable relation, Lacan frames the subject and intersubjectivity as effects of the tropological and mathematical relations that precede and produce the subject as opposed to rendering either subject or intersubjectivity as the genesis of discourse. Perhaps most significantly, Lacan's turn to math is simultaneously a turn to a new conception of rhetoric—albeit one that refigures the ways that the traditions of rhetorical studies have located rhetorical effectivity. Thus, I would like to turn to the question of rhetoric's location in the next chapter, with the goal of relocating the mathematical strand in rhetorical theory.

2
Locating Rhetoric

> My students, in reading works of rhetoric, recognized it to be their daily fare at my seminar.
>
> —Jacques Lacan, "Appendix II: The Metaphor of the Subject"

A difficulty looms as soon as one takes up the task of figuring rhetoric in Lacan's work. The difficulty is not Lacan's impenetrable writing, nor the possibility that there are lenses other than rhetoric through which one might read Lacan: the difficulty is a prevailing indecision about what exactly rhetoric is. But one might begin with a more modest question than "what is rhetoric?" The question is this: where is rhetoric located? This chapter takes up the American iterations of rhetorical theory to figure where they have located rhetoric, followed by a treatment of Lacan's tripartite scheme for the three orders of the subject's experience: Real, Symbolic, Imaginary. Because part of the confusion surrounding rhetoric is that it becomes an umbrella term for all the functions of discourse, my goal in turning to Lacan's three orders is to locate rhetoric by parsing and subsequently mapping the discrete discursive functions that are usually lumped together under the concept of rhetoric onto Lacan's triad. Next, I extend this map by treating exemplary points in Lacan's work where he reflects most explicitly on the nature and functions of rhetoric. Finally, I will conclude with a provocation on Lacan's injunction to "wring the neck of rhetoric."

Locating Rhetoric in the American Rhetorical Traditions

Largely as a result of the utilitarian leanings of rhetorical studies in composition and communication studies, rhetoricians largely defer questions regarding the ontology of rhetoric by referring to a set of standard definitions: symbolic action, a faculty for observing the available means of persuasion in any given situation, the study of the effects of discourse, and, occasionally, the study of figures and tropes. Although rhetorical studies' attempt to address the contingent and contextually bound nature of discourses is significant on its own terms, it is also significant as an exemplar of the basic options for the humanities in engaging discourse. The critical question, for rhetoricians and the humanities generally, is how one figures the effectivity of and relationship between the formal and contextual registers of discourse.

Difficulties arise when one pushes any of the readily available definitions of rhetoric for a foundation, compares them to the demands of the objects they take up, or—perhaps worst of all for the contemporary iterations of rhetoric—calls for rhetoricians to decide on or argue for a definition of rhetoric. The rag-tag mélange of objects and methods that conventionally fit within rhetorical studies might give an outsider the impression not only that rhetoric has no real content, but that virtually any practice for attending to the contextual effects of spoken, written, visual, material, and mediated discourse can be included under the rubric of rhetoric. In practice, rhetorical studies has validated Plato's infamous critique of rhetoric, which emerged virtually at the instant of its inception, that rhetoric lacks a determinate center and a firmly demarcated field of inquiry. What was formerly the grounds for a dismissal of rhetoric has been transfigured into an open secret about the nature of rhetorical inquiry, and is possibly one of the defining characteristics of rhetoric as a field (or rather, set of fields) of study: when it comes to rhetoric, both methodologically and in terms of the objects rhetoric takes up, almost anything goes. The indecision that enables this radical pluralism in rhetoric has become so central to the American iterations of rhetorical studies that many students of rhetoric have, following Robert Scott, decided it is better to not define rhetoric at all.[1]

Of course, this impulse to not define rhetoric does not translate into indecisiveness in rhetorical practice. As Scott's prescient and often misread essay argues, the impulse to not define rhetoric is dependent on a whole range of implicit phenomenological understandings of the subject, the discourses that it participates in, its relation to others, and the modes of meaning making that underwrite everyday rhetorical interaction. Even though rhetoricians assiduously avoid defining rhetoric, they nevertheless relentlessly locate it, implicitly defining it through specific framings of rhetoric's context, in operational definitions of rhetorical effect, and in defining objects of rhetorical study. Figuring the location of rhetoric, one does more than simply identify the spaces in which rhetoric is operative: implicitly defined locations of rhetoric inscribe the character of and means by which rhetoric exerts effects. There are two primary ways that the American traditions usually locate rhetoric: in contexts and objects.

Rhetorical Contexts

On a contextualist account, rhetoric's primary location lies in the intersubjective effects of speech, writing, or other forms of discourse for an audience of readers or listeners in a specific context. How was rhetoric located around this nexus? Herbert Wichelns, although often connected with the tradition of rhetoric in speech communication, inaugurated a turn to rhetoric in both communication and composition studies. Wichelns was bothered by a single-minded focus in English departments at the time on the "beautiful" and "permanent" in literary criticism.[2] Upsetting an established protocol for what counted as literature, Wichelns argued that oratorical speech was also a literary form, albeit one evaluated not by timeless aesthetic appeal, but through its persuasive and immediate effect on its audience. As an antidote to a focus on the timeless, Wichelns suggested alternative criteria for judging oratorical speech "not concerned with permanence, nor yet with beauty," but with effect, regarding "speech as a communication to a specific audience, and [holding] its business to be the analysis and appreciation of the orator's method in imparting his ideas to his hearers."[3]

In other words, rhetorical criticism became a way of doing, once again, what rhetorical studies imagines Aristotle to have called for in *On Rhetoric*—a technique for reading the available means for persuasion in any given situation, largely wrought by focusing on the audience and figuring the various means by which a rhetor might produce effects on it. A number of distinctions must come into play for rhetoric to work as a technology for unpacking the effects of discourses on audiences. First, the audience needs to be nested in a context, to be given a set of determinate historically constituted positions such as their investment in the speech or text, a setting in which it is received, and a set of dispositions toward the speaker or text. This is the thrust of Lloyd Bitzer's intervention in "The Rhetorical Situation."[4] For Bitzer, rhetorical analysis is a mode of emplotting an audience in a situation by ascribing to it a determinate context within which it receives speech, a set of contingent expectations regarding genre and the rituals of performance, and a set of predispositions and interests that dispose the audience toward or against the speaker and speech. To situate the audience effectively, one must do so in terms of the whole situation: in relationship to the exigency that makes the speech pressing for the audience, and in relation to the operative constraints that potentially block the effect intended by the speaker. Bitzer's intervention was hugely profitable for the fields of rhetorical studies, largely because it defined a privileged location for rhetorical effect, read through the tripartite division of audience, exigence, and constraint.

This is not a position that is unique to the Wichelns/Bitzer line in the discipline formerly known as speech communication; for example, in composition studies, one finds a triangular analogue in James Kinneavy's famous schema of author, text, and audience, where the elements in the rhetorical triangle define the context of rhetoric's functions.[5] What is predominantly at stake for both of these iterations of speaker (or author)/speech (or text)/audience triangle is an understanding of rhetoric nested in context and interpretively reducible to the negotiated production of meaning between addressor, addressee, and text, most notably without necessary reference to the formal charges inherent in discourse. Of course, there are good objections to Bitzer's position (for example, the speech does not simply respond to the context, but creates it), but most of the objections to "The Rhetorical Situation" do not deviate from the core of Bitzer's position, namely that speakers and speech—or rhetorical discourse—exert effects and are productively constrained by the reciprocal relations between speaker, speech, and situation, or more generally between the initiating locus of rhetorical discourse, the contents that it contains, and the context within which it is read.

This inheritance substantially influences contemporary rhetorical studies. This configuration is the dominant mode for rhetoric as the study of public address, but it even figures work in critical/cultural rhetorical studies. Critical/cultural rhetorical studies have largely moved beyond conceptions of speech, audience, and situation, replacing them with a more global conception of discursive context—and this move is beneficial to the extent that it locates what, under a different methodological dispensation, were formerly treated as insular sites of rhetorical effect by tying them into a larger cultural and discursive contexts. But even in a critical/cultural account of rhetoric, there is a tendency to reduce the work of rhetoric to a radical account of context and intersubjective negotiation without remainder.

Raymie McKerrow's "Critical Rhetoric: Theory and Praxis," which laid out an agenda for much of the work in critical rhetoric that would follow, exemplifies the tendency to read rhetoric through contextually mediated intersubjective effects. McKerrow takes up the task of articulating a practice of criticism where the critic would "have as the *text* more than traditional 'speaker-audience' scenarios in engaging critique" by focusing on "the manner in which discourse insinuates itself into the fabric of social power," and specifically by attending to the "articulation of the subject's diverse positions [as] the result of a struggle for hegemony."[6] For McKerrow "any articulatory practice may emerge as relevant or consequential—nothing can be 'taken-for-granted' with respect to the impact of any particular practice."[7] Articulation here represents so radically a contextual conception of discourse that no rule or guide for the operation of discourse can be taken as a guarantee in advance, signaling a radical structural indeterminacy in the field of discourse, bounded only by the limitations of historical habit and contingency.

Take, for example McKerrow's treatment of the idea not of the Symbolic, but of the status of the symbol. While McKerrow affords room for the productive functions of the symbol in the injunctions to "focus attention on that symbolism which addresses publics" and to account for the ways that "symbols come to possess power," what McKerrow primarily has in mind are the ways that individual symbols become sites of ideological saturation, as opposed to a more radical conception of symbolic logic that is constitutive of all utterances, including those that are explicitly marked as symbols and those that are not. The primary thrust of McKerrow's critical protocol privileges the individual ideological symbol as a contextually produced relation. As opposed to a focus on symbolization writ large, a focus on individual symbols as a site of ideological articulation instantiates the claim that there ought to be no "transcendental or universal standards" for evaluating rhetoric, implicitly rejecting the "universalizing tendencies of a . . . philosophical rhetoric" indentifying transcontextual regulatory functions for rhetorical practices.[8] As opposed to a "philosophical rhetoric" that might focus on the logics that authorize the movement of articulatory practice, McKerrow's radically "nominalist rhetoric" relies on the "sense that terms are contingently based—the reasons for their emergence are not premised on fixed, determinative models," and thus McKerrow "rejects the . . . claim . . . that everything is determined by something" and instead "celebrates [rhetoric's] reliance on contingency."[9]

Of course, one might ask: if a theory of rhetoric is to understand how subjects accommodate themselves to this contingency, and perhaps more importantly, how they might feign unicity in the context of the failure of unicity that a radical turn to undetermined context implies, then what role does a theory of rhetoric have in specifying the function of rhetoric in this context? The majority of the projects of critical rhetoric that followed in the wake of McKerrow's project would come to rely on a doctrine of contingent articulation for detailing the functions of rhetorical discourse. The question is whether there are any intrinsic components of the logic of articulation that provide articulation theory with explanatory power beyond the idea that everything in the world of discourse is a result of habits of connecting some things, practices, and concepts with other things, practices, and concepts? One might pose the question yet another way: if one were to embrace the idea that nothing in the world of discourse is given in advance, and that by implication, everything in the world of discourse is produced simply as a result of conventions of articulation, how might we understand the stunning degree of regularity that seems to inhere in discursive formations? If this view is to remain true to its presupposition that the methodological purview of rhetoric is basically to describe existing articulations, it cannot give an account of why a given formation exists—it can only defer to a description of how it functions without providing insight into the affective and discursive conditions that produce one habit of articulation at the expense of other possible configurations.

Thus, although there are points of mutual critique between a view of rhetoric as public address, and critical/cultural rhetorical studies, both visions of rhetoric share a commitment to a radical contextualism. As a result, both conceptions of rhetoric have little more to say than a somewhat circular formulation of rhetorical effect that does not diverge significantly from the ancient rhetorical conception of propriety: a given act of address or discursive articulation functions because it matches with the demands of a context, and a given context is as it is because of the accreted habits of address and articulation that produce it.[10] For both public address and critical/cultural rhetoric, the basic means for rhetorical criticism are largely dependent on identifying a context (whether naturalized in an audience or produced as an articulation) and reading rhetorical action for the ways that it confirms or interrupts the functions of this context. Even though conceptions of context differ in critical/cultural rhetoric and public address, the fundamental means for engaging criticism are virtually synonymous.

For rhetoric as public address, the contextualist commitment manifests itself as a technique for detailing the divergent means of persuasion in any given situation, or in front of any given audience. By this definition of rhetoric, context is largely a result of the practices of address that constitute the audience as it is and that set generic expectations for how a speaker should perform in a specific setting. In critical and cultural rhetorical studies, articulation embodies a commitment to radical contextuality, but the context itself is produced by the habits of discourse that a conception of context hypothetically grounds. For both public address and critical/cultural rhetoric, if rhetoric has an ontology it is one characterized by radical contextualism at the expense of any governing formal relation. Such an ontology is necessarily thin in that it never exceeds propriety as a governing function, centering rhetorical analysis on that which is appropriate or "proprietary" to, or a property of, the context. This conception of propriety suspends the question of why discourses function as they do and how the context that they are nested in was generated in the name of seeing each context in its radical specificity. An ontology of rhetoric that extends beyond the taken-for-granted, defined primarily in terms of propriety (as a means of accommodating the demands of a given articulatory situation), remains elusive for both configurations.

Rhetorical studies remains, in effect, haunted by the ghosts of Aristotle,

Bitzer, and Kinneavy, each of whom was convinced that the defining characteristic of a rhetorical analytic is its radical contextuality, although here "contextuality" is not defined as the overarching condition of possibility for the rhetorical situation, but rather by the plurality of the available "means of persuasion" in "any given situation."[11] Despite efforts to specify and even enlarge its theoretical scope, a situational conception of rhetoric largely remains the study of how specific discourses (texts or objects of rhetorical study) produce effects against the background of, and are regulated by, "situations" composed of subjects with specific social locations (in an audience or a public, for example), interests, and dispositions and a set of circumstances that mediate the reception of the discourse.

Lacan's contribution to a theory of rhetoric locates context as an effect of a transcontextual logic of discourse, situated in an economy of tropes and affects that underwrites both the sign and the concrete modes of its employment. Reading a localized discourse requires attention to the specific ways that contents, modes of address, and determinate social relations are figured within a discourse, and simultaneously to the more global functions of discourse inscribed in the function of the signifier and, by extension, the subject that employs it. A theory of rhetoric centered on context and propriety in absence of this larger frame sacrifices substantial explanatory insight: both the relatively straightforward Aristotelian explanation of rhetoric as the faculty for observing the available means of persuasion in a given context and a more contemporary critical rhetorical description of discourse as the habituated result of the operations of power ultimately rely on giving an empirical account of a context without necessary reference to the larger economy of tropes and affects that underwrite the production of discourse. Both Aristotelian and critical and cultural rhetorics can describe what happens in a given context on the basis of a reference to historically sedimented discursive practices, but neither seeks to describe how or why a given situation came into being, or perhaps most crucially, why the agents in a given circumstance are affectively invested in understanding and relating to the context as they do.

Rhetorical Objects

The question of rhetoric's location has often been implicitly resolved by reference to the object field that one takes as the aim of rhetorical practice. If a conception of context or situation fails to articulate a robust ontology for rhetoric and protocols for interpreting the effectivity of discourse, rhetoric at least has a communally sanctioned set of objects and acceptable methods for studying them. This is perhaps the most durable implication of Wichelns's dissent from literary studies on the grounds of the importance of oratory. In only a slight revision of the logic of propriety, it is not the situation but the object that implicitly calls forth a set of appropriate interpretive protocols. The object/method assemblage implies, in turn, a whole range of doctrines regarding the subject, the act of communication, and the nature of the social bonds that underwrite it.[12] The question of the rhetorical object implies a necessary, if implicit, understanding of the rhetorical subject who negotiates the meaning of a given text against the background of a specifically historically situated context. Thus, locating rhetoric's ontology in objects only invites another deferral of the context of rhetoric.

The relationship between the object and the deferral of the conditions of rhetoric has significant implications for the disciplinary self-understanding of rhetoric, animating many of the debates over the identity of rhetoric. Against the too-hasty localization of rhetoric around specific objects, one can argue for a global conception of rhetoric that takes any contextually nested and intersubjectively mediated discursive effect as a proper object of rhetorical study. Although a global conception of rhetoric's object combats the parochial location of rhetoric to specific object fields (classically defined spoken or written texts, material objects, visual images), it does so at the cost of being unable to provide rhetoric conceptual specificity. One may embrace the fact that there are a number of ways to frame rhetoric as a theory of the effects of discourse, attempting to craft a "big tent" for rhetorical practice that includes an eclectic mix of methods, objects of study, and resources for doing rhetorical scholarship. There is an understandable, even admirable, tendency within this option to "let a thousand flowers bloom," accepting that there are any number of ways that a rhetoric might be instantiated.

From Plato onward, rhetoric's critics have argued that this kind of methodological pluralism risks stripping rhetoric of any specificity. But the most significant danger for rhetoric lies not in the risk of too narrow a conception of rhetoric, nor in a conceptually flabby rhetorical globalism; it is the combination of the two risks that poses the greatest challenge for rhetoric. Even though the parochial and the big-tent options for locating rhetoric seem diametrically opposed, both dispositions work together to foreclose the possibility of a rigorously grounded and analytically precise conception of rhetoric. The simultaneous presence of rhetorical parochialism and pluralism reaffirms a particularly vexing collective indecision about what exactly rhetoric is, creating a condition where anything can be done under the sign of rhetoric, warranted by license to employ as narrow or undertheorized conception of rhetoric as one likes, and abetted by an overarching commitment to methodological pluralism that excuses anyone from having to defend a particular iteration of rhetoric.

Rhetoric *and* the Real, and Rhetoric *in* the Symbolic and Imaginary Orders

The Lacanian antidote to this indecision is to locate the place of rhetoric, by specifying both the domains of rhetoric's operations and, by extension, suggesting protocols for attending to them. To locate is both to "establish (something) in a place," and to "mark the limits of a place." Lacan establishes rhetoric in its place by parsing its functions in different orders of the subject's existence in a systematic relationship between the symbolic or tropological charge of discourse and the imaginary commitments that situate subjects in relation to discourse and one another and that provide subjects with a strategy for negotiating failed unicity. But this act of locating also marks the limit of rhetoric by revealing that there is an order of the subject's existence external to the functioning of rhetoric, posing the Symbolic and Imaginary orders against the Real.

The Real, Symbolic, and Imaginary orders, which are so central to Lacan's thought that he always renders them with a capital letter, provide a conceptual map for locating the functions of rhetoric. Were one to hazard a diagnosis of contemporary rhetorical studies on the basis of Lacan's three orders, it would go something like this: rhetorical studies has fetishized the imaginary register of rhetoric, focusing primarily on the contextually bound, intersubjective circulation of meaning at the expense of both a rigorous account of rhetoric's symbolic charge and the Real that marks rhetoric's constitutive limit. This imaginary focus both elides the centrality of the formal charge in rhetorical discourse by focusing on the intersubjective exchange of meanings and, simultaneously, causes rhetoric to exceed its "Real" limit by presuming that the world can be exhausted in representation, or more accurately, that representations effortlessly stand in for their referents.

The Real is rhetoric's limit. There are a number of different possible interpretations of the Real, although all of them circle around two central concepts: there is a world external to discourse, and the subject's understanding of this world is never unmediated and, as a result, never achieves direct adequation with it. "An adequate thought," writes Lacan, avoids adequation.[13] Although there is a world of things, relations, and effects that is mind-independent (*res cogitans* does not meet the Real, says Lacan), our access to the Real is mediated by discourses and representations that capture or present the Real for a subject.[14] Thus, Lacan introduces a distinction between *reality,* which is the way that one frames or imagines the world as a set of representations and concepts, and the Real, which names the mind-independent realm that reality attempts but fails to adequately frame. The distinction between the Real and reality rests on the idea that our understandings of reality are never quite adequate to, or more precisely, never achieve adequation with the Real. To say that the Real exists independently of our various representational framings of it is not to say that the Real does not influence the subject. One never acts outside of the influence of the Real, because the world external to discourse substantially "governs our activities."[15] Subjects inhabit a world of bodies, forces, and objects that constitute the warp and woof of everyday life. Reality, on the other hand, is fully within the purview of the subject. As soon as one attempts to figure, speak, or represent the Real, one "misses" the Real by reducing it to "reality."[16] Because conceptions of reality are mediated by an economy of trope and enjoyment—a theme that I take up in earnest in chapter 5—the interface between reality and the Real is always a "missed encounter."[17]

Lacan's first wave of readers typically understood the Real developmentally, as the point where the entry into the Symbolic cut a child off from its immediate experience. Later, as readers acclimated to Lacan's focus on the logic of limits of the sign, readers understood the Real as the name for the lack of adequation between signs, representations, and the objects to which they refer. This is the thrust of the claims in *Concepts of The Four Fundamentals of Psychoanalysis* that the Real is "the accident, the noise, the small element . . . which is evidence that we are not dreaming," an appointment that "eludes us," and most starkly, "the impossible."[18] Here the Real refers less to a pre-symbolic immediacy than to a gap that appears between representation and the world premised on the idea that symbols and representations are constitutively disconnected from the things to which they refer. Charles Shepherdson frames the relationship this way:

> Initially, the Real seems to refer to a pre-symbolic reality, a realm of "immediate being" that is never accessible in itself, but only appears through the mediation of imaginary and symbolic representation . . . later, however, the term seems to designate a lack, an element missing from the Symbolic order. . . . In the first case, the Real precedes the Symbolic and exists independently; in the second case, the Real is a product of the Symbolic order, a residue or surplus effect that comes into being only as a result of the symbolic operation that excludes it.[19]

The Real is, from the perspective of the subject, the impossible, because the Real does not reside in the Symbolic order, but is instead produced by a gap in the Symbolic order. The Real marks the gap between the world of things external to discourse and the representations that are an inadequate stand-in for it. Thus, the Real is impossible in a very specific sense: Lacan is not arguing that that which is mind-independent does not exist, nor is he claiming that it does not influence everyday life. Rather, because representational access to the Real is never direct or unmediated, the subject exists within a disconnection between its framings of the world (reality) and the actual though epistemically inaccessible Real. From the perspective of the subject of signification, the Real is simply unsymbolizable excess, which, although generated by a failure in the Symbolic order to achieve adequation with the Real, does not reside in the Symbolic. But the Real does not only exist as that which the Symbolic cannot encounter; in defining the Real as that which escapes symbolization, Lacan claims that the Real is also the unassimilable excess that marks the limit of rhetoric.[20] As I will argue in relation to the materiality of rhetoric, the Real is not a register with its own properly rhetorical logic—it is, for Lacan, defined by the fact that it resides outside of the logic of rhetoric, and is constituted by the fact that representations do not achieve adequation with it.

If the Real is the limit of rhetoric, the Symbolic and the Imaginary orders serve as both the location and habitus of rhetoric. Whenever a subject signifies—and here I understand signification in the broadest possible terms, inclusive of all possible means of representation, including speech, writing, and images—its acts of speaking, writing, and representing are constrained by a logic of metonymic linkage and metaphorical condensation that governs the modes of connection, distribution, and substitution that make speech, writing, and representation possible. This is the field of the Symbolic for Lacan, which extends the basic sensibility of Heidegger's maxim that "to speak is to respond": any act of signification relies on formal properties of discourse that precede, constrain, and make language possible.[21] Speech and signification are produced and made intelligible by logics, structures, grammars and syntactical modes that determine what can be said and how it can be said. These protocols are built into the logic of the sign itself, which presumes a correspondence between the signifier and its referent, and a differential relation between signifiers. This is an extension of the project of structural linguistics, which is founded on a distinction between the signifier and the signified and on the idea that signifiers operate through the logic of difference. As Ferdinand de Saussure and his inheritors argue, discourse is constituted in a differential relation between signs and other signs, founded on rules for combination, substitution, and differentiation. The sign rests on a three-fold operation of difference and connection, which are: the condition of possibility for signification, the enabling matrix that provides us with options for signification, and the prerequisite for the intelligibility of any sign.

Cumulatively, these functions make up the Symbolic but with a significant caveat: for Lacan, the Symbolic order is only comprehensible if one moves beyond Saussure's structural linguistics and understands the formal properties of discourse as rhetorically constituted. To say that the Symbolic is rhetorical means more than the structural linguistic insight that signifiers are governed both by relations of difference and by an arbitrary habitually repeated reference to their signifieds. The Symbolic is a quintessentially rhetorical phenomenon for Lacan because the Saussurean schema of signs constituted through differential relation and an arbitrary habitual linkage between the signifier and signified omits two functions implicit in the process of signification: that the sign is the result of artificial labor—specifically the labor of tropological connection—and that, as a result, the sign is a site of affective investment.

The Lacanian reframing of structural linguistics begins by accepting the idea that the relation between signifier and signified is arbitrary. There is nothing that forces a signifier to belong essentially to its signified or its empirical referent. The arbitrariness of the signifier is, in fact, one of the primary reasons for the subject's sense of failed unicity: the subject's use of signifiers invokes a "referential pretension" insofar as subjects can only negotiate their worlds by presuming the equivalence of signifiers and their referents. The referential pretension conceals the fact that signifiers only refer to their signifieds through the labor of a subject for whom the word invokes a signified, and by extension comes to stands in for the thing. There are three operations that are necessary in this account. First, the signifier must come to refer to a signified by standing in for it. The idea of a sign not only contains but also requires the work of metaphor to establish the possibility of the signifier referring to or standing in for a referent. Second, signifiers must be not only distinguished from other signifiers, but also combined with other signifiers to create the possibility of meaning. In other words, the logic of the sign relies on a whole field of metonymic relations, which implies both a condition of difference and one of possible connection. Finally, for a given signifier to function, as structural linguistics argues, a given signifier must be habitually repeated and therefore sanctioned by social usage. Implicit in the labor of signification is a concept of investment, because although it is a necessary condition for discourse, the abstracted formal logic of the signifier is not a sufficient condition for discourse: the economy of discourse also requires the speaking subject's investment in the habitual usage of signifiers in determinate ways. This investment in a signifier's habitual usage links and differentiates signifiers, and perhaps most crucially, it ritually repeats the labor whereby a signifier is taken to metaphorically stand in for a referent.

Lacan claims that he learned this theory of language not from Saussure, or even from other likely candidates such as Roman Jakobson (whose theory of metaphor and metonymy obviously influenced Lacan's work) or even Freud, but from Quintilian. In "The Agency of the Letter in the Unconscious or Reason since Freud," Lacan claims that his theory of signification was inspired by Quintilian's theories of metaphor and metonymy, and further, that he ultimately dissents from the structuralist account of the Symbolic on the basis of its lack of attention to the function of tropology: "The properly signifying function thus depicted in language has a name. We learned this name in our childhood grammar book on the last page, where the shade of Quintilian, relegated to some phantom chapter to convey final considerations on style, seemed suddenly to hasten its voice due to the threat of being cut off. It is among the figures of style, or tropes—from which the verb 'to find' *[trouver]* comes to us—that this name is, in fact, found."[22] At least two rhetorical functions emerge for Lacan as a result of the articulation of trope and structural linguistics. First, Lacan uses a conception of metonymy to reconfigure the basis of differential semiotics. Metonymy names the rhetorical work that connects and differentiates signifiers from one another. Second, Lacan uses a conception of metaphor to account for the possibility of reference. As opposed to the referential pretension which holds that the signifier essentially becomes the name for a real object (perhaps mediated by a mental image, as in the case of Saussure), metaphor accounts for the ways that words refer to their referents by standing in for things. Thus, the symbolic sets the basic parameters that organize human discourse, and authorizes the referential pretension.

It would be tempting to argue that if the Symbolic order accounts for the form of discourse, the Imaginary order represents all the individual and collective ways that subjects impute content to language's formal charges. More accurately, the Imaginary names the ways that a subject views its world and the modes of relation with other subjects and things that this view implies. What Lacan has in mind is not too far removed from Aristotle's claim in *De Anima* that to the "thinking soul images serve as if they were the contents of perception. . . . [T]he soul never thinks without an image."[23]

Though imaginary associations are structured by the Symbolic order, they nevertheless maintain a degree of specificity that is not exhausted by the formal properties of the Symbolic. Lacan's use of imaginary remains quite closely tied to the functions of the image, in that the Imaginary order is the site of a generalized understanding of one's status as a subject (a self-image), relations to others (an image of the Other), and of the specific character that one ascribes to oneself, others, and objects. The Imaginary is the location where the specific modes of relation to others and contents of speech are mediated for the subject—put in the register of rhetorical studies, the Imaginary is the site where specific relations of address are envisioned, and is the storehouse for the specific contents of an address.

The Imaginary figures the modes of relation that underwrite the act of addressing an other: to address an other, a subject must assign the other some determinate content, and must envision, if only implicitly, the tenor of the subject's relationship to its addressee. But the Imaginary also houses the specific contents—images, ideas, and concepts—that fill in symbolic forms. The formal structure of the sign is not enough to found the empirical life of discourse: signs also require that specific contents and concepts populate the formal structure. The Aristotelian and Kantian traditions of imagination are both at play in Lacan's conception of imagination as the specific image-content of the sign. For Aristotle, if the psyche never moves without an image, the implication is that the formal properties of thinking are never sufficient to give an account of actualized thought. Thinking requires a set of specific images that move the psyche to do all the different things that it does. Kant, in *Critique of Pure Reason,* distinguishes between synthetic qualities that make up the imagination: a "reproductive" and a "productive" imagination.[24] The reproductive imagination is essentially mimetic, presenting images to the intuition largely with the task of mediating images and concepts. The productive imagination produces original images (ones not derived from experience) and is the site of "creative" invention. Strategically muddling this distinction, Lacan's conception of imagination, which is closely allied with Freud's idea of fantasy, frames the reproductive and productive imaginations as part and parcel of the same basic movement. Images position a subject relative to its world and constitute its modes of understanding, but because the image is bound to the mediating functions of the Symbolic, it never quite achieves full adequation with the world external to it. The image is constitutively disconnected from the thing that it attempts to capture, but at the same time it is a mode of world making for the subject that employs it. Because the image is disconnected from the Real, images cannot be simply mimetic nor only reproductive, but perform both functions simultaneously.

Lacan's mirror stage represents one way of understanding the function of the Imaginary, largely because it constitutes the first place in Lacan's work where the question of the imago arises as a metaphor for the subject's relation to processes of symbolization.[25] Lacan is fond of noting that people inherit a language that they did not choose, that they can never fully control the meaning of, and that prefigures their modes of relationship to the world. This is the point of Lacan's mirror stage: subjectivity is artificially and retroactively inferred in relationship to an external image. An infant encountering its image in the mirror for the first time does not initially recognize itself as the cause of the image in the mirror's movements. As the child begins to figure out that when it moves, the child in the mirror also does so, it begins to identify with this external image. The point for Lacan is not that the child figures out that that she is the child in the mirror, but that the child requires this external image to impose a kind of unity on its experience—the image of the other child provides a retroactive totality, or more specifically an *imaginary* framing of what it means to be a subject, which helps it negotiate the split between itself, language, and the world.

The mirror stage is a metaphor for the subject's performance of a relationship to selfhood within language, and through which it negotiates the gap between experience and the subject's idealized projection of itself. Becoming a subject requires an identification with an image of one's self, which is not naturally given, but rather is the effect of a location within the Symbolic order and a specific set of historically and materially situated imaginary commitments that constitute the subject's identity. The work of the Imaginary is both the production of an image of an "I" that relates to itself, and, as a result, of a subject that can enter into relations with others. An imaginary relation, then, is the precondition for identification at two interrelated sites: identification enables a relationship with one's self—identification as taking on an identity—and a relationship with others as a site of identification, which also implicates the subject's relationship with itself:

> We have only to describe the mirror stage as an identification . . . namely the transformation that takes place in the subject when he assumes an image—whose predestination to this phase-effect is sufficiently indicated by the use, in analytic theory, of the ancient term *imago*. . . . [T]his jubilant assumption of the . . . image . . . would seem to exhibit in an exemplary situation the symbolic matrix in which the I is precipitated in a primordial form, before it is objectified in the dialectic of identification with the other, and before language restores it, in the universal, its function as subject.[26]

Consider the primacy of the Imaginary as the site through which the subject forges images and identifications from the perspective of rhetorical studies, for example in public address. The Imaginary confers a specific identity upon a subject, including the set of dispositions that a subject has, for example, as a member of an audience, and that figure the reception of speech within in a context where discursive takes on a meaning. Thus, the Imaginary is the site where persuasion and identification are active as modes of eliciting rhetorical action. If the Imaginary names the ways that a subject takes on an identity, a set of understandings of the world, and practices of relation to other subjects, then it follows that the traditional emphasis on persuasion as a means of rhetorical effect that attends to the interplay of an audience's dispositions and relations to a context primarily addresses functions that lie squarely in the Imaginary.

But the same could be said of a number of the alternatives to a view of rhetoric as primarily concerned with persuasion, for instance, in conceptions of rhetoric that rely on identification and the constitutive function of discourse. The condition of possibility for rhetorical identification (and the attendant possibility of commensuration between or even "consubstantiality" with the subject and that which the subject identifies) is the existence of an identity, which, Lacan's mirror stage demonstrates, is the paradigm for an imaginary relation. Even rhetorical theories that consciously attempt to integrate practices of subject formation into their accounts of discourse rely almost exclusively on imaginary machinations. For example, in the founding essay for constitutive rhetorics, Maurice Charland frames the rhetorical interpellation through its imaginary functions. Charland begins "Constitutive Rhetoric: The Case of the Peuple Quebecois" by noting that rhetorical studies has been unwilling to consider the subject as a "rhetorical effect," but his account of this effect is primarily based on a set of imaginary machinations, specifically identification, arguing that the subject and the collective are "interpellated . . . through a process of identification in rhetorical narratives."[27] This claim reveals a latent conflict in rhetorical studies' understanding of Althusser's conception of interpellation. As a close reader of Lacan, Althusser's conception of interpellation relies largely on an understanding of the ways that the symbolic charge determines the basic conditions of possibility for interpellation. But in Charland's rendering, a constitutive rhetoric explains interpellation as primarily a contextually bounded imaginary relation of the "moment one enters into a rhetorical situation . . . as soon as an individual recognizes and acknowledges being addressed."[28] The question is whether Althusserian hailing is primarily understood as a result of intersubjective negotiation, a function of the role of recognition in producing narratively centered meanings, or as a result of the Symbolic as a site of address. In Charland's version of interpellation, the critical interpellative moment is when a subject acknowledges and responds to the call of a specific other. In a more Lacanian account, recognition by a specific other is significant, but subsidiary to the more fundamental function of hailing's symbolic charge: what is recognized and acknowledged on this account is not the voice of the other, but rather the way that the voice of the other manifests the Symbolic in speech.

Although this is largely an analytic question whose purpose is to understand the inflection put on a discursive process as a symbolic or imaginary function, parsing the imaginary and symbolic functions is critical to crafting a theory of rhetoric that grants primacy to the Symbolic. Of course, in the empirical life of subjects, this distinction is less marked—as Lacan puts it, the three orders are woven together in a "Borromean knot."[29] The Borromean knot describes a figure that results from interconnecting three rings to each other in such a way that if one were to remove one of the rings, the other two would fall apart. The result is a figure that looks like this:

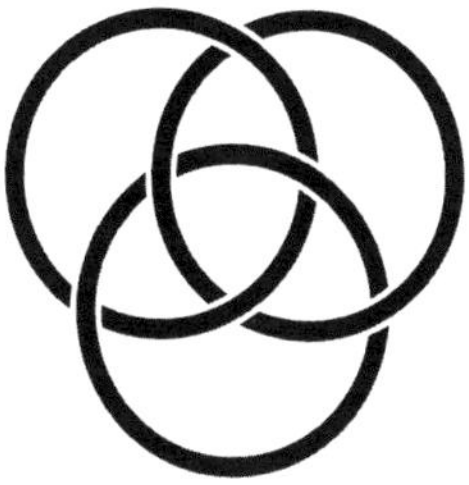

What interests Lacan about the knot is that it is a metaphor for the interweaving of the Symbolic, Imaginary, and Real as analytically distinct but empirically intertwined. Though one can analytically unpack a specific movement in the life of the subject in terms of a particular order, to remove any of the three orders from the empirical life of subjects and their discourses would collapse the integrity of the three orders as a description of the subject's existence. The question for rhetorical studies is ultimately whether the elision of the Symbolic by a reading of rhetoric that is reducible to its imaginary functions causes the knot to fall apart by severing the Symbolic ring.

Lacan and Rhetoric

Stuart Schneiderman argues that of all the disciplines to which Lacan's psychoanalysis has both an affinity and a debt, his "psychoanalysis is related most closely to rhetoric," a concept that holds a privileged position in Lacan's work.[30] One of the earliest explicit references to rhetoric in Lacan's work appears in the essay "A Theoretical Introduction to the Functions of Psychoanalysis in Criminology," a presentation given to the Thirteenth Conference of French-Speaking Psychoanalysts in 1950 in an effort to detail the usefulness of psychoanalysis for understanding criminology. The reference is brief, and almost indirect, although it is also telling in the way that it positions rhetoric. Addressing the importance of a theory of confession for criminology, Lacan refers his audience to Plato's *Gorgias,* where Socrates "refutes the infatuation with the master," and therefore critiques confession as the invocation of truth to an authoritative party.[31] This critique had been ignored, according to Lacan, because its subtitle "invokes rhetoric," and therefore is "well designed to dissuade our uncultivated contemporaries from studying it."[32] The theme embodied in this aside—the loss of, perceived obsolescence of, or perhaps most accurately, inattention to rhetoric by Lacan's contemporaries—is a common lament in the Lacanian corpus.

Lacan continues this motif in 1953's "Variations on the Standard Treatment." Calling for attention to discourse in psychoanalytic practice, Lacan argues, "the analyst will find much to borrow from linguistic research in its most concrete modern developments, with which to shed light on difficult problems posed to him by verbalization in both his practice and doctrine."[33] As soon as he announces the usefulness of linguistics to psychoanalysis, Lacan almost immediately appends an argument for the centrality of rhetoric, particularly in reflection on dreams and symptoms, gesturing toward an "outdated" form of knowledge: "we can see, in the most unexpected manner, in the elaboration of the unconscious' most original phenomena—dreams and symptoms—the very figures of outdated rhetoric, which prove in practice to provide the most subtle specifications of those phenomena."[34]

By 1957 Lacan had begun to give more content to the claim that rhetoric supplemented a structuralist understanding of language, specifically by turning to a more textured account of trope understood from the perspective of the rhetorical traditions. In the previously cited "The Instance of the Letter," where Lacan argues that his theory of signification was inspired by Quintilian's understanding of metaphor and metonymy, Lacan applies Quintilian's schemata for understanding trope to the most foundational elements of analytic practice. Out of Quintilian's schema, Lacan articulates a technology for engaging the speech of the analysand by refiguring Freudian defense mechanisms neither through an elaborate set of internal psychic mechanisms, nor through a structuralist understanding of language, but through the "rhetoric of the discourse the analysand actually utters."[35] Soon after, Lacan defines psychoanalysis as a mode of attending to signifying chains in speech, "revived from ancient rhetoric," despite a "historically motivated lacuna" that elides its place in the constitution of modern structural linguistics.[36] If rhetoric accounts for the signifying character of speech, it also accounts for the other which speech presumes and to which speech refers. Rhetoric becomes a "locus" around which both the subject and others emerge: "The locus described as that of truth serves as a prelude to the truth of the locus [of analysis]. While this locus is not the subject, it is not the other (written with a lowercase *o*) who . . . brings about the coalescences of the signifier with the signified. . . . The cunning of reason that runs through them is the refined rhetoric [that introduces] this Other (to be provided with a capital *O*) . . . invoked by anyone when he addresses an other."[37] Here rhetoric marks both the moment where a subject encounters alterity (in the form of the capital "O" Other, and a process whereby specific others emerge. Rhetoric "invokes" the Other because it names the system of signs and symbols that is the condition of possibility for this other, and invokes the specific other, because the specific other emerges as an effect of addressing the big "O" Other.

Cumulatively, if rhetoric accounts for both the character of discourse and the relations between the subject and the other(s) that constitute the whole of socially mediated reality, then it is impossible to conceive of a psychoanalysis that is not also a theory of rhetoric. Perhaps the best testimony to this fact is a claim made by Lacan in a response to a talk by Chaim Perelman on metaphor. In it Lacan argues that rhetoric and psychoanalysis are nearly synonymous: "it is on the basis of the unconscious' manifestations, which I deal with as an analyst, that I have developed a theory of the effects of the signifier that intersects rhetoric. This is attested to in the fact that my students, in reading works of rhetoric, recognized it to be their daily fare at my seminar."[38] Given the inextricable relation between rhetoric and psychoanalysis, it was perhaps unavoidable that Lacan would claim in the twentieth seminar that the "universe is a flower of rhetoric."

Though some have claimed that rhetoric drops out of the Lacanian canon as an analytic category in Lacan's later work, perhaps Lacan's most authoritative turn to rhetoric occurs in his antepenultimate twenty-fifth seminar, the second of the rhetorical bookends that I introduced in chapter 1. Lacan begins by noting that analysis relies on equivocation, or on presuming two equal voices in the production of discourse: the speech of the analysand and the symbolic charge that animates speech. Equivocation signals both the empirical fact that the speech of the analysand harbors multiple meanings and the structural phenomenon that is the condition of possibility for such equivocal speech, the whole economy of tropes that produces discourse. In seminar twenty-five, Lacan makes this argument through a reference to a prominent claim in his later career that there is "no such thing as a sexual relation"[39]: "We need equivocation for analysis . . . equivocation defines analysis, because as the word implies, equivocation gestures toward sex. . . . [That] sex is not defined by a relationship is what I declared in the formulation that 'there is no sexual relation' . . . undoubtedly because of the existence of the signifier . . . the sexual relation . . . is an empty set."[40] First, "without equivocation, there is no analysis": the fact that the analysand's speech is equivocal signals that speech cannot be reduced to its imaginary identifications. Rather, speech signifies a manifest claim and simultaneously refers to the latent symbolic connections that are the condition of speech's possibility. Were this not the case, analysis would not be necessary, because a simple transcript of the analysand's speech would be sufficient for understanding what is at stake in an analytic session. But because speech harbors and points toward a set of relationships beyond the manifest claim, analysis is necessary to connect speech with its symbolic preconditions, and ultimately to figure the function of the speech act for the analysand.

Second, sex: the claim that there is "no such thing as a sexual relation" does not mean that sex does not exist. Rather, Lacan's proclamation places a decided emphasis on the idea that there is no sexual *relation*. The lack of a sexual relation is a metaphor for the idea that even in the most intimate exchanges between subjects, there is no mutual, reciprocal, shared, intersubjective principle of consanguinity. Just as analysis cannot proceed exclusively on the basis of unequivocal speech, it also cannot proceed by taking the presence of a manifest relationship as an interpretive tool, because relationships between subjects are prefigured by the symbolic charge that produces them. Thus, the idea that there is "no sexual relation" produces an inversion of the commonsense idea that symbols are a result of the communal relation that produces them. Instead, the function of the symbol produces an Imagined intersubjective relation, and further, the Symbolic prohibits fully mutual, reciprocal intersubjective relation by introducing a mediating third term. Thus, in response to the idea that the intersubjective relation founds the symbol, Lacan holds up a conception of sex as mutual onanism—although sex involves a conception of exchange, it is less a mediated "betweenness" that characterizes this relation than an overlapping set of narcissistic imaginary practices produced by incommensurable symbolic positions. Given this metaphor, the conditions for intersubjective exchange are fundamentally equivocal, which means that the relationship between hypothetical lovers refers back to the symbolic logic that precedes the relation, and is mediated by the equivocal nature of speech and signification. As a result, even though the physical act of sex is undoubtedly a form of sharing, the relationship that underwrites it is subject to the equivocal nature of the Symbolic, and, therefore, the meaning of the relationship is not shared. Because the empirical and analytical equivocation that characterizes the sexual or communicative "relation of non-relation" is a result of symbolic prefiguration, psychoanalysis must attend to the equivocal relation that underwrites the possibility of non-relation.[41] Thus, as a technician of the relation of non-relation, the psychoanalyst "is a rhetor . . . the analyst 'rhetorifies,' which implies that the analyst 'rectifies.' The analyst is a rhetor, that is, the Latin word *rectus* is equivocal with rhetoric. One tries to say the truth, but that is not easy, because there are large obstacles to saying the truth, and it may be that when we say that we are telling the truth that we have chosen our words poorly. The truth has to address the Real, and the Real is doubled, one might say, by the Symbolic."[42] As a rhetor, the goal of analytic practice is to both "rhetorify" and to "rectify": analytic practice aims to reveal the structuring functions of the Symbolic in the speech of the subject, and, further, to reveal the ways that such speech constitutes the experience of the subject. Because there is a constitutive disconnect between speech as a representation of the life of the subject and the conditions of its existence, the analyst is a rhetor because she or he provides a suitable set of symbolically mediated representations of the Real to account for the experience of the subject. As a rhetor, the goal of the analyst is not to reveal the Real, but rather to give a compelling account of reality for the analysand that situates the analysand in relation to the generative power of the Symbolic. The analyst is less a "truth teller" who uses logical forms to square speech and the Real than a rhetorician because the main tool available to the analyst is not logically verifiable truth, but rather suggestion:

> Logic only supports a portion of things. If we do not believe, in a way, totally and freely, that words make things, logic does not have a reason for being. What I called the rhetorical impulse in analysis presents a question for the analyst, because the rhetor only operates by suggestion. Suggestion is the characteristic of the rhetor, and the rhetor does not require consistency, which is why I designated the "ex-" that supports the concept of "ex"-sistence (in the Real). How then can the analyst be a suitable rhetor? . . . That which makes truth and forgery is in the power of the analyst, and that is why I say that the analyst is a rhetor.[43]

If the idea that "words make things" is not a denial of the possibility of logic but the reason for its being, a rhetorical account of the functions of the sign is the basis for analytic practice because it figures the functions of words in generating the analysand's world. The empirical regularities of speech practice become the basis for an understanding of the overarching logic of symbolic forms. As a result, Lacan articulates a rhetorical ontology that sees words and the formal properties of the sign as the basis for the subject's engagement with the world beyond discourse. If the analyst has a role here, it is in her capacity as a rhetor, persuasively "making" some elements of the analysand's speech a forgery and others a "true" representation of the symbolic practices that precede them by simple declaration. Conversely, this is also the site where Lacan identifies an ontology of rhetoric rooted in the formal properties of signification and its effects in constituting the subject and its modes of relation. This dual function of a rhetorical ontology and an ontology of rhetoric describes why exactly an analyst must also be a rhetor: to take up speech and modes of relation between subjects presumes a logic of formal discursive interaction that grounds the human, but analysis requires the mobilization of this principle for understanding the work of the sign in producing subjects and their discourses. Lacan's psychoanalysis requires an ontology or rhetoric because it relies on an account of the trans-subjective formal properties of the Symbolic to render analytic discourse interpretable. Conversely, analytic practice requires a rhetorically situated ontology, because it understands these same forms to be the result of the subject's compensatory labor in the context of failed unicity. Thus, rhetoric is the irreducible center of analytic theory and practice.

Provocation: To Wring the Neck of Rhetoric

Despite the centrality of rhetoric to analytic theory and practice, Lacan's relationship to rhetoric has its own equivocal character. Marcelle Marini cites Lacan's quotation of Ezra Pound's maxim that one should seek to "wring the neck of rhetoric"—which is itself a reformulation of Verlaine's injunction to "wring the neck of eloquence"—stating, "Lacan's writing style belongs to the great oratorical tradition. The structure of his sentences is that of . . . long oratorical 'periods' with subordinate clauses at the beginning, interrupted by flights of oratory, reinforced by long, drawn out comparisons. . . . [W]hile style must persuade in order to convince, even paradoxical reversals belong, in part, to this cultural context which produced the oratorical tradition. . . . Ultimately, Lacan also wants 'to wring the neck of rhetoric' (*tordre le cou à la rhétorique*)."[44] Although Lacan employs the stylistic trappings of one strand of the rhetorical tradition, Lacan also writes against the grain of this tradition. This framing of Lacan's relationship to rhetoric equates "rhetoric" with something quite specific: the oratorical tradition's concern for eloquence, persuasion, and propriety. As Sacvan Bercovitch and Cyrus Patell argue, Pound's attempt to recover poetic "true art" requires wringing the neck or rhetoric because "for the modernist and New Critical generation, the charged word 'rhetoric' (which our culture still pejoratively equates with debased . . . forms of language) summed up everything that was wrong with a society given over to reductive, utilitarian, and blindly instrumental mental habits."[45] Lacan's criticism of rhetoric follows a similar strand, although it frames the target of the critique a bit differently: it is perhaps more accurate to say that Lacan would like to wring the neck of a vision of rhetoric as persuasion and propriety for the sake of establishing a new rhetoric. Lacan would like to wring the neck of a version of rhetoric reduced to its imaginary functions in the name of a version of rhetoric that attends to the Symbolic.

Lacan's impulse to wring the neck of rhetoric signifies a desire to shock rhetoric into thinking discourse differently, awakening rhetoric from its imaginary slumber to return it to a fuller, more analytically rigorous conception of rhetorical effect. Such an analytic would attend to the whole economy of trope and enjoyment that underwrites rhetoric's effects by figuring trope as the name for the labor of signification in the context of failed unicity. There are two significant implications to this claim. First, it is necessary to assign a proper analytic place for and importance to traditional staples of rhetorical criticism (exchanged meanings, context, and propriety) by locating them in the Imaginary register, and by extension as effects of a larger context for the context of specific discourses—in the work of the Symbolic in both producing subjects, regulating their conditions for exchange, and figuring their modes of relation to other subjects. Second, naming the Symbolic (and its material manifestation in the Lacanian unconscious) as the "context for the context" of rhetorical action shifts rhetorical theory's understanding of the rhetorical relation from a near-exclusive focus on what is proximate to the "situation" to the whole economy of trope and enjoyment that exceeds, underwrites, and is the condition of possibility for specific discourses.

What would this mean for practices of rhetorical criticism? Put simply, it means that as an analytic category, trope is logically prior to all the operations that stem from the Imaginary register of rhetoric. Revisiting his famous essay with Gerald Mohrmann, "Lincoln at Cooper Union: A Rhetorical Analysis of the Text," Michael Leff argues that a traditional "neoclassical," text-centric understanding of rhetorical criticism does not presume that a text "can only have one meaning."[46] Leff argues that, to the contrary, critical "argument opens the possibility of approaching the text not as a fixed artifact but as the object of rhetorical controversy whose meaning and significance change as we come to read it from different angles. . . . Recognition of the contingency of interpretive work does not prevent us from taking a position; it only makes us more aware that interpretations of texts are like other beliefs and commitments; they depend upon our historical situation, on our position in some particular time and place, and are justified through argument to some particular audience."[47] Critics have long noted that the actual empirical conditions of a specific address remain largely guesswork. A critic's vision of the actual conditions of a speech is the result of a historical reconstruction that has a dubious relationship with the original situation of a speech. Leff's tacit concession to the impossibility of recovering the moment of reception and the situational constraints that mediate the reception of a speech should shift the conventional understanding of neoclassical criticism. Instead of simply recovering the meaning of a speech in its original context, readings of a text's relationship to its original audience are necessarily filtered through the historical location of the critic and justified by argument to "some particular audience." The audience that Leff is referring to is not the original audience of the speech. Rather, the "particular audience" in this case is an audience of fellow contemporary critics, to whom a critic presents a reading of the situational constraints of a text as a matter of almost conjectural reconstruction. Thus, even neoclassical rhetorical criticism is not a reading of the work of a text in relation to its original audience. Rather, neoclassical criticism posits an original audience of the speech for the sake of reading the rhetorical effectivity of a text in the presence of a contemporary audience of critics, but this original audience never quite escapes its status as a kind of prosopopoeia: one reads a text largely by imagining and personifying an audience that receives it, and the measure of this reading is the way that it reveals the function of the text for its imagined original audience.

Paradoxically, even in the most conservative forms of rhetoric as public address that claim to recover the meaning of a text for an audience, access to the original audience is only metaphorical: neoclassical critics read texts as if the reconstructed or imagined audience seamlessly stands in for the inaccessible empirical audience of a speech. This is why some critics in this strand, such as Leah Ceccarelli, have attempted to read secondary responses to speeches in newspapers and other media commentaries: the goal is to provide the richest possible framing of the original situation of a speech.[48] Of course, to presume that more historically proximate secondary commentators are in any better position to evaluate the empirical audience of a speech is equally suspect. Historically proximate secondary commentary on the situation of a speech is bound to a logic of mediation and representation that renders access to the speaking situation problematic. As a result, even the most assiduously imaginary framings of rhetoric rely on a barely latent logic of trope to create an image of an audience that bounds the application of neoclassical critical artifice.

Alternatively, one could admit that the empirical audience of a text is fundamentally inaccessible, attempting to read a text not on the basis of the situation that it addresses, but on the basis of a rhetor's Imagined understanding of their audience. In adopting this strategy, the critic would have to assume that the empirical evidence presented by the text stands in for or metaphorically represents the intentions of the speaker in inventing the text. In either case, the critic is essentially reading the speech tropologically—that is, he or she is reading a representation of the speaker and/or situation metaphorically, as projections that stand in for the actual situation, intentions, and motivations that constituted speaker and situation around a specific rhetorical artifact. One might, following Leff, recover a sense of epistemic humility in rhetoric by wringing its neck—that is, by attending to the ways that the imaginary commitments of rhetorical criticism, although useful, are both constitutively disconnected from the phenomena that they describe, and are prefigured by the operation of the symbolic logic of metaphor. Thus relativized, even a neoclassical conception of rhetorical criticism can take up an adjusted sense of the power of imaginary framings of the speaking situation by attending to the symbolic preconditions that organize an imaginary rhetoric.

Why is it that students of rhetorical studies are so invested in the recoverability of the imaginary coordinates of rhetorical situations? In short, critics are invested in the recoverability of rhetorical situations because this presupposition reaffirms the agential capacities of the orator, the audience, and perhaps most importantly, the critic. Consider Lacan's schema of "four discourses," which defines the different configurations between the Agent, Other, Truth, and Discursive Production in the discourses of the Master, the University (or of the scholar), the Hysteric, and the Analyst. At stake in this schema are the modes of affective investment that underwrite an agent's engagement with the other that it takes as an object:

University Discourse

$$\frac{S2}{S1} \rightarrow \frac{a}{\$} \quad (\text{Impotence})$$

Analyst's Discourse

$$\frac{a}{S2} \xrightarrow{\text{Impossibility}} \frac{\$}{S1}$$

KEY:

Places:

$$\frac{\text{Agent}}{\text{Truth}} \qquad \frac{\text{Other}}{\text{Production}}$$

Symbols:

S1 - The Master Signifier
S2 - Knowledge
\$ - The Subject (Barred)
a - Surplus Jouissance/"little *a* object"

Here I will focus on the university discourse (as seen in the partial presentation of the diagram above), which represents a set of relationships that rhetorical critics grasp intuitively and inevitably encounter in making critical judgments. In scholarly or university discourses, the primary agent is knowledge (S2), and the primary other that the agent engages is an object (a). In the case of rhetorical criticism, knowledge (S2) is the agent, representing the collected insights of rhetorical theory and criticism and the taken-for-granted historical facts that describe a given situation for rhetorical action. The specific rhetorical text or set of practices that the scholar engages is the object (a) of a rhetorical university discourse.

A number of things are notable about the relation between knowledge and its object in the schema of the university discourse. First, even if it is taken for granted as a site for the application of knowledge to an object, the university discourse is anything but "objective." The site of production (represented by the lower right quadrant of the university discourse) in the schema is the $, or the subject: object of the knowledge is produced by a subject. This is a way of saying in more global terms what Dilip Gaonkar has said regarding the dialectic between object and method: because the method of reading a discourse is itself a site of investment, the object of a discourse is produced by a subject who both reads and brings the object to life as a discrete entity in the act of reading.[49] To read this schema, one should read that line separating the "a" object and the "$" subject as a site of production as both a mode of support and a site of repression. In the case of rhetorical criticism, this means that the critical subject produces the object to be read and simultaneously that the productive power of the reading subject must be repressed for the sake of the integrity of the object as a discrete entity external to the critic and meaningfully able to be assimilated to a scholarly knowledge practice.

The relationship between the critical subject and its object is therefore one squarely located in the Imaginary. The work of interpreting an object is productive for the reading subject, despite the fact that the productive nature of this relation must be suppressed to maintain the status of object as an entity endowed with its own iconic coherence. In the case of rhetorical studies, the "little *a*" object (for example, a speech) is produced by concealing the fact that what counts as a rhetorical object is itself not a pre-existent category, produced by nothing more than the application of rhetorical S2 by a subject ($) who produces a discourse in the very act of interpreting it.

All of this is a way of saying that the rhetorical object is an effect of a rhetorical reading, and is the product of applying a rhetorical artifice. There is, to be sure, a scholarly pleasure in showing how a specific speech can be usefully explained by integrating the rhetorical object (little "a") into a preexisting corpus of (S2) knowledge, whether it be the Burkean Pentad, a specific understanding of rhetoric as contextually situated discursive effect, or even in seeing the text as a node in an economy of tropological exchange. But more importantly, in taking an object of inquiry as an objectively existing phenomenon outside the ambit of discursive production, that is, in taking the object as "objective" as opposed to an imaginary projection, the discourse of the university ensures not only the validity of the forms of knowledge that it produces, but also the subjective potency of the scholar who inhabits it. By extension, the character of the object as a discrete entity enables it to be imagined as a participant in the history of negotiated meanings between text and context, independent of the investments of the scholar who ostensibly takes up an object to reveal the ways that it functions in its "native" context. Rhetoricians are invested in the recoverability of the imaginary coordinates of rhetorical situations because this investment shores up the fragile self-efficacy of the critic by assuring her or him that the meaning of a given rhetorical manifestation is accessible in its own right, and by extension, that both the critic and the critical schema maintain a kind of efficacy in reading the world and coming to terms with the presence of others in discourse.

If this shoring-up of critical efficacy is to remain effective, it must, by definition, remain concealed. Aristotle advised that in composing a speech a rhetor must "*disguise* his art and give the impression of speaking naturally, not artificially."[50] While rhetoric may be the art of observing the "available means of persuasion,"[51] one must keep in mind that "naturalness is persuasive," while explicitly marked "artificiality is the contrary."[52] If the artifice entailed in rhetorical action is too explicitly marked, the obvious presence of the artifice produces a perception in the audience that a speaker has "design against them, as if we were mixing wines for them."[53] An imaginary mode of rhetorical criticism must conceal the fact that though it exerts crucial effects in the community of rhetorical critics, it is only imaginary. It is this inflated conception of imaginary efficacy in rhetoric, one that only works by concealing its status as artifice, whose neck Lacan would like to wring—primarily by confronting the Imaginary register with its dependence on the Symbolic and the limit that it meets in the Real. But the commitment to an imaginary rhetoric is not simply a result of the work it does in shoring up the efficacy of the critic: this commitment is also part and parcel of a broader understanding of communication that has gained primacy in the reading of rhetoric.

3
Speech/Communication

Rhetoric, or the art of oration, was a science and not just an art.

—Jacques Lacan, *The Psychoses*

Lacan would like to "wring the neck" of a vision of rhetoric that locates it chiefly in the Imaginary order—a vision that focuses almost exclusively on the exchange of meanings in a context—by compelling rhetoric to attend to the Symbolic and the limit posed by the Real. In wringing rhetoric's neck, Lacan's goal is not to destroy the art of rhetoric, but to establish rhetoric as a new kind of science. Making rhetoric a science would not abandon the imaginary components of rhetorical interpretation; rather, it would contest the total reduction of rhetoric to its imaginary functions by situating the imaginary functions of rhetoric in the ground of trope, primarily by properly parsing the relation between causes and effects in rhetoric. Thus, a science of rhetoric would understand the imaginary functions of rhetoric as derived from the formal and affective properties of discourse. Wringing the neck of an imaginary rhetoric in the name of uncovering its symbolic preconditions reveals that the hermeneutic negotiation of speaker, speech, and context are not the self-sufficient causes of rhetoric's effectivity, but are effects of an economy of tropes and affects that prefigure each of them.

But wringing the neck of rhetoric also requires a critique of a concept that substantially underwrites the intersubjective fetish of an imaginary rhetoric: communication. In this chapter, I would like to take up Lacan's critique of the ideology of communication, arguing for a studied disarticulation between the idea of rhetoric and communication. Specifically, I propose that the concept of speech ought be separated from and posed against the idea of communication in the name of recovering a sense of speech that is both quintessentially scientific and fully rhetorical in the Lacanian sense of the term.

Lacan remarked with a thinly veiled skepticism that "In the present state of affairs, it's touch-and-go whether the entire theory of what goes on in living beings will be revised as a function of communication."[1] On one hand, Lacan saw substantial promise in the cybernetic model of communication, particularly as embodied in the work of Norbert Wiener. The cybernetic understanding of communication as a set of positional relations that did not require the mediation of a subject or meaning had significant affinities with Lacan's understanding of the structuring functions of discourse.[2] On the other hand, Lacan was skeptical of a view of communication that framed it simply as the transmission of messages mediated by hermeneutic understanding in the context of intersubjective exchange between subjects.

Lacan identified two basic assumptions of an understanding of communication as a mode of intersubjective "betweenness." First, an understanding of communication as betweenness puts a decided emphasis on the relation between subjects at the expense of attending to the generative power of texts or the formal elements of discursive production, by extension privileging the subject as a site of mediation and production at the expense of situating it in the whole economy of discourse. In focusing on what goes on between subjects, communication often takes for granted the givenness of the subjects between whom communication transpires. Against the metaphor of communication as betweenness, often idealized as a dyadic relation between subjects, Lacan argues for a conception of "omnicommunication" that figures the functions of discourse as the primary agents in communicative exchange, and that situates subjects engaging in communication as one node in an economy of tropological exchange.[3] The result of this practice would attend to "the omnipresence of human discourse . . . under the open sky of an omnicommunication of its text." Here, the "text" of human discourse is not the individual text exchanged between subjects, but rather the whole edifice of the Symbolic, which includes the production of the subject as a textual effect. Taking the whole edifice of the Symbolic as the "text" of the "omnicommunication of discourse" counteracts a conception of communication as an only loosely affiliated collection of dyadic exchanges. Lacan argues that while "this is the field that our experience polarizes in . . . [what] is only apparently a two-person relation," discourse should not be so conceived because "any positioning of its structure in dyadic terms is as inadequate to it in theory as it is damaging to it in technique."[4] A dyadic conception of communication localizes rhetorical agency around the subjects exchanging messages in speech, as opposed to seeing both the subject and its message as effects of the whole economy of discourse. By extension, such a view draws critical attention to the concepts and intentions expressed between agents in a communicative dyad at the expense of attending to the symbolic conditions that make exchange possible in the first place.

Second, if the model of "betweenness" understands communication as transmission, it also envisions the contents of a communicative transmission as the primary means of rhetorical action. Paradoxically, this understanding of the communicative act ignores the ways that meaning is both an epiphenomenon of the symbolic construction of the subject and its discourses, and by extension, that meaning is necessarily plural. In this model, the presence of a rhetorical interchange or "dialogue" often interpretively reduces to a mode of attending to the contents of a discourse at the expense of the tropological and affective functions that govern both the production and reception of a given speech act. Lacan implicitly poses a conception of agency distributed between addressee, addressor, and the field of signifiers to argue for an expanded conception of rhetorical effectivity beyond the transmission of specific contents:

> Dialogue . . . is played out as if between a deaf man and one who hears. That is, it represents the veritable complexity of what is ordinarily simplified, with the most confused of results, in the notion of communication. . . . [C]ommunication can give the impression, at which theorists too often stop, of conveying in its transmission but one meaning, as though the highly significant commentary into which he who hears integrates it could be considered neutralized because it is unperceived by he who does not hear. . . . [T]he message truly belongs to the dimension of language.[5]

For Lacan, the ideology of communication figures communication as an exchange between subjects mediated by a context and a negotiated practice of meaning-making. The exchange of signs represents the internal state and intentions of one subject for another subject: here the addressees of communication are the specific others who constitute an audience, treated as if they exclusively participate in communication through passive reception as opposed to active formation.

Lacan's framing of rhetoric inverts this logic. If the subject and its discourses are the effect of an economy of trope and affects that constitutes the edifice of the sign, rhetoric is the process whereby "a signifier represents a subject for another signifier."[6] That this is a tropologically inflected process is not difficult to see: a signifier metaphorically stands in for the subject in the presence of another subject who in turn metaphorically stands in for the field of signification that produces it. "Communication" purchases explanatory power largely because it elides the symbolic economy of signs, tropes, and affects by substituting the effect of this economy—the Imaginary register, or the fantasy of a subject relating to others—for its cause. If communication is constituted by the exchange of ideas between subjects via different media (writing, speech, and so on), in rhetoric the subject itself is the both the effect of and medium for the expression of the signifier. The signifier that expresses a subject is constituted both by the symbolic logic that organizes it and its material manifestation in the unconscious. By extension, this conception of the Symbolic lodges a critique of the hermeneutic conceptions of meaning exchanged between subjects as a privileged site of rhetorical action, and of the subject as the privileged locus for the cooperative communicative negotiation of meanings.

To lay out the basic structure of this critique, I would like to begin by taking up the question of meaning in Lacan's work, quickly transitioning to an account of how Lacan's conception of the unconscious reframes meaning as an effect, rather than as the cause, of rhetoric's effectivity. Second, I will introduce Lacan's reframing of the concept of speech, situating it in relation both to its role as a synecdoche for a materially situated conception of discourse and as a way of reframing the taken-for-granted logics of address presumed in a communicative understanding of speech. I will undertake a reading of the place of communication in Lacan's work, relying primarily upon his famous "schema L" from *The Ego in Freud's Theory and in the Technique of Psychoanalysis* and *The Psychoses.* What Lacan demonstrates in schema L is that the articulation of speech and communication is not without cost, and, in fact, it may be one of the primary reasons motivating an occlusion of rhetoric in the name of communication, at least if rhetoric is understood as the effectivity of trope in the context of failed unicity. Finally, I will end with a provocation on Lacan's call to return to a "science of oratory."

Meaning and the Unconscious

Lodging a critique of the reduction of meaning to the social and psychological aspects of language use (to "intentions," "ideas," "social rules, [and] conventions"), and of the linguist's tendency to reduce meaning to semantic "markerese" (to the logics of semantic markers), David Lewis calls for a conception of meaning appropriate to "the complicated, infinite entities built up out of elements belonging to various ontological categories."[7] For Lewis, the question of meaning implies two distinct questions that, although analytically separate, cumulatively account for meaning phenomena, arguing that "the description of possible languages or grammars as abstract semantic systems whereby symbols are associated with aspects of the world; and, second, the description of the psychological and sociological facts whereby a particular one of these abstract semantic systems is the one used by a person or population."[8] There are two basic kinds of work at play in this taxonomy of meaning-making functions. The first is the work of reference, that is, of associating symbols "with aspects of the world" in meaningful ways. Second, meaning requires that a subject works to situate specific referential practices in the context of an individual subject's or group's social context.

If conventional approaches to meaning largely rely on unpacking the relationships between reference and context, Lacan's foray into meaning began somewhat quirkily. Lacan's earliest work focused on obsessive thinking or on the patterns of thought that analysts of his day called "mental automatism." Analysts of the time had a readily available explanation for this problem: thoughts seemed intrusive because they came from the unconscious—from the hidden interior life of the subject. Automatic thoughts intruded on the psyche because they were a proxy for a deeply hidden desire that social or individual mores prohibited. On this account, until the desire was addressed in its naked reality, repressed desires would return in the form of automatic thoughts.

But the model of the human naturally endowed with interiority had become increasingly untenable for Lacan. Thus, a quandary: how might an analyst theorize thought that seems to come from outside the subject without conceding to an elaborate set of unquestioned internal psychic machinations that both produce the thought and hide its origins? To answer this question, Lacan argued for a reframing of automatic thought away from the question of meaning toward the systemic conditions of discourse that produce automatic thoughts. If a thought seemed intrusive, one need not posit mechanisms internal to the psyche to explain it, because automatism is a result of the analysand's relation to discourse. "My research," argued Lacan, "has led me to the realization that repetition automatism has its basis in what I have called the *insistence* of the signifying chain."[9] The automatic thought finds its genesis in two functions: a metonymic chain that connects signifiers together and an insistent habitual reassertion of this linkage. Lacan's conception of insistence relies on one of the basic insights of differential semiotics: a subject never employs a signifier in isolation from the other signifiers that give it meaning. Prior to the relationship of meaning—that is, prior to a subject's negotiation with and comportment of what a sign designates for him or her individually—sits the whole field of signifying associations that figure the place of any signifier in relationship to a field of other signifiers.

"What," asks Lacan "is the meaning of meaning?" Meaning is the labor of imputing subjective significance to words, concepts, and representations when such significance cannot be guaranteed in advance because of failed unicity. To "mean," then, words, concepts, and representations require the two forms of work identified earlier: meaning requires the work of reference to connect significance to a signified; but it also requires the work of articulating significance within a given context. As a result, meaning is both a mode of connection between a subject and a signifier and a struggle for recognition in the form of social sanction:

> Meaning is the fact that the human being isn't master of this primordial, primitive language. He has been thrown into it, committed, caught up in its gears. . . . [The subject] isn't the master in his own house. There is something into which he integrates himself, which through its combinations already governs. The passage of man from the order of nature to the order of culture follows the same mathematical combinations that will be used to classify and explain . . . a primitive symbolism which is distinct from imaginary representations. It is in the middle of that that something of man has to gain recognition. But what has to be recognized, Freud teaches us, is not expressed, but repressed.[10]

Here, Lacan implicitly opposes two conceptions of recognition. As expression, recognition is primarily conceived of as shorthand for what goes on between subjects in an intersubjective relation. A second understanding of meaning frames it as revelation, or as an uncovering of that which is repressed. On this account, meaning moves beyond the betweenness of the intersubjective relation, gesturing toward the signifying economy that produces subjects and the artificial means through which subjects feign significance.

A signifier functions because it is habitually repeated, and therefore is a site of investment: subjects develop virtually automatic attachments to signifiers that remain largely invisible to them. Cumulatively, these two functions (signifying articulation and investment) locate repetition automatism as a function of the "signifying chain." Lacan's insight supplants the conceptions of meaning that framed mental automatism as the expression of an unresolved inner conflict in the psyche—as an internal meaning-making negotiation—with socially situated signifying relations that are neither explicitly intended nor secretly forged by the psyche of the subject of the automatic thought. Automatic thought does not have meaning in and of itself, if meaning is understood as a specific designation that a subject assigns a signifier. Rather, signifiers impose themselves on subjects as a correlative of the idea that subjects do not speak a language that they create, but rather uneasily inhabit one inherited from the symbolic edifice that renders signs intelligible. Therefore, the automatic thought can be located both outside of and manifest in a given subject, as an "*ex-sistence* (that is, the eccentric place) in which we . . . grasp by what oblique imaginary means the *Symbolic* takes hold in even the deepest recesses of the human organism."[11]

Though this dynamic is condensed in the automatic thought, it is also the condition of possibility for language. For example, one cannot assert the concept of "patriotism" without also relying on a range of associations that saturate the concept of patriotism: love, a concept of "fatherland," the virtues of home, and a vision of all the specific actions that patriotism entails. Invoking patriotism, one simultaneously operationalizes a constellation of other concepts against which patriotism takes on a determinate meaning, such as complacency regarding one's fatherland, infidelity to the nation, and that other nations that are not the "fatherland." Signs invoke a plurality of explicit and latent associations that give them a determinate character. Second, borrowing from Heidegger's concept of insistence (most clearly articulated in "On the Essence of Truth"), Lacan's conception of mental automatism explains the way that representational practices exercise a kind of sway on the subject who employs them. Automatic thought insists, via the force of accumulated social habit, on certain meanings that impose themselves on the signifying subject. The signifier is the agent in this relationship, and the subject is the one who is subjected to the force of the insistent sign.

As a result of his engagement with mental automatism, Lacan engages in a subtle but significant reframing of meaning. On a classical Saussurean reading of the meaning of the sign, a signifier refers to an image of a thing, and the image correlates with the actual existence of the thing in reality. The act of forging mental correspondences between signifier, signified, image, and reality locates meaning in a very specific place—meaning is the province of a subject who either properly or improperly correlates signifier, signified, image, and reality, and further, who interpretively ascribes meaning to these relations. Lacan's intervention breaks with the Saussurean conception of the signified as a referent for the signifier. Outlining the difference, he cautions that "the trap . . . one must not fall into, is the belief that signifieds are objects, things. The signified is something quite different—it's the meaning . . . it always refers to meaning, that is, another meaning. The system of language . . . never results in an index finger pointed at reality; . . . reality . . . is covered by the entire network of language."[12] Signifiers refer to meanings, and these meanings, in turn, refer to a network of differentially articulated other meanings. The "repressed" aspect of meaning is that intersubjective practices are not the efficient cause of meaning, but meaning is an extension of asubjective mediation that is the extension of the basic logic of articulation and differentiation that constitutes signs.

Where is the signified object or concept in this relation? It is present as represented by a meaning, but this is only a representation—the actual thing is absent. What sustains the relationship of reference in signification is not things, but rather other meanings implied in other significations: "no signification can be sustained other than by reference to another signification. . . . [W]e will fail to pursue the question further as long as we cling to the illusion that the signifier answers to the function of representing the signified, or better, that the signifier has to answer for its existence in the name of any signification whatever."[13] This explanation seems not only counterintuitive, but maybe even impossible: if signifiers function because they seem to refer to things, how can the logic of signification as reference be sustainable in the absence of the signified? By Lacan's account, "we are forced . . . to accept the notion of an incessant sliding of the signified under the signifier."[14] The referential pretension is sustained only by a specific act of labor in signification—the speaking subject "slides" the signified under the signified, or, as Lacan puts it later, the speaking subject "stuffs" the symbolic contents of the signifier into the place of the signified.[15] Thus, out of a theory of mental automatism Lacan refigured the meaning of meaning. His intervention engages in a three-part critique of structural linguistics, refiguring the sign as a product of the labor of sliding signifieds under the signifier, the referential relationship by substituting meaning as the referent of the signifier, and meaning by distributing it outward from the subject toward a whole network of signs.

But Lacan's framing of mental automatism does more than upset the conventional understanding of signs, reference, and meaning. The turn to the whole network of signification as a reservoir for and condition of possibility of meaning made a reinvention of the Freudian unconscious a virtual inevitability: "In our time, in the historical period that has seen the formation of a science that may be termed human, but which must be distinguished from any psycho-sociology, namely, linguistics, whose model is the combinatory operation, functioning spontaneously, or itself, in a presubjective way—it is the linguistic structure that gives its status to the unconscious."[16]

As opposed to a vision of the unconscious as the subjective interiority of the individual or collective, Lacan's unconscious comprises all the latent associations that inhere in the accreted history of a signifier, and by extension, the whole network of meanings. Thus, "the remembering at stake in the unconscious," using the word in the Freudian sense, "is not related to the register that is assumed to be that of memory, insofar as memory is taken to be a property of a living being. . . . [I]n doing without this subjection, we can find in the ordered chains of a formal language the entire appearance of remembering, and especially of the kind required by Freud's discovery. . . . The program traced out for us is hence to figure out how a formal language determines the subject."[17] There are only three formal preconditions for the existence of the Lacanian unconscious, and they have the benefit of being somewhat conceptually minimalist, even elegant: the unconscious requires that signifiers are differentiated from and associated with other signifiers in a network, that signifiers are associated with referents via a relationship of meaning, and that these connections are socially routinized. The conditions for language are exactly the same as the conditions for the existence of the unconscious. As with language, the logic of the sign in the unconscious is ultimately dependent on the function of trope. The sign depends on metonymy, in that some things are ritually connected with other things, and not with other things. Some connections become routinely habituated, or, better yet, saturated, such that they organize a series of metonymic connections around a central point of investment—that is, some connections become metaphorical. The unconscious names the whole field of tropological connections that is the condition of possibility for a sign to have an intelligible meaning. Notably, these conditions require neither a subject nor a conception of interiority.

If the unconscious, or "the discourse of the other," represents the field of possible metonymic connection that might stem from the employment of any signifier, concealment—which largely replaces the orthodox Freudian account of repression—is the result of the subject employing a signifier with a particular relation of meaning inscribed in it at the expense of foregrounding other possible connections, a phenomenon inhering in structures of signification.[18] To insist on a specific metonymic connection that inheres in a sign displaces other possible lines of metonymic connection that, though latent, are not explicitly invoked in a given employment of a sign.[19] Although such connections are temporarily displaced, they are still operative in the enunciation and reception of a signifier. Here, Lacan replaces the orthodox Freudian account of repression as the compensatory work of the ego with something akin to the Heideggerian conception of insistence invoked earlier: the investment that raises an insular metonymic connection to the status of a metaphor conceals or renders latent the other metonymic connections that also inhere in the accreted history of a sign. But the condition of this concealment is the whole field of latent connections that are both accreted and expressed in the social use of signs.

A conception of the unconscious as tropological accretion lies at the core of the Lacanian maxim that "the unconscious is structured *like* a language."[20] To say that the unconscious is structured like a language marks two complementary qualities. First, the unconscious, while a linguistically mediated phenomena, does not operate along the lines of the structural linguistic account of signification that presumes an unproblematic referential relationship between signifier and signified. Second, the unconscious is wrought through the labor that has been done by the subject in sliding a signified under the signifier, or in bringing trope to bear in creating meaning.[21] As a result, "the unconscious is structured like a language" because "before any experience, before any individual deduction, even before . . . collective experiences . . . something organizes the field, the initial lines of force. . . . Before strictly human relations are established, certain relations have already been determined. . . . Nature provides . . . signifiers, and these signifiers organize human relations in a creative way, providing them with structures and shaping them."[22] The unconscious is structured like a language because it is a result of the structural possibilities for polysemous meaning in any act of signification, but it is not a language because it does not obey the conventional rules of reference that an instrumental conception of the sign presumes. Reference is always distributed across multiple signifying possibilities. Freud's famous "Rat Man" case is instructive here: the signifier "rat," Freud asserts, invokes not only a furry rodent, but a whole set of sedimented connections, including the dirty conditions one imagines rats to live in, and the sense of immorality associated with dirtiness.[23] Following Freud's lead, Lacan exteriorizes the unconscious by locating it in the connections implied by past usage of the word "rat," highlighting the metonymic associations it invokes in a signifying chain, even when they are displaced by the metaphorical operation that insists on a specific meaning for the word "rat." The unconscious exists beyond the subject's specific use of a sign and is simultaneously present in the subject's speech as a series of latent metonymic associations.

As a result, the unconscious is also the speech of the other, or, rather, of two kinds of others: the big "O" (or "A" in French, for *Autre*) and the little "o" (or "a") other. The unconscious is the speech of the big "O" Other (which I will address in detail later) because it is the material manifestation of the logic of combination and substitution that governs the sign and the whole field of signifying relations sanctioned by social usage. But the unconscious is also the result of the accreted speech of little "o" others, or specific others who also speak, producing the chains of signifying associations that are present in any act of speech.

Given this characterization of the unconscious, there is a constant tension in the gaps between langue and parole (between the structural logic of signification and the embodiment of speech in the subject), and between the subject and the other, because the moment of speech always and necessarily contains a set of unexpected associations that belie the possibility of consummating a communicative exchange through shared meanings. Speech both says too much and not enough: it says too much because any act of signification is overburdened by a plurality of metonymic connections, and not enough because the mere fact of sliding a signified under a signifier ensures that the connection between the two is never fully saturated or without polysemous possibility.

But why call this the unconscious, as opposed to simply saying that individual discourses always find their meaning in relation to the whole field of discourse? Because accreted metonymic connections have a specific relationship to the field of discourses from which they emerge. Although metonymic connections are not repressed by the intentional action of the ego (as in the orthodox Freudian understanding of repression), they are both durably latent in the field of discourse, and are concealed but nevertheless still present in the subject's employment of a given sign. Lacan invokes the Freudian unconscious because he would like to mark that although not all the associations in any given sign are employed in a given use of a sign, all these latent connections are present, historically accreted in the usage of a given fragment of discourse, imposing themselves tropologically in every employment of the sign—insisting with the charge of the signifying chain. From this insight, and the doctrine of the unconscious that it founded, Lacan took up anew the question of meaning. On first glance, it may seem that this understanding of the insistence of the signifying chain eliminates the need for recourse to the social mediation of meaning. After all, one need only attend to the various structuralist projects that frame the Lacanian moment to find theories of discourse that argue that meaning is wholly subsumable and solely determined by structural effects. But more accurately, one might say that the insistence of the signifying chain provisionalizes meaning, locating it in a very specific register: meaning is both a tropologically determined effect of reference and an imagined disposition toward the signifying chains that a subject inhabits.

Thus, for Lacan there is a tight complementarity between the subject and meaning, such that "only a subject can understand meaning; conversely, every meaning phenomenon implies a subject."[24] Meaning is experienced by a subject, but the subject is not the efficient cause of meaning. Rather, the subject is the site at which meaning is manifest. A reduction of meaning to an intersubjective account of the social field elides the symbolic economy that prefigures meanings and the subjects who experience them. If meaning is an effect of the signifying functions that produce language, to take the shared social charge in meaning at face value frames meaning as an exclusively imaginary phenomenon, severing the link with the symbolic economy that produces it. As Lacan argues, "while the image equally plays a capital role in our own domain, this role is completely taken up and caught within, remolded and reanimated by the Symbolic."[25] The point of provisionalizing meaning by situating it in the Symbolic is to figure meaning as a manifestation of the logic of trope that prefigures it, while simultaneously asserting that the rhetorical situation is not reducible to the social exchange of shared ideas.

By extension, meaning is a retroactively inscribed function of the Symbolic. The usual framing of ego-oriented psychology argues that the goal of analytic practice is, following Jaspers, to "restore meaning to the chain of phenomena."[26] While for Jaspers chains of phenomena are intrinsically meaningful, and meaning is lost only in pathological circumstances, for Lacan meaning is always imposed after the fact: the meaning of a sign or practice is determined by a set of "conventions or rules of the moment" that exert a regulatory symbolic function. For example, Lacan takes up the hypothetical case of a sibling hitting a child. "Was that a slap or a pat?" asks the child, and the answer determines whether the child cries or returns the favor in response to the sibling.[27] The point is that understanding is an "ideal relation," one premised on the ways that symbolically figured conventions and rules of the moment retroactively inscribe meaning. The moment of understanding is an "ideal relation," and thus "as soon as one tries to get close to it, it becomes, properly speaking, ungraspable."[28] To situate meaning solely within the bounds of a contextually bound imaginary intersubjective exchange makes understanding ungraspable, because understanding is also symbolically determined.

Speech and the Other

In figuring the relationship between the Symbolic and Imaginary, Lacan turns to an account of speech: "for some years all my effort has been required in a struggle to bring to the attention of these practitioners the true value of this instrument, *speech*."[29] Lacan's turn to speech originally began as an attempt to detail the function of attention to trope in analytic listening, which Lacan understood to be an intrinsic part of analytic practice. "It is the analyst who knows better than anyone else," writes Lacan, "that the question is to understand which 'part' of this speech carries the significative term, and this is exactly how he proceeds in the ideal case: taking the recital of any everyday event for an apologue addressed to him who hath ears to hear, a long prosopopoeia for a direct interjection, or on the other hand taking a simple lapsus for a highly complex statement, or even the sigh of a momentary silence for the whole lyrical development it makes up for."[30] The strong parallels between this understanding of analysis and rhetorical criticism and the use of a vocabulary drawn from rhetoric ("apologue," "prosopopoeia," "lapsus") will not be lost on rhetoricians. The tools of a good psychoanalyst and a good rhetorical critic, both in taking up speech as an object, and in reading its figural properties, are virtually indistinguishable.

For the analyst, however, attention to the figural properties of speech points beyond the specific contents of a speech and gestures toward the whole edifice of discourse, which forces a movement beyond the contents of a speech to the conditions of its utterance. "The fact that one says," argues Lacan, "remains forgotten behind what is said in what is heard."[31] Speech is the site where language moves through a subject, and where the economy of signs takes up a specific material position, mode of address, and social context. But first and foremost, speech is the making manifest of the symbolic function in a specific relation of address, and it refers to a set of unconscious connections that although manifest in an individual speech act are not exhausted in it.

"To speak," claims Lacan, "is first of all to speak to others."[32] The question is which other or others speech invokes. When taken from the perspective of an unquestioned articulation between speech and communication, that speech is a relation to others (or a "betweenness") might imply the possibility of establishing an intersubjective relation that could both account for the genesis of speech and read speech without reference to an external structuring principle; after all, even the most basic conception of speech as communicative dialogue also begins with the idea of speech addressed to an other. Lacan's understanding of the addressed relation refutes the idea that speaking to others is a sufficient condition for a mutual, reciprocal, and potentially transparent relation. There are two issues here: the character of the specific other to which one speaks, and the issue of "other" others who are also present in and addressed in speech. By other others, I do not mean that speech might also aim at a group, but rather that speech is addressed to at least three different kinds of others: not only a specific bodily manifest audience member, but also to the self as an other and to the big "O" Other:

> Speech . . . hooks on to the other. . . . Without doubt, speech is . . . mediation between subject and other, and it implicates the coming into being of the other in this very mediation. An essential element in the coming into being of the other is the capacity of speech to unite us to him. . . . But there is another side to speech—revelation. . . . [T]he unconscious is not expressed, except by deformation, *Enstellung,* distortion, transportation. . . . I wrote *The Function and Field of Speech and Language,* intentionally without using the term "expression," because the whole of Freud's work unfolds in the dimension of revelation, and not of expres-

> sion. Revelation is the ultimate source of what we are searching for in the analytic experience.[33]

First, "speech runs entirely along the slope by which it hooks on to the other." Here Lacan renders "other" with a lower case "o," so in this instance speech hooks onto specific others. Lacan's description of this relationship as hooking is radically different from conversation, dialogue, or negotiation. "Hooking" implies an appropriative capture or comportment more than reciprocal exchange. Because the unconscious, as the reservoir of socially accreted signifying relations or the "discourse of the other," is the matrix from which speech is generated, speech always presumes exchange with others. But, hooking implies that what is at play in speech is not a relationship of mutual exchange between interlocutors, but a form of indirection where a relationship to a specific interlocutor is scripted by other others who are only present in the discourse in historical accretion of speech.

Second, speech hooks onto an other because the condition of speech is that it be addressed to a specific other, but this hooking does not attach to a pre-existent other. Rather, speech constitutes the other. "Speech is mediation between subject and other" because speech produces both addressor and addressee by constituting their identity, modes of subjectivity, and assigns each a role relative to the other.[34] Thus, speech is by necessity tropologically constituted because the symbolic conditions of address constitute the ground from which interlocutors emerge. The point of Lacan's critique of mediation is not that mediation between the addressee and addressor does not exist, rather the point of the critique is that one cannot account for speech simply on the basis of this mutual mediation of meaning: as a manifestation of symbolic processes, speech produces both the interlocutors and the conditions for locution.

Thus, intersubjectively mediated speech is not the cause of rhetorical action; it is the effect of rhetorical action whereby symbolic speech elicits the "coming into being of the other in . . . mediation."[35] A conception of communicative exchange that sees speech as disclosive, expressive, or even strategic misses the mark if it presumes that the speaker and recipient pre-exist the act of speech. The other is both constituted by and framed for the speaker in the act of address. If the other is "revealed" in speech, revelation points to the fact that speech is not a site of shared meaning, but of math, or the routinized combination and substitution of signifying elements that prefigures the emergence of the other. Thus, the emergence of the other reveals the durable, formal significative properties inherent in the metonymic operation of the unconscious. The concept of revelation comports closely with a conception of rhetoric as an "analytic finding" of the formal relations that constitute discourse as opposed to "hermeneutic seeking." Finding is, for Lacan, a specifically rhetorical mode that invokes the rhetorical tradition's conception of *inventio* as discovery: "You cannot fail to see that in the celebrated expression of Picasso, 'I do not seek, I find,' that this finding (*trouver*), the *trobar* of the Provençal troubadours and *trouvères,* and all the schools of rhetoric, that takes precedence over the seeking."[36]

Even though speech does not express the contents of the unconscious by expressing their movement in transparently accessible form, speech instantiates the symbolic function in the movements of "*Enstellung,* distortion, transportation" that arise naturally from accidental metonymic connection and metaphorical condensations of meaning, and subsequently unfold "in the dimension of revelation." Speech overflows with possibilities for meaning because of the beyond from which it flows. It "is instituted within the structure of the semantic world . . . of language. . . . [S]peech never has one single meaning, nor the word one single use. All speech possesses a beyond, sustains various functions, [and] encompasses several meanings."[37] What is the nature of this beyond? For Lacan it is the big "O" Other.

Lacan's conception of the Other borrows from the continental tradition of a generalized alterity that functions in the life of the subject, producing for it an exterior point that founds the logic of relation. The Other is the locus of the signifier, figuring the Symbolic as the ex-sistence of an exteriority exceeding the subject. But what is crucial about the Other is not so much its existence as its function. The idea of the Other marks the relationship of reduction, simplification, and comportment in the object relation: to relate to something as an object is to render it both intelligible and representable in ways that occlude the broader set of affective and signifying relations that produce it. An object is a stand-in for the Other, which is itself a placeholder for the signifying relation writ large. Dylan Evans frames this relationship between the specific and generalized Other like this:

> The little other is the other who is not really other, but a reflection and projection of the Ego. . . . [It is] simultaneously the counterpart and the specular image . . . entirely inscribed in the Imaginary order. . . . The big Other designates radical alterity, an other-ness which transcends the illusory otherness of the imaginary because it cannot be assimilated through identification. Lacan equates this radical alterity with language and the law, and hence the big Other is inscribed in the order of the Symbolic. Indeed, the big Other *is* the Symbolic insofar as it is particularized for each subject.[38]

Defining the Other as the locus of the sign is less about imputing a positive existence to the Other than providing a counterpoint to the idea of the object relation as a necessary reduction. In the initial phases of Lacan's work the idea of the Other represents the locus and hypostatization of the alterity of the sign and the conceptual foil to the object. As Lacan's understanding of the sign evolves, so too does the character of the Other/object relation. In seminar eight, *The Transference,* instead of seeing the Other as the foil to the other/object, Lacan begins to see the idea of the object as contained within the Other. Although there is still a relationship of reduction present in the idea that the object is a specification of the Other, this move changes the nature of the reductive relationship substantially by admitting that the relationship of reduction also entails a relationship of dependence and mutual determination. Jacques Alain Miller notes in his essay, "Extimacy," that "the Other, in [*The Transference*], is no longer only the place of the signifier, there the object is included in the Other. . . . Something has been introduced in Lacan's teaching which has only been understood recently, i.e., the devalorization of the Other of the signifier. That is what allows us to understand . . . how [the object] as [surplus] founds not only the Other's alterity but also what is real in the Symbolic Other. It is not a matter of a link of integration, of interiorization, but of an articulation of extimacy."[39] The Other is extimate to the object in that instead of a relationship of exclusion, where the object and Other were defined by a dialectic of interiority and exteriority, "extimacy" defines the nature of the relationship between the object/other and the generalized Other by seeing them as mutually determined but not necessarily mediated. If intimacy implies a conception of internality, extimacy implies that what critics would locate as internal, as seemingly at the core of a conception of identity, is, by nature, in excess of identity. Extimacy does not mean the same thing as saying something is "external" to identity, because that which is extimate is included both in the constitution of an object and in the identity of the subject. Thus, extimacy implies the paradoxical internalization of a relation of non-relation. Here, the idea of other as locus or hypostases recedes in favor of an understanding of an Other that does not "exist," but that is constituted functionally in the articulation of an extimate relation. Lacan "could thus say," argues Miller, that "'the Other does not exist,' which does not prevent the Other from functioning, for many things function without existing. . . . [T]he sentence, 'The Other does not exist,' is meaningless if it does not imply that a . . . exists. . . . [T]he Other that functions is not [R]eal."[40] That the Other does not exist does not mean that it does not exert regulatory effects in the life of the subject. Although the Other exerts a constitutive function for subjects and discourses, purchasing for them a degree of stability, this quality is less a result of the existence of the Other than the rhetorically figured investments that situate the subject in relationship to the economy that constitutes it. This articulation of the Other drives rhetoric toward an understanding of the relationship between the formal rhetorical functions that constitute subjects and discourses and the concrete practices of speech that figure the subject in relation to these practices. More importantly, one might extend Miller's claim to lodge a critique of structuralist understandings of Lacan's work that rely on making the "big Other" the ground of symbolic forms. If the relation between the object and the Other is extimate, then the Other only comes to play the role that it does in the discourse of the subject as a function of its empirical grounding in the subject's practices of relation to objects.

Schema L, or the Others of Speech

The simplest model of communication has often been schematized like this:

Sender ⟶ Receiver

This model embodies the basic presuppositions Lacan identifies in the ideology of communication: dyadic relation, transmission, etc. Of course, there are many attempts to render the model in a more nuanced way, either by drawing the arrow to imply reciprocal interaction or by figuring the arrow as more than a channel for communication but as a medium. Despite such attempts, Lacan argues that there is something fundamentally broken about the model.

To speak is to speak to others, but one cannot forget the presence of a specific other: the self. When one speaks, it is not only other others, or the big "O" other of the sign that serves as an addressee. The fact that when one speaks one not only hears one's own voice but also serves as one's own addressee is the most crucial failing of the model. As Lacan frames it: "The phenomenon of speech can't be schematized by the image that serves a number of what are called communication theories—sender, receiver, and something that takes place in between. It seems to have been forgotten that among many other things in human speech, the sender is always a receiver, and at the same time, that one hears the sound of one's own words. It's possible not to pay attention to it, but it is certain that one hears it."[41] Why would an almost banal realization about speech figure so prominently in Lacan's critique of communication? Consider two splits that Lacan presents in a schema for communication that illustrates "the problems raised by the ego and the other, language and speech":[42]

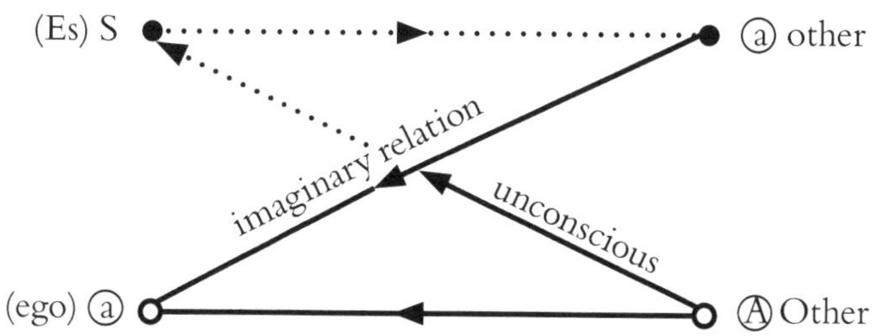

The first split, which lies between the material position of utterance that one inhabits and the "statuesque" projection of identity that Lacan identified in the "mirror stage," is located on what has traditionally been understood as the "sender" side of the model. In Schema L, this split is represented by separating the sender side of a traditional diagram of communication into two points: a point representing what Freud called the *Es* (or the "it") S and a point labeled (ego) a. As introduced briefly in chapter 1, the essence of the mirror stage is that a subject is split between the disorganized material, biological, and experiential reality of having a body and a retroactively inscribed imaginary image of the self. The split labels the uncoordinated existence of a body prior to its articulation as a subject and the ego, figured as an image of identity that retroactively imposes both unity and meaning on the field of the Es. Lacan argues that "the big S whose medium is speech . . . is not what a vain people thinks it is. . . . There is the real person who is before you . . . who manifestly captivates you and is capable of making you jump up and hug him . . . [in] an ill-considered act of the Imaginary Order."[43] In conflating these two points, the traditional model of communication misrecognizes what is at stake in speech because it elides the fact that the ego is an imaginary projection, and therefore is not only constitutively disconnected from the *Es*, but is itself a product of rhetorical artifice.

The second split occurs on the "receiver" side of the traditional model, which Lacan also splits into two discrete analytic foci: one that represents the apparent addressee of speech, the little "a," and the big "O" (or "A") Other. Understanding the Lacanian framing of the Other's relation to the subject and desire requires careful reference to his use of capital letters. The French word for other, *autre*, begins with an "a." So, for example, Lacan's famous formula for the fundamental fantasy, which is the most basic representation of the imaginary relation, ($ ◊ a), hypothetically names the way that the split subject ($) relates to its object or other by desiring it (a). But this little "a" object or other can only be read if one also reads the enthymeme; that the small "a" in the formula, the *objet petit a,* implicitly refers to a necessary reduction of the Other to an object.

Lacan is uncharacteristically clear on this point. In the seminar *On Feminine Sexuality,* Lacan argues that "the aim of [his] teaching is, insofar as it pursues what can be said and enunciated on the basis of analytic discourse, to dissociate *a* and *A* by reducing the first to what is related to the Imaginary and the other to what is related to the Symbolic."[44] The purpose of the analytic dissociation of *a* and *A* is to interrupt the easy slippage between the order of the Imaginary and the order of the Symbolic as a way of highlighting the primacy of the (A) in the production of the subject, as opposed to seeing the subject as a function of the intersubjective relation with little "a" others. Therefore, even though the subject's ($) desire is for the "desire of the Other," specific others are epiphenomenal in some sense; they mediate the more primary relationship for the desire of the Symbolic order, or for a transcendental foundation in the order of language, even if this relationship cannot inhere by definition.

In an argument with fellow psychoanalyst Daniel Lagache, quoted by Anthony Wilden, Lacan writes, "[Our divergence] lies in the actual function which he [Lagache] confers on intersubjectivity. For intersubjectivity is defined for him in a relation to the otherness of the counterpart, a symmetrical relation. . . . [T]he subject learns to treat himself as an object through the other. My position is that the subject has to emerge as from the given of the signifiers which cover him in an Other which is their transcendental locus."[45] Lacan's dissent from an all-constituting intersubjectivity replaces a bilateral, symmetrical, and reciprocally constitutive direct relation between subjects with a tripartite, asymmetrical relation of indirection. Schema L contains four points, but only three of the points are others in the proper sense of the term. The broken lines on the diagram represent a relationship of immediation between the Es (S) and its three others. The relationship represented in Schema L breaks the symmetry of the intersubjectivity by assigning priority to the symbolic capital "A" Other, rendering the other others as little "a" and little "a" prime. In more practical terms, the primacy of the A is a nod to the disproportionate effectivity of the Symbolic in shaping the contours of the derivative others. Finally, Schema L replaces the direct relationship of mutual constitution between the self and other that characterizes intersubjectivity by seeing the terms of the relations between the S and its others both in terms of symbolically mediated indirection, and as the site of a fundamental blockage imposed by the imaginary relation.

The three others that serve as the addressees of speech emerge from the three distinct gaps in the order of discourse: between the subject's ideal "I" and the "it" (as revealed in the mirror stage), between the subject and its object or localized addressee, and between the big "O" Other and the little "o" other that serves as its proxy. The three others in speech then, are: the subject's imaginary understanding of itself is addressed in speech by virtue of the fact that when one speaks, one hears the sound of one's own voice; the image of the specific other (a) who serves as the manifest addressee of speech (the image of the audience); and the big "O" Other, or the representation of the alterity of logic of symbolization and sign.

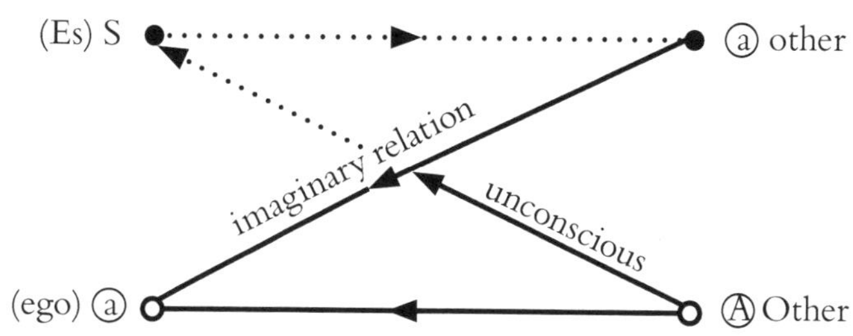

What schema L reveals is not simply that these three others are present in and constitute the situation of speech. The point of Schema L is to show how the relations between these three others implicate communication.

Two significant points stem from this account, both of which interrupt the idea of the intersubjective relationship. First, the specific (a') other is also an object; and second, privileging the specific other or set of others in speech elides the function of the big "O" Other. That one also hears one's own voice when one speaks does not simply indicate a kind of foundational narcissism in speech, nor does it simply prove that speech is self-interested. Rather, Lacan is pointing towards the tight complementarity between the Imaginary as a way of figuring the self, and the Imaginary as a mode of figuring who the other is when he says that "the subject loses himself in the machinations of language, in the labyrinth of referential systems made available to him by the state of cultural affairs in which he is more or less an interested party. . . . [T]he ego isn't even conceivable without the system, if one can put it this way, of the other. The ego has a reference to the other . . . [and] is constituted in relation to the other. It is its correlative."[46] Imaginary engagements with the other demonstrate that subjects do not seek to relate to a specific other in its irreducible uniqueness, but rather by projection—subjects do not relate to the other to know it, but subjects figure the other in ways that are functional for them, which is an elaborate way of saying that subjects address others as objects to confirm their pre-existent understandings of the world.

The ego is both the means by which the subject and specific objects are constituted and put into imaginary relation with others. Through analysis, argues Lacan, we learn "that the ego is an absolutely fundamental form for the constitution of objects. . . . [I]t perceives . . . its fellow being in the form of the specular other. This form of the other has a very close relation to the ego, which can be superimposed on it, and we write it as *a'*."[47] As a result, images of the other retroactively shore up the identity of the subject who addresses them. This is the point of Lacan's maxim that in speech "the subject receives his message from the other in inverted form."[48] When one addresses another, the act of address has implications for both the addressee's and the addressor's identities; for example, when I refer to someone as my student, I imply that I am their professor. As Lacan puts it, "communication [makes] the other speak as such."[49] The implication of this argument is that the relation with another is less a mode of accessing the other on its own terms than a means of retroactively constructing the equivalence of the Es with the ego, and therefore of constructing and performing a relation to one's own subjectivity that imputes coherence to the self.[50] That the sender is the receiver is another way of saying that the act of speaking (or even of receiving speech, for that matter) is framed by an imaginary projection of who the sender and the receiver are.

In this sense, the producer of speech never has access to its addressee on its own terms, but instead only speaks to a projection of the addressee, and this projection does more than provide an understanding, for example, of a speech's intended audience: speakers are invested in an image of the audience because such a picture is effective not only in theorizing the available means by which a speaker might persuade an audience, but also because this picture figures and renders the social world intelligible for the speaker or addressor. One could reverse the polarities and say basically the same thing about the act of reading. A reader of a text, audience member of a speech, or critic of either never has access to the point of a text's production, nor to the intentions that animate it, but only has access to the text as framed through an imaginary relationship saturated with investments in sustaining a picture of the reader's world: "If speech is founded on the existence of the Other, the true one, language is so made as to return to us in the objectified other, to the other whom we can make what we want of, including thinking that he is an object. . . . [L]anguage is as much there to found us in the Other as to drastically prevent us from understanding him."[51] Put differently, communication fails because intersubjectivity is impossible. If subjects and their discourses are produced symbolically, and if subjects engage others only through the mediating principle of the sign and by reducing them to objects, a condition of shared intersubjectivity can never inhere in human relations:

> [W]e think there are subjects other than us, that authentically intersubjective relations exist. . . . [W]e in fact address A_1, A_2, those who we do not know, true Others, true subjects.
>
> They are on the other side of the wall of language, where in principle I never reach them. Fundamentally it is them I'm aiming at every time I utter true speech, but I always attain *a', a"* through reflection. I always aim at true subjects, and I have to be content with shadows. The subject is separated from the Others, the true ones, by the wall of language.[52]

Privileging the relation between the ego and the specific other occludes the subject's relationship with the big "O" symbolic Other. The pivotal point of schema L lies at the broken intersection of the crossed lines in the middle of the diagram, where the imaginary relation intersects the line representing the unconscious. At this crossing the imaginary relation between subjects interferes with the revelation of the unconscious because "what pertains to the ego is always perceived, appropriated via the intermediary of an other, for whom the subject always retains . . . the fundamental image of the ego. Hence the misapprehensions [*méconnaissances*] thanks to which misunderstandings no less than ordinary communication—which itself rests on the said misunderstandings—become established."[53] As "the plane of the mirror" and "the symmetrical world of *egos* and of the homogenous others," the imaginary relation gains a "false reality" in the life of the subject, by establishing relations of identification.[54] This false reality intersects the movement between the Symbolic and the Es by sealing off attention to the ways that the subject and its others are produced by a symbolic logic. Put more simply, the imaginary functions of rhetoric foreclose attention to the Symbolic by ascribing to the imaginary plane a "false reality, which nonetheless is a verified reality. . . . When the subject talks to his fellow beings, he uses ordinary language, which holds imagined egos to be things that are not simply *ex-sisting,* but real."[55] We might consider three analogies for what happens at this intersection, two of which are drawn from Lacan's work, and another inspired by contemporary theorist of technology Friedrich Kittler: the tessera, the palimpsest, and the computer.

The tessera was a form of coinage made of wood, bone, or ivory that ancient Romans used to identify themselves and to exchange for goods. Like all coins, the more that the tessera was used, the more the markings that made it distinctive, and therefore more valuable than an unmarked fragment of wood or bone, were effaced. Lacan notes that the "analyst's art" does not aim at an understanding of the specific contents of speech, but "on the contrary" it "involve[s] suspending the subject's certainties until their final mirages have been consumed. . . . [H]owever empty this discourse may seem, it is so only if taken at face value—the value that justifies Mallarmé's remark, in which he compares the common use of language to the exchange of a coin whose obverse and reverse no longer bear but eroded faces, and which people pass from hand to hand 'in silence.' "[56] Completing the analogy, Lacan notes that "speech, even when almost completely worn out, retains its value as a *tessera*."[57] If the markings on the tessera represent the Imaginarily derived contents of discourse, the effaced tessera represents the material functions of the symbolic in speech—the more one attends to the numismatic markings that give the tessera its distinctiveness, the less one is able to engage the material conditions of exchange that allow the tessera to be so marked in the first place.

Of course, one could argue that it is in fact possible to pay attention to both the markings on the tessera and their material substrate. Employing the metaphor of the palimpsest in the "Response to Jean Hyppolite's Commentary on Freud's *Verneinung*," Lacan frames the chiasmus in Schema L not simply as a distraction, but as an erasure. Because parchment was a rare commodity in antiquity, writers often reused it by erasing what was written on it, producing a palimpsest, a blank space for writing. For Lacan, the palimpsest represents the fact that "immemorial forms" of the "symbolic text" are erased in the "palimpsest of the Imaginary" to make room for the specific contents and modes of relation that constitute the Imaginary.[58] As palimpsest, the imaginary text is only "communicable" if it efficiently effaces the symbolic text that precedes it.

Inspired by Friedrich Kittler, one might also think of the relationship between the Imaginary and Symbolic in speech through an analogy to the personal computer.[59] Our primary points of interface with the computer—the screen, the images and sounds that it presents, the keyboard, and the mouse—provide us with a familiar and easily navigable communicative environment. Usually, the user is not conscious of the other processes (both material and digital) that are constantly working to make the experience possible: the software, binary coding, and the hardware that support the digital interface. This is not to say that use of a personal computer necessarily excludes attention to these things (we are often made painfully aware of them, when, for example, the system crashes). Rather, the problem is the way that our comfort with the digital interface lulls us into taking for granted the vast array of symbolic and material processes that cause words to appear on the screen. Communication, of course, is the "interface" par excellence—if "communication" represents the interface with the computer screen, the more one is drawn into these interfaces, the less one is attentive to the codes and processes, or to the tropes and points of investment that enable the interface. The ideology of communication often works at cross-purposes with attention to rhetoric, or to the function of trope and investment in prefiguring the subject's encounter with discourse.[60] Thus, a question emerges: what kind of interpretive practice would be up to the task of reading both the logic of the Symbolic *and* the imaginary contents and modes of relation that populate it?

Provocation: Returning to a Science of Oratory

One of the most hallowed maxims of rhetorical studies is that rhetoric is an art—a techne for engaging discourse in the properly Aristotelian sense of the term. Techne implies a systematic mode of experiential knowledge, but often in declaring that rhetoric is an art, the accent of this declaration falls on the intuitive and the experiential facets of techne at the expense of the more systematic charge inherent in it. While for much of the rhetorical tradition, techne has primarily taken the valence of a prudential guide for intuitive judgment, Lacan turns to rhetoric to confer on psychoanalysis a scientific status.

Lacan's claims to the "science" of rhetoric respond to a number of critics who had framed psychoanalysis as an alchemical mix of unfounded theories, intuitions and inherited practices. Borrowing from Karl Popper's philosophy of science, such critiques of psychoanalysis argued that analytic practice was non-falsifiable, resting on the idea that no empirical evidence could be mustered to refute it. Any claim to evidence to the contrary of Freudian theories could always be elided by generating another explanation with dubious empirical grounding to account for potential exceptions. In drawing on rhetoric as a systematic mode for theorizing the nature of the sign, representation, and the logic and social functions of discourse, Lacan rescues Freudian categories from non-falsifiability. Rhetoric, which is so squarely rooted in "art," became one of Lacan's most powerful allies in articulating psychoanalysis as a science, providing a vocabulary for attending to the repeatable elements of signification that might be held up to empirical verification.

Lacan vacillated at different points in his career on psychoanalysis's status as a science, arguing at points that it was clearly a science, at others that it was not, and at others that it was a special kind of science.[61] Generally, Lacan's early career embodied the strongest claim for the scientific status of psychoanalysis, while in his later career he became less invested in the idea, arguing that it need not attempt to assume scientific status to validate itself.[62]

What is most interesting about the ambivalence toward science in Lacan's thought is that at each instance where the relationship between psychoanalysis and science is at stake, the question of rhetoric is never far from the conversation. For example, in *The Psychoses* and *The Four Fundamental Concepts of Psychoanalysis,* Lacan argues that psychoanalysis is a science on the basis of its attention to a set of repeatable logical forms, specifically to trope as a way of specifying the possible connections underwriting discursive and representational practices. Other accounts read Lacan as eventually giving up on the idea that psychoanalysis is a science, but do so, once again, with explicit reference to rhetoric. For example, Stuart Schneiderman argues that by 1977 Lacan had given up the quest to prove psychoanalysis as a science, that "after having posed the question of the scientific status of psychoanalysis for so many years, he had come to the conclusion that it was not a science. The reason was one offered by Karl Popper, namely that psychoanalysis was 'irrefutable.' Lacan said that analysis was closest to rhetoric. . . . Thus analysis seeks to persuade but not convince, to persuade the analysand to recognize things that he knows already and to act on his desire."[63] Of course, one might take issue with the account of rhetoric that is implicit in this claim, particularly on the grounds that the framing of rhetoric in Schneiderman's account affirms an understanding of rhetoric exclusively through reference to persuasion, contingency, and probability—a conception that is, as I have been arguing, at odds with Lacan's understanding of the work of rhetoric. More accurately, rhetoric affords Lacanian psychoanalysis a status as a special kind of science by providing it with a set of techniques for paying attention to the mathematical qualities of discourse. Regardless of how one understands the moniker "science," rhetoric drives psychoanalysis toward a systematic account of the possible modes of connection that animate actually existing discourses, and toward an observation of the concrete functions of trope in the social life of the subject.

Lacan derives this understanding of psychoanalysis as the systematic science of attending to discourse from Freud. For example, in *The Interpretation of Dreams* Freud argues for a practice of reading dreams that revised received methods for interpreting dreams. Prior to Freud's intervention there was a long-standing tradition that held that an image in a dream correlated with an unconscious meaning in much the same way that a word in a dictionary correlates with a definition. In order to found his mode of dream interpretation, Freud dissents from a definitional understanding of dreams by distinguishing between manifest "dream content" and the underlying logic of a dream, or the "dream-thought."[64] Although the manifest content of a dream may seem utterly random, it is driven by the dream-thought expressed in it, investing the specific contents of the dream with a meaning dependent on the thought that articulates it. For Freud there is no universal protocol for the expression and interpretation of dream contents, but rather a set of associations unique to an individual which, although not uniform in content, are bound by a more universal logic of expression.

It is tempting to see in Freud's presentation of the interpretation of dreams a cognitive semiotics that verges on a proto-presentation of Saussure's conception of differential signification, albeit sixteen years prior to the publication of the *Course in General Linguistics.* Each element in a dream means something not because it has an intrinsic referent, but rather because it is defined by a relationship of difference to other elements in the dream content, and cumulatively the structure of differentially related signs allows for an interpretation of the underlying dream-thought. Naturally, this is the reading of Lacan's employment of Freud's *Interpretation of Dreams* by those who see Lacanian psychoanalysis as an integration of Freud's unconscious and the insights of Saussure.[65] The difficulty arises when one tries to determine what exactly Lacan is attempting to do by reading the regularities of structure that animate dreams and, by extension, discourse. On one account, this reading produces a logic of dreams and discourse that emphasizes structure at the expense of the empirical. But a second account replaces the structuralist poetic account with a rhetorical conception of trope, inventing a science of rhetoric that forces attention to the interchange between form and its empirical manifestations. To instantiate a rhetorical relation between the logics and manifestation of dream contents, Lacan turns to a science of oratory that drives analytic labor toward the empirical life of discourses.[66]

"What specifies a science," writes Lacan," "is having an object."[67] To say that a science must have an object elicits an objection that specifying an "object" presumes a science engages something given in advance as opposed to contingently made. But approaching an object requires equal parts analytic rigor and prudence: "we must be very prudent, because this object changes . . . as the science develops. . . . [W]e cannot say that the object of modern physics is the same now as at its birth."[68] Attention to a changing object implies a relationship of mutual determination between the mode of inquiry and the objects that such a mode takes up. A science is not a general theory to be mapped onto reality because sciences are parasitic on the specific. As Lacan argues, science always begins with the particular: "To be sure, analysis as a science is always a science of the particular. The coming to fruition of an analysis is always a unique case, even if the unique cases lend themselves . . . to some generality. . . . [A]nalysis is an experience of the particular."[69]

But what is the particular object around which a science of oratory might emerge? The answer is the economy of trope and enjoyment. Claiming that Freud drew attention to a "fundamental" opposition between metaphor and metonymy in "mechanisms of dreams," Lacan argues that "what Freud calls condensation is what in rhetoric one calls metaphor, what one calls displacement is metonymy."[70] That this reference to a rhetoric of trope frames Lacan's application of the vocabulary of structural linguistics is clear from the concluding sentence of this paragraph: "It's for this reason that in focusing attention back onto the signifier we are doing nothing other than returning to the starting point of the Freudian discovery."[71]

In "The Function and Field of Speech and Language in Psychoanalysis," Lacan argues that the core insight of *The Interpretation of Dreams* might be fruitfully applied to more than just unpacking dreams. The logic that inheres in dream work is the same logic that underwrites the function of speech generally. If, following Lacan's reading of *Interpretation of Dreams,* one is inclined to agree that speech serves as a synecdoche for rhetorical processes generally; by extension one might conclude that speech offers privileged insight into the functioning of everyday discourses. Thus it is no surprise that Lacan recommends instruction in rhetoric as an indispensable component of analytic practice. According to Lacan, this realization should compel attention to the function of "*rhetoric* . . . ellipsis and pleonasm, hyperbaton or syllepsis, regression, repetition, apposition—these are the syntactical displacements; metaphor, catachresis, antonomasis, allegory, metonymy, and synecdoche—these are the semantic condensations in which Freud teaches us to read the intentions . . . out of which the subject modulates his oneiric discourse."[72] This extension of Freud's dream work to speech by means of a globalization of trope founds the possibility of psychoanalysis as a science, via recourse to the scientific properties of oratory:

> At the bottom of the Freudian mechanism one rediscovers these old figures of rhetoric which over time have come to lose their sense for us but which for centuries elicited a prodigious degree of interest. Rhetoric, or the art of oration, was a science and not just an art. We now wonder, as if at an enigma, why these exercises could have captivated whole groups of men for such a long time. If this is an anomaly it's analogous to the existence of psychoanalysis, and it's perhaps the same anomaly that's involved in man's relationships to language, returning over the course of history, recurrently, with different ramifications and now presenting itself to us from a scientific angle in Freud's discovery.[73]

Why wonder at the "enigma" of a science of oratory and the "exercises" that constituted it? The "exercises" that Lacan is most likely referring to were the progymnasmata—the graduated sequence of somewhat formulaic pedagogical practices that introduced the student of oratory to the inventional moves one might make in composing and/or delivering a speech. This attention to form, embodied in both a theory of arrangement and delivery, attuned the budding orator to the regularities in speech that render inventional moves not only intelligible, but potentially eloquent. Oratorical practice had foreseen and, long in advance of contemporary linguistics, "discovered" the formal properties animating discursive practice.

There are two senses of the word "formal" for Lacan: one that relies on quantification and another that relies, if not on math as we typically understand it, then on the mathematizable, or that which can be symbolically rendered as a repeatable relation.[74] A science is defined by mathematization, as opposed to quantification: "what is distinctive about positive science, modern science, isn't quantification but mathematization and specifically combinatory, that is to say linguistic, mathematization which includes series and iteration."[75] The oratorical tradition discovered that rhetorical invention was scientific: in discovering the progymnasmata, the tradition articulated a conception of *inventio* (invention) as the discovery of repeatable symbolic forms. Lacan prefers the first sense of "formal" because it comports with oratorical pedagogy's insight that language is mathematizable (amenable to a description of its repeatable formal properties), which is the condition of possibility for a science of oratory. The science of oratory discovers a mode of knowing that would eventually make "linguistics the most advanced of the human sciences" by specifying that which is formally repeatable in the life of the subject and its discourses.[76]

This understanding of rhetoric moves it from a prudential "art" of the intuitive intersubjective judgments to the symbolic science of forms. For Lacan, an art premised on the disciplining of critical intuition does not move beyond the Imaginary because "everything intuitive is far closer to the Imaginary than the Symbolic."[77] In place of the art of intersubjectively grounded intuition, Lacan calls for attention to the trans-subjective apparatus of the Symbolic: "the important thing here is to realize that the chain of possible combinations of the encounter can be studied as such, as an order which subsists in rigor, independently of all subjectivity. . . . [T]he symbol is embodied in an apparatus—with which it is not to be confused, the apparatus being just its support. And it is embodied in a literally trans-subjective way."[78] This understanding of rhetoric as science does not abandon the subject; rather, it decenters the subject as a taken-for-granted interpretive maxim, replacing attention to what goes on between subjects with the formal movement of tropes, a movement that is mathematizable, and therefore amenable to a formal scientific account of its effects:

> In as much as he is committed to a play of [the Symbolic], to a symbolic world . . . man is a decentered subject. Well, it is with this same play, this same world, that the machine is built. The most complicated machines are made only with words.
>
> Speech is first and foremost that object of exchange whereby we are reorganized. . . . That is how the circulation of speech begins, and it swells to the point of the symbol which makes algebraic calculations possible. The machine is the structure detached from the activity of the subject. The symbolic world is the world of the machine.[79]

The world of the symbolic is machinic in a very specific way: only insofar as it relies on the set of regularized, logically possible connections between words and other words. In other words, the Symbolic is machinic because it is tropologically constituted. But because the Symbolic is tropologically constituted, its machinic nature is premised on the various failures in unicity that invite the trope as a compensatory function. Thus, if the Symbolic is a machine, it is a machine that fails. In the next chapter, I take up the paradox of the failing machine by suggesting the metaphor of *economy* as a way of parsing the relationship between the machinic (or automatic) and its failure in the life of the Symbolic.

4
Toward an Economy of Trope

> When one reads the rhetoricians, one realizes that they never get to an entirely satisfactory definition of metaphor, or of metonymy.
>
> —Jacques Lacan, *The Psychoses*

Though the proper object of rhetoric has proved historically malleable, Lacan centers rhetoric as a science on the economy of tropes and investments that constitute the subject and its discourses. As Gilbert Chaitin has pointed out, the basic operation at play in this economy is deceptively simple. According to Chaitin, Lacan's account of the economy of trope is organized around two basic exchanges, to which I will add a third. First, a signifier is exchanged for the "original nothingness of the subject . . . the catachretic substitution of something—a signifier—for nothing."[1] This exchange is catachretic because in it the subject is virtually created ex nihilio, essentially "troped" into existence by the metaphorical substitution of a symbolically constituted form for the emptiness that precedes it. Second, as a subject begins to take on concrete empirical form, it accretes habits of relation and identity by substituting "another signifier for the first."[2] Put in more concrete terms, if the subject is an "empty signifier" in the first act of substitution, in the second exchange, a subject takes on a determinate identity that defines who it is, what it believes, and that situates it in a field of meaning. Although such identitarian commitments are the product of rhetorical artifice, they function as if they are an intrinsic part of the subject's being as an extension of the formal properties of metaphoric substitution. Third, as an extension of the subject's metaphorical assumption of an identity, the subject positions itself and assumes modes of relation to others, thereby entering into exchanges with others in the field of discourse.

There is an elegance to this framing of Lacan's economy of trope: a subject is substituted for the nothingness that precedes it; an identity is substituted for the empty form of the subject; and finally, the subject among others, who takes on specific modes of social relation, is substituted for the only apparently insular subject of identity. This model could be rendered in even more concise fashion: as Victoria Kahn notes in a treatment of Quintilian, the trope metalepsis represents the substitution or "transumption" of one trope for "another which is itself figurative."[3] The whole of Lacan's theory of trope could be accounted for as an elaborate version of metaleptic substitution of tropes for other tropes, although reducing Lacan's conception of trope to metalepsis would entail a risk: it elides the specificity of metaphor and metonymy as different modes of signifying articulation. But what distinguishes metaphor and metonymy? For Lacan, the difference between the two is not simply formal: while the distinction between metaphor and metonymy maintains a formal character, the distinction also relies on the differences in labor and investment that inhere in metonymic and metaphorical connections.

In this chapter I highlight the relationship between trope, labor, and investment at two distinct but inextricably intertwined locations of signifying labor. I will refer to the first, inspired by the work of Jean Joseph Goux, as the "general economy" of tropological exchange.[4] The general economy refers to the exchange of a signifier for the nothingness of the subject, and thus it is the site of the subject's relation to and production in discourse writ large. The general economy is the site of a number of elements of failed unicity that I identified earlier, including the trauma of entry into the Symbolic, the gap between subject and sign, and the impossibility of the social relation that stems from the intervention of the logic of signs.

If the general economy of tropological exchange marks the relationship between the sign and the genesis of the subject, it also serves as the regulatory principle for the specific economies of tropological exchange that constitute the subject and its imagined modes of social relation. Specific economies of tropological exchange are discrete configurations of tropes that individuals and groups take up in assuming public identitarian commitments. The specific economy names the space where subjects invest in texts and narratives about their relation to other subjects, where public discourses circulate, and where a subject takes on specific imagined modes of relation to others. Specific economies of tropological exchange encompass the second and third moments in the condensed economy of tropological exchange I introduced earlier, where subjects assume an identity and concrete modes of relations to others.

The distinction between the general and specific economies marks the difference between two sites of tropological labor and investment, but it also figures the modes of relation through which localized discursive practices refer to and are figured by the transcontextual work of the general economy. But the relationship between the general and specific economies is not unidirectional: specific economies of tropological exchange supplement the failed unicity that marks the general economy. The tropological exchanges that follow from the original substitution of the subject for the nothingness that precedes it not only make possible but demand the inscription of determinate identitarian content to the empty form of the Symbolic.

This demand is an extension of both "Schema L" and the "mirror stage," both of which hold that imaginary identifications shore up the subject in the face of the failed unicities that elicit the tropological production of the subject. Arguing for a distinction between general and specific economies of tropological exchange, I would like to draw attention to the ways that the Imaginary register of rhetoric presumes, relies on, and supplements the general economy of tropological exchange while simultaneously constituting the ground of the general economy. Figuring the general and specific economies as mutually implicated authorizes a rhetorical reading of individual discourses subject to the relation between signification, subjectification, and the localized practices that instantiate these relations. The distinction between the general and specific economies of tropological exchange allows rhetorical theory to connect the functions of the two orders in an analytically precise way: the specific economies of exchange are not slavishly determined by the general economy, but neither are they independent of tropological functions that ground rhetoric's ontology.

To figure the implications of this distinction for rhetorical studies, I begin with a schematic treatment of strategies for conceiving tropes in contemporary rhetoric. Second, I provide a reading of metaphor and metonymy (the primary tropes for Lacan), beginning with a treatment of the sign as an accident, tracing the implications of trope as a mode of accommodating this accident in Lacan's seminar *The Psychoses* and in "The Agency of the Letter in the Unconscious." From there, I turn to a treatment of the constitution of the subject and its modes of relation to other subjects, situating a subject as one node in the economy of tropological exchange. Next, I argue for the virtues of understanding Lacan's work through the metaphor of economies, primarily by reading his categories of *tuché* and *automaton* as a way of addressing the relationship between structure and contingency in his work. Finally, I conclude with a provocation on the idea of reading in psychoanalysis, gesturing toward the rhetorical analytic that this theory of trope authorizes.

Trope in Contemporary Rhetorical Studies

How does the contemporary iteration of the rhetorical tradition address trope? There are a number of easily identifiable places where trope has been afforded the status of a generative ontological category at the borders of the rhetorical tradition. Four come to mind almost immediately: Nietzsche's famous aphorism that truth is a mobile army of metaphors;[5] Giambattista Vico's theory of metaphor, metonymy, synecdoche, and irony as the four phases of historical *ricorso* (return);[6] Hayden White's analysis of trope as the "deep structural form of the historical imagination";[7] and Kenneth Burke's declaration of the "four master tropes" at the slippery line or "evanescent moment" between the "figurative and literal" conceptualization of the truth.[8]

Although there are moments where trope achieves a place of privilege in the rhetorical traditions as represented in communication and composition studies, the contemporary iterations of the rhetorical tradition tend to demarcate trope as a special class of rhetorical action as opposed to the general condition of possibility for rhetoric. In practice, American communication studies typically relies on one of three options for framing trope. One option largely continues the Ramist tradition of understanding trope as mere ornament, as a particularly artful and potentially persuasive way of saying something that could otherwise be said in direct denotative language. In this framing, figurative language can be significant insofar as it is publically persuasive, but it is subjugated to either the ideational content that the trope carries or to the ways that a troped presentation of an argument fits with the demands of a rhetorical situation. A second option understands trope as a range of associations that cohere around a signifier, usually indicated by the formulation "the trope of X," where X represents a specific set of discourses (for example, the trope of war). "The trope of X" identifies language that draws attention to its figural status and intervenes in a field of otherwise denotative discourses and therefore understands trope as a deviation from more direct employments of discourse.[9] Finally, following Burke's extension of Vico's "four master tropes" in the appendix to *A Grammar of Motives,* elements of the rhetorical tradition in communication studies engage tropes through their "role in the discovery and description of the truth."[10] In this approach to trope, critics primarily attend to the epistemic consequences of tropological framing. While the epistemic vision of trope sees it as an ineradicable element of human discourse, this approach does not make an a priori claim to the ontological status of trope in constituting language.

One might read the rhetorical tradition as an attempt to account for the effects of discourse around one of two poles: trope or persuasion. Paul de Man has argued that this is the essential antimony that gives rhetoric "the appearance of a history."[11] What is at issue in de Man's aporia is the relationship between the formal charge in rhetoric (represented by "trope") and the contextual charge (represented by persuasion). While an elegant solution suggests itself in arguing that rhetoric is about both trope and persuasion (which is one extension of the act of locating rhetoric around the Symbolic and Imaginary poles suggested in the first chapter), the question is this: when standard accounts of rhetorical theory locate the nexus of rhetorical effect, does the context or form of speech take primacy? To the extent that a theory of rhetoric emphasizes the contextual charge, it is less able to account for the transcontextual functions of trope; conversely, to the extent that a theory of rhetoric emphasizes the quasi-structuring functions of the formal charge, it forfeits attention to that which is unique to a given rhetorical situation. Extending de Man's insight, Peter de Bolla argues that this split enumerates the two basic approaches to rhetoric in a broad historical account of the rhetorical traditions: "What is rhetoric? Rhetoric, as it has been conceived from classical times to the present, is habitually defined in two distinct ways: the first concerns what might be called its substance and the second its effects. In terms of substance, rhetoric is defined as a system of tropes, the list of names such as metaphor, metonymy, and so forth, which refer to a number of different modes of substitution of words within the linguistic system."[12] But defined "in terms of its effects," argues de Bolla, "rhetoric is . . . the art of persuasion."[13]

Put in the context of the whole rhetorical tradition, the three predominant options for understanding trope in American communication studies implicitly decide in favor of persuasion, understood as the proprietary accommodation of discourse to its context, as the privileged bearer of rhetoric's effects. From its inception around Wichelns's call to attend to the persuasive effects of speech, an intersubjective account of a contextually mediated theory of persuasion constitutes the dominant history of rhetoric in the American tradition of speech communication. This history renders another possible history that employs trope as a strand organizing rhetoric around the formal charge in language as a minor history of rhetoric.

One might object that rhetorical studies' account of persuasion references tropes all the time. But it is not really the generative ontological status of trope that is at issue in readings of rhetoric as persuasion; instead, it is the persuasiveness of individual figures that becomes the object of analysis for conventional rhetorical studies. Contemporary rhetorical praxis holds, argues de Bolla, that "in order to identify the presence of metaphor—the trope that has determined a figurative use—we must look at a specific use of language. We do not see metaphor as such . . . but its effect in language. . . . [W]hat we see are words that are used metaphorically."[14] Lacan's conception of trope as generative of all signs and, by extension, meanings represents an alternative understanding of trope that views the tropes as generative as opposed to simply ornamental and as constitutive of discourse as opposed to being a discrete manifestation of it. For Lacan, trope does not only mark the formal charge in language but is the condition of possibility for speech, the subject, and the social.

Metaphor and Metonymy

For Lacan metonymy describes any contingent connection between a sign or representation and its intended referent, between series of signs, or more broadly as any point where signs and representations are articulated to one another as a point of investment. Metonymy has two discrete functions: it marks the difference between individual signifiers, and it organizes them in contiguous relation by connecting them together. Metaphor also describes two discrete but interrelated processes. First, metaphor describes the function whereby a metonymically generated signifying connection comes to stand in for its referent. Ludwig Wittgenstein argues in *Culture and Value* that "the limit of language is shown by its being impossible to describe the fact which corresponds to (is the translation of) a sentence, without simply repeating the sentence."[15] Language is limited by the impossibility of generating an extrinsic grounding relationship with that which is external to it. What holds true of the sentence also holds true of signifiers and representations more generally: signifiers and representations do not automatically or effortlessly refer to an external Real. Words and representations only function when subjects invest in them by acting or speaking as if speech stands in for the thing. For Lacan, metaphor marks the "standing in" function. Second, metaphor is a particularly affectively saturated connection that organizes a field of metonymic connections around a central figure. Metaphor names rhetorical processes whereby certain signifiers and representations take on disproportionate weight in a signifying chain via condensation. When specific metonymic connections become particularly significant points of investment, organizing a set of subsidiary metonymic connections around them, such connections become metaphors.

Even this treatment is a bit too schematic. One way of articulating Lacan's basic insight is to say that all signification is accidental. Signification is accidental because there is no origin point for language that can found a direct and descriptive referential relation. Given the classical definition of metonymy as an "accidental connection," the concept of metonymy is particularly well suited to defining a connection between sign and referent that is simply the result of artifice as opposed to some preordained principle of connection. But accidental connections need some principle that would make them durable: signifiers need to meaningfully stand in for referents if they are to be effective. Like metonymy, metaphor is uniquely positioned to describe this relationship, given the longstanding tradition of defining metaphor as a word, concept, or image that "stands in for" something else. As soon as the human signifies, it is implicated in the symbolic economy of trope: all language is "troped" because it relies on the functions of metonymy to establish differentiation and connection and on the work of metaphor to establish condensation and reference.

There is, claims Lacan, no "zero-degree" descriptive discourse.[16] All signs and representations are tropologically inflected in that they rely on the basic metonymic connection of a signifier with its referent, with other signs, and on the work of metaphor to establish the possibility of reference. Here, Lacan's theory of trope relies on the original Greek understanding of trope as *tropos.* Hayden White's exegesis of the concept of trope captures the conceptual richness of the varied elements contained in the idea of trope under the rubric of turning. In Classical Greek, tropos means to turn, but later Koiné usage also implied the idea of a "manner" or "way" of doing something.[17] This conception of trope "comes into modern Indo-European languages by way of *tropus,* which in Classical Latin . . . meant [a] 'figure of speech,' and in Late Latin . . . [meant] 'mood' or 'measure.' . . . All of these meanings . . . sedimented in the . . . word trope, capture the force of the concept."[18] As turning, for Lacan, trope takes on a globally constitutive discursive function, encompassing the manner of signifying, a mode of figuration, and a mood or affective disposition within discourse.

A Lacanian tropology encompasses all these functions of trope. Also by seeing all language as turning, there is no direct reference or description but only the work of trope in attempting to turn the signifier toward its referent in the absence of an automatic referential relation. If turning is the essence of the language, this essence is not a result of structure: metaphor and metonymy are not pre-given structures that are internal to language but are instead the basic forms that signifiers can take in turning toward their referents. Lacan's conception of trope names a relation that emerges in situ as opposed to a transcontextual apparatus that exists apart from the subjects that employ it. The Symbolic only seems to take on the character of a preordained structure in theorizing the "emergence" of language because such theorizing is already caught up in the basic network of moves that authorize signification. Thus, a vision of language as structure is less a result of ascribing trope a metaphysical character than a constraint imposed on use by our dependence on the artifice of the sign: "We imagine that there must have been a time when people on this earth began to speak. So we admit of an emergence. But from the moment that the specific structure of this emergence is grasped, we find it absolutely impossible to speculate on what preceded it other than by symbols which were always applicable. What appears to be new thus always seems to extend itself indefinitely into perpetuity, prior to itself."[19] Here Lacan is extending Jakobson's argument that trope is a natural result of the subject's experience in the field of language. Lacan claims that the relationship between metaphor and metonymy is fundamental to discerning the operations of discourse, a realization that he roots in Freud's reading of dream logic. But this fundamental feature is not a result of a prestructured form as much as it is an implication of the fact that the signified is missing or of the lack of an automatic referential relation between the signifier and signified: "what Freud calls condensation is what in rhetoric one calls metaphor, what he calls displacement is metonymy. The structuration, the lexical existence of the entire signifying apparatus, is the determinant . . . since the signifier [is] the instrument by which the missing signified expresses itself. . . . [I]n focusing attention back onto the signifier we are doing nothing other than returning to the starting point of the Freudian discovery."[20] But what is the character of this relationship? In *The Psychoses,* Lacan undertakes his fullest treatment of the relationship between metaphor and metonymy. Lacan begins by noting "metaphor is not the easiest thing in the world to speak about" because so many accounts of metaphor simply understand it to be "an abridged simile."[21]

Here Lacan is implicitly criticizing conceptions of metaphor as merely ornamental speech and as a simple comparison between two already established concepts. Lacan admits that there is something to this reading, noting that one might understand this function under the psychoanalytic category of "identification," but there is something more profound at play in metaphor: "our use of the term *Symbolic* leads us to restrict [metaphor's] sense, to designate only the metaphorical dimension of the symbol."[22] The connection between metaphor and identification introduces a crucial distinction between metaphor as a taken-for-granted similarity and identification as a mode of feigning similarity. Chaitin argues that "metaphor is a matter of identification rather than similarity" because metaphor is the precondition for producing similarity as opposed to simply naming similarities that inhere in signifieds.[23] Given a distinction between identification and similarity, a symbolic reading of the metaphor undoes the conception of metaphor as ornament, revealing that meaning is not the primary function in the metaphor: meaning is only "datum." The symbolic function of metaphor is a precondition for the intelligibility of the datum because the metaphoric relation simultaneously "deflects and commands" the signifier.[24] The metaphoric relation deflects the signifier as an extension of its character as a trope, which by necessity entails a "turning" toward a referent, but it commands the signifier because this act of turning constitutes both the signifier's direction and the effects that it will exert.

Lacan's theory of metaphor turns critical attention away from a rendering of metaphor as a bearer of meaning toward the logic of predication that underwrites the referential pretension. Metaphors work because they organize and attribute meanings, not simply because they rearrange already existing meanings. Prior to what a metaphor means, the metaphoric relation assigns meaning and "aligns signifiers," a fact that is often "neglected when symbolism is discussed . . . the dimension linked to the signifier's existence [and] organization."[25] Metaphor is symbol taken to the level of "metalanguage," which is another way of saying that the relation of similarity that underwrites the operation of metaphor is not simply a result of the transference of characteristics that are latent in signified but rather similarity is a result of the system of signifying relations.[26] Because metaphor names the operation of language as a "system of positional coherence," Lacan's theory of metaphor and metonymy aims at a theory of "signifying articulation."[27] If metaphor names the globally constitutive symbolic relation of predication and reference in this theory of articulation, metonymy names the principle of articulation that encompasses both contiguity and difference, which like metaphor is a kind of substitution, albeit one that functions by displacement and relates more to accidental connection than the condensation of meaning. For Lacan, metaphor and metonymy are opposites in at least one regard: while metaphor aims at the centralization or specification of determinate meanings via symbolic articulation, metonymy both articulates signifiers against other signifiers and produces new relations of contiguity. Where metaphor substitutes centripetally, for the sake of condensation, metonymy substitutes centrifugally by referring signifiers outward toward other signifying relations: "The rhetorical form that is the opposite of metaphor has a name—it's called metonymy[, which] involves substitution for something that has to be named—we are in fact at the level of the name [where] one thing is named by another that is its container, or its part, or that is connected to it."[28] Metaphor and metonymy are diametrically opposite movements from the perspective of their respective relations to meaning, but they are also crucially dependent on one another. While metonymy names the proliferative functions of signification, it is also the condition of possibility for articulating metaphor. Alternatively, although metaphor attempts to arrest the proliferation of meanings invoked by metonymy, the centripetal force of metaphor both relies on and never efficiently occludes the centrifugal movement of the metonymic connection.

Lacan frames this dynamic in the "Instance of the Letter," taking up Quintilian's famous example of the sail as a metonym for the ship:

> The properly signifying function in language has a name . . . metonymy. I shall refer only to the example of it given there: "thirty sails." . . . [T]he connection between ship and sail is nowhere other than in the signifier and that metonymy is based on the word-to-word nature of this connection. I shall designate as metonymy the first aspect of the actual field the signifier constitutes, so that meaning may assume a place there. . . . The other aspect is metaphor. . . . Metaphor's creative spark does not spring from the juxtaposition of two images, that is, of two actually equalized signifiers. It flashes between two signifiers, one of which has replaced the other by taking the other's place in the signifying chain, the occulted signifier remaining present by virtue of its (metonymic) connection to the rest of the chain.[29]

Metaphor and metonymy constitute two sites where the links in the signifying chain tend to fall apart. The first precarious link is the one between the subject's "intentional meaning and the apparatus of signifiers."[30] The tropological functions of language both introduce a divorce between intention and signification but are also, paradoxically, the means by which the subject negotiates this gap. The second precarious link is a "link of dissolution internal to the signifier. . . . [T]here is a sort of regressive decomposition [where] . . . language isn't reducible to the ideally primary language of the infant—but through a veritable *turning.*" The resonance between "turning" and tropos should not escape our attention: the signifier is not simply the domain of referential meanings but is instead constituted by the labor of trope in turning signifiers toward their signifieds.

In *The Psychoses,* Lacan poses metaphor and metonymy as the sites where "man [uses] speech to . . . get his bearings . . . as a function of his natural tendency to decompose in the presence of the Other."[31] A theory of the subject's investments in signifiers supplements the formally defined distinction between metaphor and metonymy, framing the difference between the two in terms of degree of investment. If the proliferative character of metonymy represents the condition of possibility for decomposition, metaphor represents a site where the subject labors to get its bearings, to centralize meaning around points of metaphorical condensation for the sake of imputing stability to the subject, others, and the modes of relation that inhere between them.

In "The Instance of the Letter in the Unconscious or Reason Since Freud" Lacan employs four algorithms to represent the relationships between signification, metaphor, and metonymy and the (de)composition of the subject. Despite claims that Lacan replaces a focus on rhetoric with a focus on math, here one finds an unambiguous metaphorical transposition of trope into math: the trope is still present in its mathematical erasure because math serves as a metaphor for the logic of sign. The first formula defines the "topography of the unconscious," the most basic material form that discourse takes. The "algorithm" is a repeat of the Saussurean sign, although Lacan is playfully equivocal about the terms in this schema. The capital "S" represents both "Subject" and "Signifier," and as detailed earlier, the unconscious "slides" the signified under the signifier and the subject: the metaphor of reference holds the signifier and subject in concrete relation to their signifieds,[32]

$$\frac{S}{s}$$

The relationship between, on the one hand, the signifier and subject and, on the other, the signified as a referent is crucially dependent on the "—" or the bar between the signifier and the signified. Unlike Saussure's bar, Lacan's is not a neutral placeholder simply marking the difference between the signifier and signified. The Lacanian bar implies both a relationship of difference, mutual dependence, and perhaps most importantly a literal bar to or blockage in correspondence that implies a site of labor: "A signifier is first of all that which has a meaning effect. . . . [B]etween the signifier and meaning there is something barred that must be crossed over."[33] Lacan specifies the first formulation of the subject/sign with a second more precise one:

$$f(S)\ \frac{1}{s}$$

Embodying an understanding of the signifying relation as a kind of work, Lacan refers to the relationship between the signifier and the signified in terms of a mathematical function. This formula details the function (f) of the signifier for the signifying subject (S), which slides the signified under the bar, producing representations that generate unicity for the subject (1). This formula marks the relation between reference to signifieds and the production of unicity, but the bar is also equivocal: reference to the signified both underwrites a conception of unicity but also structurally bars representations of unicity from ever being adequate to the signifieds that they represent.

This formula for the signifying relation requires two supplementary formulae: a formula for metonymy and a formula for metaphor. Lacan formulates metonymy via calculus:

$$f(S \ldots S')\ S \cong S(—)\ s$$

This formula can be read as follows: metonymy is the function (f) of the signifier (S) that ties together a chain of accidental connections (S . . . S'), and this function is homologous with (≡) the introduction of a bar between the signifier (S) and the signified (s). The signifier-to-signifier connection "allows for the elision by which the signifier instantiates lack of being in the object relation, using signification's referral value to invest it with the desire aiming at the lack it supports."[34] Here, Lacan has moved well beyond the formalist account of metonymy. The bar (—) is, as in all the preceding cases, equivocal, representing the "maintenance of the bar" as an act of labor that produces the material conditions for signifiers to be both differentiated and connected.[35] But, the bar (—) also "denotes the irreducible . . . resistance of signification as constituted in the relations between signifier and signified."[36] This definition of metonymy moves beyond a formal articulation of the metonym, primarily by figuring the place of desire as a form of investment that differentiates metaphor and metonymy.

What is desire here? Desire is not a result of internal or biological processes, but rather it is an effect of the lack entailed in failed unicity. There is no intrinsic connection between a given object and a subject's desire. Objects are not the natural referent of desire, but rather objects are a cause of desire, emerging in the context of a field composed by other subjects who also desire objects. Humans desire mimetically, or by desiring objects desired by the other: human "desire" writes Lacan, "is the desire of the other."[37] Desire is the desire of the other because the other lies tantalizingly beyond our reach—our impulse toward the other is a result of the unattainability of an authentic, transparent relation with both specific others and the Other. Thus, subjects do not desire as a result of intrinsic biological impulses (Lacan categorizes such impulses as "needs"), but rather subjects learn to desire mimetically, that is, by seeing what it is that others desire. I will return to this formulation in more detail in chapter 7, but for now I would simply like to point out that one of the defining characteristics of metonymy is that it refers the subject to the field of desire, to the accidental connections that in the face of utter ontological lack, teaching a subject what it is that it wants.

Metaphor represents an alternative function within signification, represented by the following algorithm:

$$f\left(\frac{S'}{S}\right)S \cong S(+)\,s$$

This formula should be read as the function (f) of the signifier for the subject (the S to the right of the brackets) that makes one signifier (S') stand in for another signifier (S) that is roughly equivalent to (≡) the subject and signifier (the S to the right side of the isomorphism sign) crossing the bar that separates them from the signified (s): "this crossing expresses the condition for the passage of the signifier into the signified, whose moment [was] playfully pointed out above by provisionally conflating it with the place of the subject."[38] If metonymy is constituted by a centrifugal function that refers the subject to a virtually infinite field of possible significations and produces desire, metaphor names the principle whereby a subject acts as if a signifier refers to delimited sets of objects, and therefore metaphor largely functions by disciplining signifying connections in the name of meaning. But like metonymy, metaphor is also a function: it is the mode of labor whereby a subject and the others and objects to which it relates are granted a kind of stable, provisional coherence.

Thus, what distinguishes metaphor from metonymy is not simply a formal difference, but it is also an affective difference: metaphor names the kind of habitual investments that subjects make in signs and representations. If metonymy is what makes a subject "uncertain because he is divided by the effects of language," metaphor names the ways that a subject invests in an account of itself "through the effects of speech," producing an ideal conception of itself as a coherent totality laid over the fragmentary experience of the individual, and through which a subject takes up modes of relation to others.[39] The subject is caught in a dialectical tension between metaphorically realizing itself as or in an other subject to the Symbolic and the metonymic deferral of a feigned unicity: the subject "realizes himself more in the Other, but he is already pursuing there more than half of himself. He will simply find his desire ever more divided, pulverized, in the circumscribed metonymy of speech. . . . [T]he subject proceeds from this synchronic subjection in the field of the Other."[40] As Lacan puts it in one of his more poetic moments, citing Monsieur de La Palice: "Naïve mouth—whose eulogy I shall spend my final days preparing—open up again to hear me. No need to close your eyes. The subject goes far beyond what is experienced 'subjectively' by the individual; he goes exactly as far as the truth he is able to attain—which will perhaps come out of your mouth again. Yes, this truth of history is not all contained in his script, and yet the place is marked there in the painful conflicts he experiences because he knows only his lines, and even in the pages whose disarray gives him little comfort."[41] This poetic account of the tension between "the script" and the "painful conflicts" that a subject experiences "because he knows only his lines" is the driving impulse behind the mirror stage. As already noted, in the mirror stage Lacan uses the metaphor of an infant looking in a mirror for the first time to explain the trauma of entry into the Symbolic. The infant in the mirror is an "it" (*Es*) and does not yet have a concept of a unified self or causality, and it is therefore puzzled by the fact that when it moves, the child in the mirror also moves. As the child begins to figure out that when it moves, the child in the mirror also moves, it begins to identify with this external image. The image provides the child an imaginary retroactive totality that renders a coherent ideal form of the self. From this encounter, Lacan infers the existence of two loci that characterize the subject: an ego or a statuesque projection of an "ideal I" and the phenomenological experience of an unformed Es or "it."

Despite the developmental vocabulary that drives Lacan's account of the mirror, the mirror stage is not intended to be a literal account of the stages through which a child must pass to gain an identity: rather, it is a metaphor for the subject's continuing negotiation with the general economy of tropological exchange. Anthony Wilden has argued that the French word for "stage" (*stade*) implies not only the developmental but also the theatrical stage as a space of performance.[42] What is performed in the mirror? The mirror reveals that subjectivity is a tropological exchange. The mirror is a metaphor for two movements: it is a metaphor for the relationship between the trauma of entry into the Symbolic and feigned subjectivity, and it demonstrates the means through which an imago stands in for the experience of the Es. This performance relies on a set of progressive metaleptic substitutions. First there is a metonymic connection between an unformed subject who is not integrated into the Symbolic and a symbolically given representation of who the subject is supposed to be. As the subject attempts to manage this gap, they inhabit the space between their own experience and the given image of what it means to be a subject; they do so by moving this metonymic (or accidental) connection to a metaphor that explains who they are. The experience of being a subject is the experience of identifying with an image of one's self that is not naturally given but rather given by a specific location within the Symbolic order and a specific set of historical and material factors that articulate a notion of identity that a subject assumes or, better yet, inhabits. But this assumption or inhabiting of a frame for identity is never completely effective, nor is the subject ever fully able to exorcise the gap that constitutes it because this gap between the subject and the Symbolic is the precondition for the subject's emergence. Thus, the subject is a placeholder for the movement of tropes that constitutes it.

That the subject is a placeholder in the economy of signification sheds light on Lacan's aphorism that "the signifier represents a subject for another signifier."[43] As noted earlier, this formulation of the subject's relation to language inverts the conventional wisdom that preconstituted subjects use language as an instrument to communicate their subjective intentions. Subjects are articulated through language, within the differential space of signification, and are subsequently related to other subjects only by assuming an imaginary relation to them. The articulation of the Imaginary both allows the subject to assume a coherent image of the self and creates a conceptual structure for dealing with the other. This imaginary structure gains efficacy by suppressing the subject's relationship with its constitutive gap, or as Lacan puts it, "the mirror stage . . . manufactures for the subject . . . the armor of an alienating identity."[44] The armor of an alienating identity does not only negotiate the subject's relation to itself, it also imposes the narcissistic structure of the ideal I on the other, figuring the other as the mirrored reflection of the self in a "guiding grid for a method of symbolic reduction."[45] This attempt to control the other by framing it through the narcissistic misidentification is a driving force in the reiteration of the ego: "thus, to break out of the circle of the *innenwelt* [inner world] into the *umwelt* [outer world] generates the inexhaustible quadrature of the ego's verifications."[46]

A subject is not the cause of, nor is it reducible to an effect of, discourse's formal properties. Rather, a subject is an individual node in an economy of tropes sustained by a conception of affective investment as a practice of metaphorical condensation. If the subject is a result of tropological functions, it is but one node in the economy of tropological exchanges. This view implies that agency is distributed across the whole economy of discourse and present not only in the subject's affective investments but also in the movement of tropes themselves. The "Instance" in the "Instance of the Letter" can also be translated as "agency," as a number of early translations of Lacan's essay rendered it. If the letter is also an agent, subjects are only agents as a result of the nodal functions of an economy of trope, while tropes are agents in and of themselves. As Lacan argues by detailing the etymology of the verb *agir*: "to act' has more than one resonance . . . beginning with that of actor. *Actionnaire,* 'shareholder' . . . is made from action. . . . [D]oesn't the activist properly speaking define himself . . . [as] the instrument of something?"[47] This reading of agency accounts for the relations of mutual imbrication between the general and specific economies of tropological exchange and the texts that at least partially animate them by figuring each moment in the economy of trope as a site of agency, albeit without necessary reference to the subject as the privileged agent.[48]

An economically figured practice for reading trope can provide rhetoric with an account of the force of individual texts, primarily by attending to the intertextual tropological exchanges that animate and exceed them. An economic theory of trope and affective investment (primarily in the form of enjoyment, as I detail later) provides rhetoric with the capacity to understand the imaginary commitments that subjects hold, the modes of public relation that they imply, and the specific tropological configurations that animate public discourses. By extension, if the general economy marks the relationship between the trauma of failed unicity, trope, and affect that arises at the level of signification, then one can read the specific economies that underwrite the circulation of texts and tropes at specific sites of economic exchange both as the result of what is unique to a tropological configuration and simultaneously in reference to the work that such configurations do in accommodating subjects to the traumas of the general economy. Imaginary relations and their instantiation in specific publics can be profitably read as structures of performance through which subjects negotiate the problems of the general economy generated at the three distinct moments of failed unicity: in the constitutive gaps that characterize a subject coming to life in processes of signification; in the impossibility of communication and a communicative account of the social; and in the imaginary framing of others. In each of these moments, subjects are forced to comport themselves toward the constitutive functions of trauma in producing and addressing these gaps and toward the surplus enjoyment generated by these modes of comportment. Collectively, these processes constitute both a general economy of tropological exchange, read as the set of processes that subjects must negotiate generally when moving in the realm of representation, and a specific economy of tropological exchange, or the set of specific imaginary commitments and tropological exchanges that root a subject within a specific social formation and in relation to individual texts as nodes of exchange that negotiate a relationship to the general economy.

Why an Economy of Trope?

The concept of discourse as an economy appears frequently in Lacan's corpus. As early as his first seminar a conception of discursive exchange supplants communication as communion and transmission. For instance, Lacan draws on Augustine to establish the difference between communication as the unidirectional transmission of a signal and as "the exchange of interhuman speech."[49] In the same seminar he also first introduces the concept of discourse as "labor."[50] In the second seminar, Lacan introduces the metaphor of economy as a characterization of the exchange between the Imaginary and the Symbolic, noting that if "the imaginary economy has meaning, we gain purchase on it, only insofar as it has been transcribed into the Symbolic order, where a ternary relation is imposed."[51] By the third seminar these concepts are combined into a full-fledged treatment of discourse as an economy. Taking up the question of how an analyst makes delusional speech intelligible, Lacan turns to an account of discourse: "We can let ourselves be taken in by our first initial contact with the subject. . . . [This] brings us to the point of going beyond [meaning] and positing the term *discourse.* For to be sure, these patients speak to us in the same language as ourselves. Without this component, we would be in total ignorance. It's therefore the economy of discourse, the relationship between meaning and meaning, the relationship between their discourse and the common organization of discourse, that allows us to ascertain that a certain delusion is involved."[52] This conception in turn becomes the basis for reading the sign as a form of currency in the seventh seminar on *The Ethics*: "The sign here is very close to a representative currency."[53] This theme continues through most of the seminars, appearing for example in seminar seventeen, *The Other Side of Psychoanalysis,* which refers to the "economy" within which the "signifier can be located," and even as late as seminar twenty, *On Feminine Sexuality,* where Lacan refers to the "economy of enjoyment."[54]

Why does Lacan treat discourse through the metaphor of an economy? In large part, Lacan's turn to a conception of economy frames trope as an extension of rhetoric as opposed to a reiteration of structuralist poetics. One of the most common criticisms of the Lacanian reinvention of Freud is that it imports a hypertrophied structuralism, popular among some of Lacan's French contemporaries, into psychoanalytic work. This criticism was first forwarded by Maria Ruegg, who claimed that Lacan erred in posing metaphor and metonymy as structurally determined antithesis.[55] For Ruegg, posing such an antithesis ontologizes it, rendering it immune from the contingency that marks the field of discursive production. While Ruegg's criticism has difficulties in accounting for the relationship of mutual dependence and differential investment between metaphor and metonymy that I have argued for here, versions of this criticism have reemerged in the recent post-structuralist attempts to characterize psychoanalysis as an old ontology in a new wineskin. For example, Andrew Robinson argues that psychoanalysis's fascination with "constitutive lack" ontologizes lack, framing it as a new foundation and authorizing the creation of a new structure based mostly on violence. Derrida's criticism of the *arche* in psychoanalysis works this argument out in a little more careful detail in *Archive Fever,* although he maintains a kind of ambivalence about the "beyond" of psychoanalysis in his later work.[56]

What are the characteristics of and problems with a structuralist account for Ruegg, Derrida, and Robinson? Structuralism is flawed because it overdetermines fields of action and signification—put differently, structure eclipses contingency, a category that is at the very heart of rhetorical theorizing. The basis of this criticism is that structuralism reads specific phenomena as epiphenomenal, in that individual phenomena are meaningful only because they reveal and are determined by the underlying logic of the structure. Here, structuralism implies a kind of overdetermining automaticity to individual phenomena, and therefore it endorses both a form of determinism and centers a new form of unicity on the concept of structure. Reconstituting unicity around structure poses both an ontological and an interpretive problem. The ontological problem is that there is nothing that grounds a conception of structure in most structuralist accounts—structure is presumed to be autopoetic. The interpretive problem is that individual phenomena are always read through the frame of the self-generating structure, so that there is a kind of non-falsifiability built into a structuralist account. Structuralist readings may even be tropologically inflected, but a structuralist account of trope necessarily operates at the expense of an account of contingency in figuring tropological operations as automatic extensions of a structuring logic. This criticism repeats the basic Popperian charge against psychoanalysis that there is no criteria for testing it because it generates an all encompassing and ubiquitous set of general explanations that are not amenable to empirical testing.

The most classic rendering of both of these arguments about the ontological and interpretive problems of structuralism is found in Derrida's "Stucture, Sign, and Play in the Discourse of the Human Sciences." Derrida isolates two specific paradoxes for structuralism: that structure is itself a kind of event, and play in structures is governed by a center that is exempted from the rules that govern the rest of the structure.[57] In the final analysis, the force of Derrida's criticism is that structures themselves are historically determined by a field of play that provides them with a kind of intelligibility in their specific epoch, and as a result, references to ahistorical structures are haunted by the specter of their own historicity or eventfulness. The implication of this claim is that structure cannot, by definition, have a transcontextual purchase because structure itself is determined by the context within which it arises.

These criticisms are incisive in their diagnosis of structuralism, but the question remains if criticisms of structuralism are applicable to Lacan's psychoanalysis. So, the nexus question: is Lacan's conception of economy structuralist? Lacan's conception of economy maintains some of the tenor of the concept of structure, in that it seeks to describe persistent regularities in the life of the subject that exert substantial regulatory force. However, Lacan's conception of economy is premised on the failure of unicity or on the idea that the structuring functions of the sign fail in scripting the Real. In structure's place, a Lacanian economy sees the contingent but highly regularized rhetorical functions of trope as emerging from the failing of structure: because trope emerges at the limits of speech as a result of failed unicity, trope cannot be an expression of unicity but of the turning or indirection that inheres in employments of signifiers. Lacan's concept of economy also interrupts the tendency of structuralist accounts to elide contingency: if, as I argued earlier, trope emerges as a post hoc account of the burdens language use imposes on the subject, and of the empirical effects of this burden, an economic account differs from a structuralist explanation because the contingent nature and empirical life of the signifier are the genesis of the "structuring" function, as opposed to an epiphenomenon of structure. As a result, economy confronts structure with the necessity of grounding the functions of discourse in the interchange between rhetorically (that is, tropologically) constituted structuring functions and contingent localized rhetorical (that is, situational) effects. This is an extension of the basic logic of the Borromean knot, which reveals, more than anything, that the regularities in the Symbolic are dependent on their imaginary instantiation in the concrete modes of discourse and social relation that configure the relationship between subjects.

One can render the metaphor of the economy as simply a preexisting formal structure or, alternatively, in the spirit of Lacan's Borromean knot, as a set of contingent regularities in exchange that can only be understood heuristically—that is, after the fact of exchange. Put more simply, the question is if structure is a foreordained reality or an emergent association of regularities in exchange. The first definition of economy as structure is familiar to those who study the more market fundamentalist orientation of some neoliberal descendants of Adam Smith: the term "economy" represents an unavoidable logic of material exchange, guided by invisible hands and invariable self interests. As critics of neoliberalism are quick to point out, the metaphor of the economy seems structuralist in all the most dangerous senses of the term: individual exchanges are expressions of a governing logic exempt from the vicissitudes of history and specific context. But even within discourses of the free market there is a second possible rendering of an economy as a contingent set of regularities in exchange that, although they produce structuring functions, do not require positing a structure that is given in advance.

Milton Friedman's "The Methodology of Positive Economics" argues that the goal of a methodologically positivist economics is not the perfect prediction of behavior in every possible instance on the basis of economic laws, nor is it the articulation of hypotheses that mirror reality.[58] Instead, economic theorization is a post hoc heuristic that accounts for what must have been the conditions of exchange that underwrite an economic interaction as opposed to the description of the inevitable outcomes of specific economic assumptions in any given case. The core of Friedman's claim is that a truly "realistic" theory of economic behavior that presents a seamless account of all the assumptions and inputs in an economic exchange and their outcomes is impossible:

> A theory . . . cannot possibly be thoroughly "realistic." . . . [A] completely "realistic" theory of the wheat market would have to include not only the conditions directly underlying the supply and demand for wheat but also the kind of . . . credit instruments used to make exchanges; the personal characteristics of wheat-traders such as the color of each trader's hair and eyes, his antecedents and education . . . ; the kind of soil on which the wheat was grown, . . . the weather . . . ; the personal characteristics of the farmers . . . and . . . consumers . . . ; and so on indefinitely. Any attempt to . . . achiev[e] this kind of "realism" is certain to render a theory utterly useless.[59]

Instead of a theory of economics as a structure that mirrors economic behavior, Friedman frames economics as a discourse in autobiography, maxim, and example: "the construction of hypotheses is a creative act of inspiration, intuition, invention. . . . The process must be discussed in psychological, not logical, categories; studied in autobiographies and, biographies, not treatises on scientific method; and promoted by maxim and example, not syllogism or theorem."[60] Economic praxis is more a rhetorical mode for reconstructing the conditions of exchange than an automatic application of economic laws in order to understand the precursors for an exchange. Friedman goes so far as to claim that post hoc accounts are more useful when they do not match the realities of economic exchange because they grant us new insight into the formal possibilities of economic logics.

One cannot help but read the resonance between Lacan's account of the relationship between the Real and reality in Friedman's call to retheorize economics. Although Friedman holds out for the eventual promise of a positivist validation of such maxims and examples, Friedman's economics suggest an analogy for a psychoanalytic economy: a psychoanalytic economy has a special relationship with structure not based on an automatic relationship between structure and phenomena but instead premised on a post hoc hypothesizing of the regularities of an economy in the context of structure's failures. Lacan describes the role of an economy of the sign in exactly this manner by introducing the distinction between tuché and automaton in *The Four Fundamental Concepts of Psychoanalysis.* Borrowing from book 2 of Aristotle's physics, Lacan's category of tuché embodies the uncanny randomness of the Real, the category of chance, and automaton designates the automatic functions of nonhuman agents (later configured as the very definition of automaton as machine that unfailingly works according to its own logic). For Lacan, the psychoanalytic account of subjects is not about the inevitable unfolding of the automatic structures of the Symbolic in the subject's action; instead it embodies the contingent interface of the subject that is both thrown into the Symbolic and simultaneously into the tychic realm of chance.[61] The Real is unruly in the same ways that Friedman's wheat market is—it is inherently unspecifiable and unrepresentable from the vantage point of the automatic logic of the structure.

Lacan frames the relationship between the tuché and automaton as a missed encounter. Automaton, which is an iteration of the structural logic of the Symbolic order, attempts to orient the subject toward its world as a systematic unity. But this systematic presentation of the subject's world is constantly thrown against the hard "kernel of the Real."[62] Every automatic act of world framing is a missed encounter with the tuché of the "unassimilable" Real, and this produces a kind of trauma for the subject by revealing that the operations of the Symbolic are accidental and arbitrary.[63] On Lacan's reading, symbolic automaton attempts to address this missed encounter through strategies of repetition, constantly attempting to make the symbolic logic map on to the contingent Real. But this repetition is not sustained simply as a result of the formal structural properties of the Symbolic. Instead, repetitive practices only gain a purchase in the life of the signifying subject because they elicit affective investment in feigning the efficacy of the automatic function. The execution of structuring functions is never automatic, but it is always the result of the concrete labor subjects do to negotiate a condition of failed unicity, a quintessentially tychic process. Psychoanalytic economies are a kind of tertium quid in the simple binary of structure and contingency, refusing reduction either to decontextualized structure or to the infinite play of contingent production.

Lacan provides an analogy that helps explain the relationship between psychoanalysis and structuralism in his Baltimore address, his earliest and most significant engagement with structuralism. The lecture, titled "Of Structure as an Inmixing of an Otherness Prerequisite to Any Subject Whatever," employs the analogy of counting as a representation of the structuring functions in a psychoanalytic conception of economy, primarily by reasserting the failure of unicity.[64] If the commonsense logic of counting represents it as a set of externally determined quantities, the condition of the possibility of counting is that the one who counts treats counted elements as if they can be included in the set of things to be counted a priori. It is this presupposition of "sameness" that reveals the structuring functions of counting as artifice and not simply as the description of preexisting quantities of equivalent elements:

> Sameness is not in *things* but in the *mark* which makes it possible to add things . . . [without consideration for] their differences. The mark has the effect of rubbing out the difference, and this is the key to what happens to . . . the unconscious subject in the repetition. . . . If the "thing" exists in this symbolic structure, if this unitary trait is decisive, the trait of the sameness is here. In order that the "thing" which is sought be here in you, it is necessary that the first trait be rubbed out because the trait itself is a modification. It is the taking away of all difference, and in this case, without the trait, the first "thing" is simply lost. The key to this insistence in repetition is that in its essence repetition as repetition of the symbolical sameness is impossible.[65]

For Lacan, numbers are a second order representation of things in the world. The number is not naturally contained in the things in a given set. The sameness that allows things to be counted is only wrought through an assigned "mark" that includes things counted into a conceptual unifying category. Conceptual commerce in numbers requires eliminating the difference between things counted, presuming their sameness for the sake of authorizing their inclusion in a set. But the function of this sameness is only made possible by fully transposing the thing into the conceptual automaton embodied in the act of accounting. There is, however, excess in this relationship—the act of assigning consecutive numerals to objects in a set does not fully suppress the difference between the objects, or "in its essence repetition as repetition of the symbolical sameness is impossible."[66] Every act of identifying and repeating sameness is inextricably tied to and articulated against the contingent operation of tuché or to the contingent differences that belie the unity of the set. Thus, the psychoanalytic economy requires the presupposition of ineradicable difference among different elements integrated into the Symbolic. Far from suppressing plurality under the rubric of economy as a structure, psychoanalytic economies are a mode of articulating the subject's negotiation with the plurality of the Real, because a Lacanian economy presumes its own failure in fully assimilating any given phenomena into a structure.

Provocation: Reading Psychoanalytically

Though Lacan argued that trope functions as if it were a metalanguage that ordains the operations of discourse, he was also adamant in claiming that there is no metalanguage. Instead of acceding to the structural linguistic tendency to focus on the synchronic pole of language, the site where one might locate a metalanguage, Lacan insisted on locating the functions of trope in relation to the contingency of signifying bodies and the concrete investments that subjects make in reproducing and repeating signifying practices: "I still maintain that there is no metalanguage," because "anything that one might think is of the order of a search for the meta in language is simply, always, a question about reading."[67] The point of this claim is that the seemingly "meta" structuring functions of language are not the result of a formal determination but are always situated in a concrete subject reading discourse. If this claim has significant implications for reading the status of structure, it has equally significant implications for analytically inspired reading practices.

One strand of psychoanalytic method in literary studies holds that the Freudian tradition affords a mode of reading or, better yet, of *psychoanalyzing* individual texts. Reading in this way, one puts a text and its author on the proverbial couch, subjecting them to a set of analytic tools for unpacking the latent meanings of the text and the hidden interior processes that governed the text's invention. An understanding of the relationship between text, author, and invention authorizes this work: literary production is the outward manifestation of an only thinly veiled set of mental processes that produce the text as a token of the internal state of the author. This tradition promises the possibility of access to the psychic economy of the author via an exegesis of the unconscious logic of signs and desires that are *really* writing the text. Flavors of this rendering of psychoanalysis are not unique to the Freudian tradition, and they range from utterly naïve to excruciatingly sophisticated.

To varying degrees, readers of Lacan almost always affirm that there is something a bit too easy in this mode of interpretation, especially in the ways that it insulates both subject and text from the broader economy of tropological production within which they are situated. Nevertheless, there is a more nuanced strand of the thesis of an essential and reciprocal complementarity between author and text that inheres in many readings of Lacan. Citing Ben Stolzfus's *Lacan and Literature: Purloined Pretexts,* Ehsan Azari characterizes the presupposition that underwrites this understanding of complementarity as a misunderstanding of Lacan's maxim that the unconscious is structured like a language, arguing that too tight a coupling between the individualized unconscious and its manifestation in the form of a text figures "literature as a mirror reflection" of "the unconscious."[68] Although Azari rejects this configuration, he unintentionally recreates a version of this coupling in arguing that "any orientation for reading . . . has to be grounded in the . . . text itself" because "everything in literature . . . should be interpreted in the way that the author himself wanted it to be."[69]

It is easy to understand why a particular configuration of subjectivity as interiority and writing as symptom or token of the unconscious raises the ire of critics of the psychoanalytic tradition in a more general sense, since this configuration implies a commitment to a doctrine of the subject as stable interiority and as given in advance. This critique of the subject is largely in line with the Lacanian reframing of the Freudian tradition, which also argues against this configuration of the subjectivity as interiority in favor of a distributed conception of agency. The problem with the more generalized psychoanalytic conception of literature as reflective of the psyche, and of parallel Lacanian interpretations that assert the mutually reflective nature of the text and the unconscious, does not necessarily lie in the fact that such a view overdetermines literary production, since in both the Lacanian and in the more general psychoanalytic traditions writing may be understood through any number of metaphors that work against the grain of absolute determination, including the idea of a bilateral relationship between text and the figuring of the unconscious or of a struggle for mutual recognition between the two.[70] Nor does the problem simply lie in the ways that such a configuration evokes the intentionalist fallacy: whether located as function of interiority or as a product of a more general system of tropological labor, the point of the unconscious is that manifest intentions always and inexorably gesture toward a set of dynamics that both produce and exceed them.

For critics of a certain strand of an "applied psychoanalysis," there are two interrelated objections to psychoanalysis as a mode of reading literature: an applied psychoanalysis fetishizes the literary object, and therefore, it decontextualizes the literary object from the economy of trope that produces it. For example, Jean Michel-Rabate argues that "Lacan refuses to psychoanalyze either the author or the works. This would be too easy and would miss the mark."[71] Rabate cites an essay in which Lacan argues against posing too tight a complementarity between texts and the unconscious on the grounds that such a reading strategy erases the specificity of the individual literary text and ignores the relationship of mutual production between texts and the unconscious: "It is because the unconscious needs the insistence of writing that critics will err when they treat a written work in the same way as the unconscious is treated. At every moment, any written work cannot but lend itself to interpretation in a psychoanalytic sense. But to subscribe to this, ever so slightly, implies that one supposes the work to be a forgery, since, inasmuch as it is written, it does not imitate the effects of the unconscious. The work poses the equivalent of the unconscious, an equivalent no less real than it, as it forges the unconscious in its curvature."[72] Rabate concludes that "what [Lacan] does with texts, then, is similar to what he does with patients:

he treats 'the symptom as a palimpsest' and tries to understand the 'hole' created by the signifier, into which significations pour and vanish."[73] The invocation of the palimpsest shows that for any given text there is a relation with structure, but structure does not determine the contents of the text in a simple one-to-one relationship. Texts and the unconscious are caught up in relation of mutual economic exchange, and, as a result, one cannot simply read the text as an epiphenomenon of the unconscious, nor can one read the unconscious as independent of its textual manifestations. Instead one must read economically, that is, at the site of exchange between the two; a "text" is never readable on its own terms but must be situated in relation to the whole field of intertextual discursive effects. As a result, a psychoanalytic reading strategy is as interested in the tropes that are manifest in, move through, and point beyond the individual text. An individual text has a kind of integrity that is only purchased by its reference both to the specific economies of tropological exchange from which it inherits specific tropes and to the more general economy of tropological exchange that constitutes it as a site of affective investment. Texts intervene into the field of the unconscious, and as a result, what is perhaps most interesting about an individual text is the tropological transpositions that it enacts. In an economy of trope one reads as much for the ways that tropes are reorganized and rearticulated in and across texts as for the intrinsic function of a trope at a node in the economy of exchange.

To read economically is to read the work of trope in situ, as a site of exchange and production that alters the field of discourse into which it intervenes. Thus, as Rabate notes, literary production, literary poetics, and even literature occupy a more ambiguous place in the Lacanian system than the idea of psychoanalysis as an applied structuralism would suggest: "literature cannot be just an object caught up, traversed or exhibited by a discourse seeking a simple justification through exemplification, it inhabits the theory" from within.[74] As a result "The literary work . . . only exists in that curvature which is that of the structure itself. We are left then with no mere analogy. The curvature mentioned here is no more a metaphor for the structure than the structure is a metaphor for the reality of the unconscious. It is Real, and, in this sense, the work imitates nothing."[75] The questions implied here are how this metaphoric structure achieves a measure of durability in discourse despite the fact that it is premised simply on the exercise of artifice, and by extension, what the relationship is between this metaphoric structure and the Real. Thus, in the next chapter, I take up the question of the relationship between the Real and trope as a kind of curvature toward a referent.

5
Reference, Enjoyment, and the Materiality of Rhetoric

> The late nineteenth century form of psychology that claimed to be both scientific and forced itself even on its adversaries, thanks both to the apparatus of objectivity and the profession of materialism, simply failed to be positive, excluding from the outset both objectivity and materialism.
>
> —Jacques Lacan, "Beyond the Reality Principle"

One of the most frequent targets of Lacan's critical sensibilities is ego psychology, which holds that the goal of the talking cure is to square the function of the ego with the demands placed on it by desire. Ego psychology attempts to give a scientific account of symptoms as bearers of meanings produced by the subject's interior life, understood through the lens of the desiring body. The talking "cure" works by revealing the meaning of the symptom to the analysand, thereby offering the analysand an opportunity to rearticulate their true desires in a more socially acceptable form. Ego psychology claimed both scientific objectivity in arguing for a systematic mode of attending to the meaning of symptoms and a form of materialism in attending to the body as a cause of desire. For Lacan, ego psychology fails because it presumes a subject that is given in advance, conceiving of it outside of the symbolic matrix that precipitates it. As a result, by ignoring the work of the Symbolic and the imaginary nature of the subject itself, the project of ego-oriented psychology excluded "from the outset" the very conditions that would afford it a claim to scientific status or attention to materiality.

Although the analogy between rhetorical theory and ego psychology is not exact, the parallels are evocative: contemporary rhetorical theory is largely centered around practices of meaning making, it is interested in squaring meaning making with the demands of a subject negotiating discursive contexts, and it too would like to claim an understanding of the materiality of its processes. And if rhetorical studies fetishizes the Imaginary register, it too may "exclude from the outset" the conditions that would afford it a claim to materialism.

The question of the materiality of rhetoric, first heralded in Michael Calvin McGee's "Materialist's Conception of Rhetoric," represents rhetorical studies' continuing effort to define the persistence, durability, and scope of rhetorical processes in the social construction of reality. The primary question that debates over rhetoric's materiality harbor is this: how much of reality is ultimately reducible to rhetorical effect? By implication, a second question emerges: if the field of rhetorical effects has a boundary, is it correct to imply only that which is beyond the boundary is necessarily "material"? For example, a strand of the debate surrounding the materiality of rhetoric thesis critiques what it identifies as a certain rhetorical imperialism that would seek to reduce every phenomenon to the operation of discourse, arguing that a global conception of rhetoric elides attention to the historically situated, extra-rhetorical, material processes that constitute the world.[1] Yet, caution is in order: framing the debate over the materiality of rhetoric in a simple binary between a global account of the discursive production of the world and a dissent on the basis that some phenomena are external to the operation of rhetorical discourse invites a conceptual slippage. This framing conflates two senses of the concept of "materiality," confusing one definition of the material as that which exceeds or exists independent of human discourse and cognition with another that frames materiality as the durable social character of discursive formations.

Thus, one might reframe the binary conception of the materiality of rhetoric by posing two Lacanian questions that parallel these two senses of the term material. First, what is the relationship between rhetoric and the Real? Second, what is the relationship between rhetoric and the material? My goal will be to demonstrate why these questions ask two radically distinct things, and why an account of enjoyment is necessary to proffer an answer to both questions.

In chapter 1 I asserted that the Real is rhetoric's limit. If the Real is independent of or, more accurately, beyond the rhetoric, it follows that the Real exists outside of the symbolic and imaginary operations that relate a subject to its world. Although the Real can be effected by the movements of the Symbolic and Imaginary orders (as the Borromean knot demonstrates), the Symbolic and Imaginary cannot internalize it. For example, Lacan argues that as a result analytic practice must place "speech in a kind of suspension in relation to what amounts to a purely imaginary relation. There is nothing present, . . . nothing Real in [it]."[2] This claim does not mean that rhetoric cannot exert material effects, nor does it mean that rhetoric does not rely on materially situated processes. Far from it: in parsing the question of the Real and the material for rhetoric, I would like to both reassert the case for the Real as the limit of rhetoric and introduce an argument for a conception of the materiality of rhetoric as an economy of trope and enjoyment that exerts durable historically situated effects by placing the subject, which is always a product of discourse, in an (im)mediated (or, as I will argue later *metaxical*) relation to both the body and "materiality," specifically by "enjoying a body."[3]

Lacan's understanding of the materiality of rhetoric centers on two issues: on the logic of reference that relates discourse to the world and on the distinction between the Real and "reality." The imaginary and the symbolic logic of the sign figure the world for subjects, but the gap between representation and referents ensures that the Symbolic and Imaginary orders fail at efficiently shaping the world in their image or by their logic: there is a Real that is external to these orders that can only be engaged through the mediating capacities of signs and representations. The referential relationship between the order of signifiers and the order of things fails, never quite achieving adequation with a world external to discourse. Yet, rhetorical processes supplement this fundamental inadequacy in the subject's attempts to engage the Real by providing it means for feigning a referential relationship with the world in the form of "reality," which is a substitute or stand-in for the Real. As soon as a subject names things, whether they be objects, social processes, or phenomena, rhetorical processes organize its relationship with them. This claim does not mean that everything that exists is a product of rhetorical processes: rather, it forces a theory of the relationship of mediation between a subject's image of reality and the Real toward which it gestures but never achieves adequation. The rhetorically inflected processes of becoming a subject, naming and enframing the discrete set of objects that populate reality, and inhabiting speech tend to occlude access to the Real, which exists with a degree of autonomy from rhetorical effects. Defining the materiality of rhetoric requires attention to the Lacanian cut between "reality" as an imaginary picture of the world governed by the logic of the sign and the Real that escapes symbolization.

Presuming that a subject can directly encounter the Real via the mimetic function of the sign elides the analytic distinction between the Real and reality. Such an encounter would take a representation of reality as more "real" than the Real. That the Real is the impossible means that subjects only have indirect access to the Real via the mediation of symbols, representations, and signs or, more directly, when the sign fails and the logic of the symbolic is interrupted. The Real does not exist, but it *ex*-sists: it stands outside of the subject's conceptualization of it, embodying the persistence and durability of material relations independent of any act of conceptualizing them. If the subject is to encounter the Real directly, it is only as a result of its intrusion in the form of events that cause the representational faculty to falter.[4]

Alternatively, "reality" is fully reducible to rhetoric. Discourse shapes reality insofar as reality is exclusively a product of the rhetorical logic of the troped sign and the image. Reality is a quintessentially imaginary field, figured by the constitutive role of the Symbolic. If reality and the Real never quite achieve adequation, how might one account for the persistence of reality in attempting to engage the Real? What sustains and, perhaps more importantly, ensures for the subject a presumed relationship between the reality that it configures and the Real that escapes it? The answer lies in enjoyment, a principle of investment in reality that provides the social world with a degree of durability in the face of the ultimate instability that characterizes the terms of the non-relationship between reality and the Real.

My task in this chapter is to detail the implications of the split between reality and the Real and to figure the implications of this distinction for the materiality of rhetoric by providing a substantive account of enjoyment. To do so, I obliquely engage two general trajectories for characterizing the materiality of rhetoric: one trajectory frames the formal qualities of discourse as a durable productive system embodying the materiality of rhetoric;[5] another locates rhetoric's materiality as a "natural social phenomenon" relying on processes of "residual and persistent" communicative exchange.[6] This chapter rereads these two presuppositions of the conventional account of the materiality of rhetoric with the aim of avoiding a reduction of rhetoric to the Imaginary register or to discursive operations and contextually nested sets of communicative habits without remainder. Simultaneously, I would like to argue that locating rhetoric in the Symbolic and Imaginary orders also provides an account of the complex relationship between rhetoric and the Real as its constitutive limit. To develop this reading, I briefly introduce a distinction between *taxis* as a model of rhetorical mediation and *metaxy* as a studied practice of non-mediation, thereby lending specificity to the concept of the "relation of non-relation" introduced earlier. Taking metaxy as inspiration, I will provide a Lacanian interpretation of the materiality of rhetoric articulated through a conception of failed unicity. Next, I draw out a few conclusions regarding the problem of rhetorical interpretation suggested by this reading of rhetoric's materiality. Finally, I conclude with a provocation on the implications of this theory of the materiality of rhetoric for the relationship between theory and practice in a materialist rhetoric.

Love and *Metaxis*

Reading Plato's *Symposium*, the political theorist Eric Voegelin discovered something remarkable about the term "metaxy," a preposition meaning "between." Voegelin's reading turns on Diotima's claim that Eros is a "great daimon . . . between (metaxy) god and mortal."[7] Even though daimons move the divine and the human, daimonic metaxy does not constitute a midpoint between gods and humans. Metaxy is the unmediated suspension between two opposites: daimons participate fully in both the divine and human but are more than a simple combination of the two. Metaxy is thus taken by Voegelin to mark an ontological condition noteworthy enough for him to render it in the nominal form: "the metaxy" or metaxis. Metaxy parallels one crucial point of Lacan's critique of the ideology of communication: the simple presence of two entities that are brought into relation does not necessitate that the relation be premised on direct mediation between the two; rather, the metaxical intermediary that prohibits direct relation between two entities suspends them in an (im)mediated relation to one another.

As Nancy and Lacoue-Labarthe argue in *Retreating the Political,* psychoanalysis often thinks in terms of a "relation without relation" or a "relation of non-relation," for example, in articulating narcissism as a social bond or the concept of the object as a mode of encountering the other.[8] At both of these sites, subjects are bought into relation precisely because they refuse relation to other subjects, but the impossible presence or withdrawal of the other exerts a mutually constituting effect on subjects who are positioned relative to one another in a "non-relation."[9] The two terms in a relation of non-relation are only brought into relation by their mutual relation to a third term. In what seems on first glance to almost be a needless exercise in theoretical pyrotechnics, the terms of the relation of non-relation become the grounds for a triangulated mode of relation that supplants the original non-relation. What redeems this move from dismissal on the grounds of its almost comic nature is the insight that it produces regarding the terms of relationship among subjects: the relation of non-relation reveals that the Sign is the primary agent in relating subjects, and that the terms for intersubjective relations rest largely on supplemental practices that preclude authentic intersubjective exchange. If, by the same token, metaxy is a form of betweenness, it is one that can only feign mediation: metaxy refuses a simple logic of mediated exchange in the name of (im)mediacy or of a kind of co-presence in which the terms of a relation are not primarily about bilateral, negotiated, shared interactive exchange but about the mutual production of difference without mediating betweenness. Thus, Augusto Boal's definition of metaxis as "the state of belonging completely and simultaneously to two different, autonomous worlds: the image of reality and the reality of the image."[10]

This is exactly what is at issue in Lacan's reading of Plato's *Symposium* in *The Transference,* which addresses love as a mode of unicity. For Lacan, love serves as a synecdoche for the possibility of union between subjects and subjects and between subjects and things. For Plato too, a conception of love served as the means for addressing the relationship between the human and divine realms in the *Symposium,* a concern that is ultimately less theological than indicative of the (im)possibility of humans grasping the ideal forms that constitute reality. Love, on Lacan's reading of the *Symposium,* has the strange character of being the mediator of things human and things divine, but it neither belongs to the human or the divine: "let us not forget that Diotima had introduced love at first as being not at all of the nature of the Gods, but that of demons, insofar as it is, an intermediary between the immortals and the mortals."[11] Love suspends the human "between *episteme,* science in the Socratic sense, and *amathia,* ignorance, this intermediary which is in the Platonic discourse, [called] *doxa,* [or] true opinion insofar no doubt as it is true, but . . . the subject is incapable of accounting for it, in that he does not know why it is true."[12] If, for Plato, love is only properly the domain of the daimon, humans are not able to give or receive it and are therefore not in a position to encounter the divine in a direct relationship of mediation—or they are not able to access the necessary preconditions by which they might grasp divine knowledge. Platonic love positions the human in the untenable position of trying to encounter the divine by means of a logos that it does not have: "to give the formula, 'the logos, without having it' . . . [echoes the] formula . . . of love which is precisely 'to give what one does not have.'"[13] Put differently, the metaxical status of love as a mode of producing ontological and epistemic unicity places the human in a relation of non-relation to the objects of its love. Interestingly, in *Transference* Lacan frames this relationship as ultimately a result of the signifying properties of rhetoric: if "we are going to hear about this divine love, we are going to hear about its effects . . . [that] reveal . . . [a] theme which has become a little worn out since in the developments in rhetoric, namely the fact that love is a bond against which every human effort will come to grief."[14]

Love, Rhetoric, and Articulation

If rhetoric reveals that love is an impossible bond for Lacan, the implication of this argument is that attention to rhetoric reveals the fundamental moments of immediation between subject and itself, subject and subject, and between the order of the signifier and the order of things. As Joshua Gunn has pointed out, the impossibility of love as uninterrupted union with the other in their alterity implies the impossibility of consummating a relationship of identification: this is the logic of Lacan's understanding of love applied to the Imaginary order, and, as a result, all identifications are, by definition, misidentifications.[15] In the same way, the critique of love as union also produces a reading of the immediation between discourse and the order of the Real. Discourse is never adequate with the world but is condemned to address it through the mediating work of producing reality, which does not describe the Real as much as it imposes a subjectively invested representation of reality on it. Although discourse produces reality, reality only relates metaxically to the Real: as an extension of the Platonic metaphor in the *Symposium* for the relation between the divine, daimonic, and the human would have it, reality belongs to a different order than the relatively autonomous Real.

This conception of metaxy stands in somewhat stark contrast to the common understanding of articulation in rhetorical studies, especially in critical and cultural variants where discourses configure the world by means of mediated production: discourse produces "real effects" on the order of the world external to it, and the material world conditions the functioning of discourse. For example, taking up the tradition of taxis—traditionally arrangement but also a mode of textual articulation—as a way of understanding articulatory processes, Nathan Stormer has suggested that the core issue in the rhetorical tradition is the relationship between the "order of discourse and the order of things."[16] Stormer's formulation exemplifies the telos of rhetorical materialism as technology mediating not only discourse and reality at the level of their production but simultaneously as a theory of discourse as a referential tool uniting the order of the sign with the order of things to which it refers. Stormer exemplifies the ultimate goal of a version of rhetorical materialism that asserts the social productivity of discourse, arguing that articulation theory serves as a principle of taxis, mediating the divide between the order of discourse and the order of Real by reading them as mutually imbricated and co-productive.

Though articulation as taxis is a productive metaphor, what does framing the relationship between discourse and the Real as taxis prevent rhetoric from thinking? Current iterations of the materiality of rhetoric do not attend to the immediation between the order of discourse and the Real, deferring to a taxical mediation of the two: the most commonly posited solution sees discourse as a force that intervenes into the Real to configure it according to a logic of habit or practice. Against the seductive mediating tendencies of taxis, Lacan's conception of rhetoric asserts the productivity of metaxis as studied (im)mediation, as a site of enjoyment that flows from the gap between discourse and the world it describes, providing the material support for the subject, rhetorical discourse, and reality.

Lacan's work offers a technology of metaxis that details the relation between the image of reality and the reality of the image by pointing to the reasons why it is perhaps not words, discourses, or communicative contexts but processes of signification and representation that shape reality. These processes do not only describe, frame, represent, or explain reality: they also fail in the task of engaging the Real. However, this failure is unequivocally productive because it necessitates a turn to strategies of trope and practices of enjoyment that collectively produce subjects and their worlds. The domain of trope and enjoyment is the site of metaxy, reducible neither to the contextual operations of a discursive system nor to the social as a shared space of meaning. Rhetoric, on this reading, requires attention to the remainder that escapes the taxical reduction of reality to systems of discourse or social context and to the excesses produced in the failure of mediation.

Immediation and Failed Unicity

Many of Lacan's critics take proclamations such as "the universe is a flower of rhetoric" as evidence of Lacan's antirealism, therein identifying him with the most radical versions of the discursive turn. The danger of this dispensation for understanding rhetoric is, as Dana Cloud puts it, that under the dispensation of an extreme version of the rhetorical construction of reality, "discourse not only influences reality, it *is* . . . reality."[17] Admittedly, Lacan's declaration that "it is the world of words that creates the world of things. . . . Man speaks, then, but it is because the symbol has made him man" seems to confirm the instinct that Lacan reduces the world to discourse.[18] But despite this nod to the radical discursive turn, there are other possibilities in Lacan's work for framing of the relationship between the world of words and the world of things.

There are three sites of discontinuity that disrupt the seamless unicity of subjects within language relating to their world. Though I have already discussed each of these at length, it would be useful to recap them in abbreviated form for the sake of identifying the metaxical moment in each of them. First, unicity fails in the relationships between the subject and the Symbolic and, by implication, in the relationship between the subject and itself. For subjects, the failure of unicity lies in a requirement for external principles to order and give sense to an already ongoing experience of existence. The principles that unify one's own subjectivity are not given internally but are received from an external reservoir of images of the self and practices of self-reference. Subjectivity is a retroactive process that both names and organizes the experience of an individual in discourse in the presence of others; as a result, practices of subjectivization are split between one's lived experience and external semantic referents that both identify and defer one's uniqueness as a subject. The gap identified in the mirror stage between the subject position (understood as a set of identificatory discourses, practices, and habits that comport an individual to the world) and the individual (understood as the unorganized body) is essentially metaxical, or configured as a non-mediated relationship only held together by practices of affective investment.

Unicity also fails in the gap between subject and other, best exemplified by the chasm between speech and the other's reception of it. Lacan frames this problem in two ways. The first framing notes that all speech is both addressed to specific others and a general or big "O" Other. For instance, this chapter is both aimed at a reader but also implicitly aims at the Symbolic order in attempting to bring to bear a set of recognizable semantic moves and identifiable content. This is a problem in the order of discourse's reception: misreading is simple misunderstanding, but it is also a constitutive condition given that one can never be sure that there is a seamless overlap between a reader, audience, and the Symbolic order. This gap is related to a second one between the subject and the Symbolic: there is an irreducible gap between the speech of a specific subject and the order of discourse as an external set of logical relations. The split in discourse extends beyond the order of reception—inhering in the classical distinction between langue and parole, which I explore in greater depth below. The metaxical relation at this site of failed unicity resides in the gaps between the subject and other subjects and between the subject and the Symbolic. The subject requires discourse as a medium for its articulation and action, but subjects are never quite fully at home in it.

Finally, unicity fails in the relationship between the Symbolic and the Real, which ultimately names the tragic confrontation between the sign and its ontological limit. Foundational ontology presumes the possibility of grounding a thing in the Real, articulating the possibilities and modalities of its existence, but only succeeds in grounding beings in a representation of reality. If the Real is uncodable, ontology is impossible on its own terms: there is no adequation between the Real and the Symbolic processes that code the Real in the order of language and reality. Put in terms of reference and representation, the conventional doctrines of sign and representation hold that signs and representations refer to objectively existing entities. But it is equally plausible that acts of representing and acts of naming also produce the realities to which they refer. Framing the problem in this way does not require that words literally generate the substance of things; rather it requires that the terms of the relationship between discourse and the world cannot be understood as automatic—representation requires artifice and labor to sustain itself. Put in terms of metaxis, since the relationship between words, the reality they generate, and the Real is not automatic, rhetoric is in need of enjoyment and trope as erotic daimons that feign unicity in the context of its ultimate and necessary failure.

What is it that sustains the subject and its discourses despite the condition of failed unicity? If rhetoric is signifying in a condition of failed unicity, a metaxical materiality hinges on two functions: rhetoric is material because signifying in a condition of failed unicity requires trope as a specific instantiation of the material durability of the sign despite its failings, and rhetoric is also material because it finds its life in enjoyment as a practice instantiating subjects and discourse in the economy of trope. Rhetoric is material because it is tropological: if failed unicity implies that all signification is rhetorical in the absence of a "One" signifier grounded in the Real to which all signifiers refer, then tropes provide the means through which discourse works through the failure of reference. That is to say, where a referential relationship to the Real fails, metaphor and metonymy fill in, founding all the durable historically situated relations that characterize the materiality of discourse, including, most significantly, the unconscious. Here, if the rhetorical function of trope underwrites both the failure of unicity and simultaneously founds a means of feigning unicity, then rhetorical theory might be recast as the formal study of how discourse copes with referential failure.

But trope alone is insufficient. If a formal account of discourse or of communal mediation cannot overcome the condition of failed unicity, a principle is needed that accounts for the persistent feigned unicity of subjects, signs, and communicative contexts. How can Lacan affirm a repetition, regularity, and logic in discourse while simultaneously asserting that discourse is constantly and constitutively failing as a structure? The answer is a specific kind of labor done by the subject: enjoyment. An economy of trope produces the formal possibility of speakers, acts of speech, and communication, but an economy also requires labor and investments. Enjoyment is the name for the labor done by the subject's investments in the practices of signification and subjectivity that grant an economy of trope durability and regularity.

Affect and Enjoyment

I would like to define enjoyment by distinguishing it from two related terms: affect and emotion. Further, I would like to distinguish affect from emotion by figuring emotion as an epiphenomenal manifestation of the economy of affects. By extension, I would like to define enjoyment as a specific affective modality that could be characterized as "repetitive affect," that is, as a name for specific forms of affective labor that organize the subject and comports it to the world through practices of repetition. But what is affect? One common usage of the term in rhetorical studies reads affect and emotion as synonymous.[19] Reading emotion and affect as equivalent reflects a bias rhetoric inherits from close textual criticism: a critic takes a display of emotion (here an "affect"), reads it in relation to a context and intention, and explicates the way it functions. But affect is a richer term than emotion in a number of ways. Affect can also mean to influence something, as in Spinoza's famous distinction between *affectio* and *affectus,* later put to productive use by Deleuze. Deleuze claims that one can only avoid a "disastrous" confusion in theorizing affect by properly parsing the terms: "In Spinoza's . . . *Ethics* . . . one finds two words: affectio and affectus. Some translators, quite strangely, translate both in the same way. This is a disaster. They translate both terms, affectio and affectus, by 'affection.' . . . [W]hen a philosopher employs two words, it's because in principle he has reason to, especially when French easily gives us two words which correspond rigorously to affectio and affectus, that is 'affection' for affectio and 'affect' for affectus."[20] As affectio, affect means something like the affections or sentiments. Affectus names a state of potentiality. To be situated in the field of affectus means that a thing can both be affected and affect something else. For Deleuze, this conception of affect as affectus remedies a tendency in humanistic scholarship to read every interaction in relation to a subject who experiences and mediates it representationally by reading lines of force that are not exclusively mediated by a subject operating within a field of representations and that, by extension, turns critical attention toward "the virtual."[21] Although useful, the Deleuzian distinction also risks stripping affect of some of its specificity—affect risks becoming a name for all the possible interactions that constitute the world. Lawrence Grossberg argues for a more specific conception of affect's relation to emotion than a global affectus, suggesting one way of parsing the distinction between affects, signs, and emotions: emotions are "the product of the articulation of two planes: signification . . . and affect."[22] But what are the terms of this articulation? While emotion requires a subject to experience and display it, and a regime of signs to give it meaning, affect serves as a trans- or asubjective economy of forces that produces the subject, its emotions, and underwrites the economy of signs that lend emotion a logic.

There is resonance in Grossberg's solution with a Freudian motif, namely with Freud's insistence that to understand the manifest life of the subject, it is necessary to engage the set of forces that precede the manifest content of the subject's actions and investments. One might object that a Freudian turn only moves the work of the subject to a deeper, more hidden level of operation and thus does not capture the desubjectivizing move intended by Deleuze and Grossberg in theorizing affects. This criticism has merit, but it partially misses the significance of Lacan's recovery of the Freudian unconscious, which was not that it revealed a new frontier for the interiority of the subject. Rather, the unconscious proffers a rule for interpretation: do not take discourses at face value but interrogate what is obscured, condensed, or displaced in the manifest meaning of a discourse. In Lacan's reading of Freud, the unconscious is essentially exteriorized, becoming a site for the exchange and articulation of ideas, commitments, and intensities, figured under the economic operation of tropes of connection, articulation, displacement (via metonymy), and condensation (via metaphor).[23] Addressing the relationship between emotion and affect under a Freudian dispensation means that instead of asking "what does this public manifestation of emotion mean," as a close reader might, one might instead ask: "what are the conditions of possibility for a specific emotion to be manifest given the specific economy of tropes that organizes the experience of emotion?"

Affect, especially as affectio can be a synonym for emotion, specifically for the external manifestation or display of emotion. But affect can also mean to put on a false show, imitate or simulate something, as in an affected accent or way of speaking, and it can capture the range of forces that produce a subject. The psychoanalytic concept of affect invokes all of these: affect is a line of influence that produces the subject and its actions; it is related to the display and subjective experience of emotion; it is a line of force and logic that organizes subjects and their relationship to the world; it is a condition of possibility for a subject's experience and display of emotion. The psychoanalytic concept of affect is divided from emotion by arguing that felt and displayed emotion is external or epiphenomenal to the movement of affect, but it also asserts an inextricable link between affect and emotions as an economic exchange.

Lacan tends to deemphasize affect, especially when compared to affect's significance in the rest of the psychoanalytic traditions. In seminar ten, *Anxiety,* Lacan addresses critics who fault him for deemphasizing affect by emphasizing what affect is not: "Those who follow the movements of affinity or of aversion of my discourse by frequently letting themselves be taken in by appearances, think no doubt that I am less interested in affects than in anything else. This is quite absurd. On occasion, I have tried to say what affect is not: it is not Being given in its immediacy, nor is it the subject in some sort of raw form. . . . My occasional remarks on affect mean nothing other than this."[24] Here Lacan positions his understanding against a prevalent reading in the psychoanalytic tradition that reads affect as the direct expression of the bodily energies of the subject, a view primarily forwarded in the Freudian traditions' protophatic concept of affect, which frame affect as a manifestation of the bodily functions of the nervous system and more often than not as a site of repression by cognitive processes. In the protophatic account, the intrinsic difficulty of being human is that our cognitive and social schemas often work against the direct expression of visceral impulses—for the sake of comporting with social norms, one cannot always do what one feels compelled to do by the body. Arguing that affect is not "being given in its immediacy," Lacan is making a claim that affect, understood as all the forces that impinge on and move through the subject (social, material, and bodily), is itself organized for the subject by the function of the signifier. The signifier works to organize the expression and character of affective impulses, primarily by transposing and translating them into an economy of rhetorical production: "What, on the contrary, I did say about affect is that it is not repressed; and that is something that Freud says just like me. It is unmoored, it goes with the drift. One finds it displaced, mad, inverted, metabolized, but it is not repressed. What is repressed are the signifiers which moor it. . . . Where best does Aristotle deal with the passions? . . . [I]t is in Book Two of his *Rhetoric*. The best thing about the passions is caught up in the reference, in the net, in the network of the *Rhetoric*. It is not by chance. This is the net."[25] Lacan's conception of the rhetoric as a net comports in suggestive ways with the Deleuzian idea of "affective capture." Although rhetorical processes do not produce every movement of affect, they comport affective flows, which are, in turn, effected in part by the operation of the signifying economy. If the primary focus of Lacan's engagement with affect is largely in response to the psychoanalytic traditions' configuration of affect as the subject's bodily energetic charge transposed by repression into the expression of emotion, Lacan's primary reticence to address affect largely stems from a desire to move beyond the idea that affect represents the direct bodily immediacy of Being. He argues for a conception of affect as a set of forces organized, captured in, and mediated by the rhetorical functions of the Symbolic and the Imaginary. This is the basic strategy that Lacan takes in referring to affect, almost indirectly, as affectus: as the name for the field of relations that produce the subject, signification, the Real, and simultaneously the specific modes of affective capture that underwrite the reconstructive labor that grants a subject the appearance of wholeness. Thus, as opposed to framing the analytic practice as a simple reliving of experience, "the restitution of the subject's wholeness appears in the guise of a restoration of the past. But the stress is . . . placed more on the side of reconstruction than on that of reliving, in the sense that we have grown used to calling *affective*. The precise reliving—that in the subject remembers something as truly belonging to him, as having been truly lived through, with which he communicates and adopts . . . is not what is essential."[26]

What is essential, if a bit unclear on Lacan's account, is to understand that affect can be situated in the Real, although not necessarily at the site of the body. Lacan would like to argue that affect cannot be situated in the body because he would like to respect the character of affect in the broader sense of affectus—as a set of relations of force that move through the body instead of originating in it. But more importantly, Lacan refuses to situate affect exclusively in the body because to concede to the body as the exclusive site of affect would hold open the possibility of bodily experience not mediated by the presence of the signifier: "I don't need to do more than remind you of the confused nature of the recourse to affectivity; . . . it always leads us toward an impasse. . . . [I]t is not a matter of denying the importance of affects. But it is important not to confuse them with the substance of that which we are seeking in the [unorganized body], beyond signifying articulation of the kind we artists of analytical speech are capable of handling."[27] But were one to locate the movement of affect outside the reduction to the body or subjective practices of meaning, and in the "ground" of the Real, affect can take on an important role in an analytic quasi-ontology, albeit one that escapes seamless representation in the regime of signs. This is why it is so difficult for Lacan to talk about affects: he agrees with Freud that they are conventionally produced (that is, that they are the result of contingent configurations), that they are artificial, and that they exert effects in the life of the subject. But there is a limit in Lacan's work that makes it impossible to account for the empirical functions of affect beyond simply defining affect's theoretical character and defining what affect is not. If affect exceeds the regime of the sign, one cannot comport it representationally without fundamentally disfiguring affect by translating it into the economy of signs. Affect is a *signal* for Lacan, but the character of this signal means that it is both irreducible to the sign and cannot be integrated into the economy of signification without displacing it. "As far as . . . affect is concerned," writes Lacan, "Freud always manages . . . suggestive hints. He always insists on their conventional and artificial character . . . not as signifiers but as signals, to which in the last analysis they may be reduced. This character also explains their displaceable significance, and, from the economic point of view, presents a certain number of necessities, such as irreducibility. But affects do not throw light on the economic or even dynamic essence which is sought at the horizon or limit from an analytical perspective."[28] Even though this reading attributes an uncharacteristic degree of indecisiveness to Lacan in theorizing affect, one that is largely reflective of his own ambivalence to the term, this account of affect pays a significant dividend for rhetoric in engaging the contemporary theoretical humanities. For example, the contemporary turn to theorizing affect without recourse to regimes of representation or signification forwards an aggressive critique of rhetoric on the grounds that it reduces everything to the function of language. Borrowing inspiration from Deleuze and Guattari's *A Thousand Plateaus,* critics in this line argue that signification is one regime for ordering affect among many others, and that to reduce the movement of affects to the economy of the sign both overdetermines it and conceals the status of the order of signification as a "command" that reduces the world to the structuring functions of language.[29] Indeed, in Lacan's reading, the Deleuzian attempt to escape the reduction of reality to representation and subjective mediation in the name of recovering a global sense of "affect" is impossible. The human, both in terms of its genesis as a subject and in its symbolic interaction with the world and others and objects is always, perhaps even tragically, given over to the rhetorical logic of the sign not only in spite of but *because* of the constitutive failings of the sign and representation. Of course, one could gesture toward a global conception of "the affective" outside of representation and subjective mediation, but such a conception of affect must see the field of affectus as Real in the full Lacanian sense of the term. As soon as one names these relations they would cease to be "Real" and would become "reality" and would, by extension, be caught up in the signifying net of rhetoric. To argue that there are movements of affects external to the sign is reasonable, but because such affects function in the Real, significant problems arise as soon as one attempts to arrest the movements of affect by naming them. As a result, such a reading of affect is effective only when it resides squarely in the Real, but as soon as one reduces it to reality by naming and enframing it as a conceptual object, one is accountable to the structuring principles of the Symbolic.

As a result Lacan claims that "from [this] perspective . . . there is only one affect, which is, namely, the product of the speaking being's capture in a discourse, where this discourse determines its status as object."[30] If affect is at first an uncoded "signal" when captured in the net of discourse, it is subsequently transposed into the economy of signs that animates the subject's production and movement within discourse. By extension, the discursive capture of affect is both the condition of possibility for and a means of modulating the production of emotion. But what are the terms of the exchange between affect as productive force, discourse as a translational principle, and manifest emotion?

For Lacan, the answer is enjoyment, which both names the process of producing a subject and the set of habits, investments, and relations that orient a subject toward its world. Enjoyment organizes affect, representing a subject's "useless" repetition of its habits of subjectivity and the subject's ritual organization of its affective investments and the means of organizing these practices. Enjoyment is the underlying condition of possibility for a manifest emotion, because enjoyment names the investment that both constitutes a subject and aids it in organizing its world, and therefore it regulates the conditions under which an emotion might be experienced or displayed. Enjoyment is distinct from pleasure: as opposed to the experience of delectation, enjoyment signals both an affectively charged state and a ritually repeated habit or compulsion that may as often be received as annoying or unpleasant as pleasurable. Enjoyment gives coherence to the subject's world by investing it with an identity and a set of predicable habituated relationships to its world. For example, take hypochondria, not as pathology but as a discourse. One reading of the hypochondriac interprets complaints of pains and bodily anomalies as a call for diagnosis and palliation. But the manifest complaint conceals something else: the hypochondriac's discourse functions as more than a call for help. Although the manifest emotional states of the anxiety and bodily states of pain are significant, the process of lodging the complaint creates an enjoyment that is external to a call for a cure. Perhaps the medical demand purchases the hypochondriac a sense of control that stands in for another more significant and difficult to articulate anxiety, perhaps there is a pleasure in figuring one's self as the object of care and concern. While the hypochondriac does not find their symptoms pleasurable per se, the process of lodging the complaint does work for the hypochondriac that organizes affects, practices, and anxieties, so that even though the hypochondriac may not find pleasure in their disorder, by definition they enjoy it.

The Lacanian term for enjoyment is jouissance, intended to capture the tensions and pleasures of sex, something that is overwhelmingly powerful, something that generates satisfaction, but also something that is not necessarily pleasurable. How can enjoyment be all of these? First, jouissance is an agent. It is not a characteristic of a subject, deterministically responding to the subject's drives or intentions: enjoyment underwrites subjectivization through discourse, but it is also the material substrate within which the performance of subjectivity is situated.[31] Jouissance is, in one sense, prior to subjectivity. It is not ontologically or temporally prior, but it can be read as a prior material condition for the production of subjectivity.

Enjoyment is a mode of affective organization that does not aim at the production of a specific end but that revels in mere fact of its repetition. It is the repetitive character of affect that induces Lacan to claim that enjoyment "is what serves no purpose."[32] Enjoyment is useless in a very specific sense: although the effect of the habitual capture of affect in the form of enjoyment purchases a sense of unity for the subject, enjoyment is useless in regard to the specific site of its exercise. When a subject enjoys a relationship to an object, or a specific habituated practice, it is tempting to read the subject's investment in the object or practice as a validation of the fact that the subject values the thing in and of itself. But, if Lacan's account of enjoyment is correct, enjoyment in an object or practice is less about the dignity of the thing invested in than the ways that the object or practice serves the subject in negotiating a relationship to the general economy of exchange. Thus, the exercise of enjoyment is often somewhat counterfactual: the subject invests in objects or practices for the sake of something that is beyond the object or practice and for the sake of accommodating to failed unicity. Even when situated against this broader context, enjoyment is useless, because, ultimately, in a condition of failed unicity the subject is useless: it does not aim at an ultimate end; rather, the subject is constituted by and for nothing more than the enjoyment of its own subjectivity. Thus, jouissance does not intentionally aim at the production of anything but paradoxically produces everything in the subject's world, including its subjectivity.

What does this have to do with the sign, trope, and materiality? Consider the relationship between enjoyment, trope, and materiality at the three sites identified earlier: at the site of the subject's constitutive split, the subject's split with the Symbolic, and finally where language mediates the impossibilities of reference. These three moments cumulatively define the materiality of rhetoric by defining the materiality of speech, the materiality of the speaking subject, and finally the materiality of discourse as a set of durable and sedimented metonymic relations, which I will frame in terms of the unconscious.

First, the split between the subject and the Symbolic: Lacan's critique of structural linguistics is that Saussure pays insufficient attention to speech as a paradigmatic representation of the subject's symbolic labor. Lacan argues for the distinctiveness of speech as the "key" to the analytic experience and by extension to discourse, claiming that psychoanalysis finds "in speech . . . its instrument, . . . material, and even the background noise of its uncertainties."[33] Invoking the letter, or the "material support that concrete discourse borrows from language," Lacan distinguishes between langue, the operations of symbolization, and parole, the specific speech acts of speakers.[34] At the level of langue, an economy precedes the speech acts of any given speaker, bounding speech with a set of logical semiotic operations—either metonymic combination or metaphoric substitution. Second, speech acts cannot be understood as solely produced within the bounds of language as an intersubjective exchange. The logical structure implied by signification exceeds any given context in generating speech acts.

As I argued earlier, there are two ways of reading the classical structural linguistic algorithm for the relationship between the signifier and the signified:

$$\frac{S}{s}$$

The main point of contention between Lacan and Saussure is not the "S" representing the signifier, nor the "s" representing the signified, but the "—," the bar dividing the two. For Saussure, the "—" represents a conceptual distinction between the signifier and the signified that enables differential signification, but the distinction is mediated by a relationship of reference, by a "bi-univocal correspondence between the word and thing, if only in the act of naming."[35] The psychoanalytic framing of the "—" reads it as a *bar,* as a prohibition or productive repression of the thing that is signified by the signifier. The bar provides an antidote to presuppositions of effortless reference: Lacan's bar marks the fact that reference is labor, a site of jouissance where the signified is constantly being slid under the signifier via the movement of trope and contra the structural linguistic sign. Rhetoric's materiality lies in the labor of desire that underwrites signification by "sliding" the signified under the signifier. In practical terms, because signification is irreducibly rhetorical, relying on a logic of trope and investment as support, it is also material, producing the economy of tropological exchange that is the condition of possibility for discourse.

What is it that labors, enjoys, and desires? The split between langue and parole returns us to the second site of rhetoric's materiality: the materiality of the subject. But for many theorists of rhetoric's materiality, the subject is the problem. Ron Greene is correct in noting that the subject is a privileged site for rhetoric as a "politics of representation," rejecting the latter because it occludes the materiality of rhetoric by ignoring the means of production that elicit both the subject and its representational commerce.[36] The psychoanalytic strategy for engaging the subject as a material and rhetorical practice takes the opposite approach: it presumes the constitutive ineradicability of the subject and its referential pretension, or the subject's obsession with and enjoyment in making reference work as the critical question of rhetoric's materiality. Paradoxically, instead of abandoning the subject and a representational politics in the name of rhetoric's materiality, a rhetorical theory should focus all the more intently on the representation, because it is precisely in representation's failure that the subject is produced and thrown into an economy of signs that materializes and exceeds it, making the subject "subject to" tropes and practices of enjoyment that produce, prefigure, and move beyond it.

Subjects are material rhetorical artifice or nodes in a tropological economy produced by the split between speech and the Symbolic. Subjectivity is this experience of identifying with an image of one's self that is not natural but mirrored by a specific location within the Symbolic order. The structure of mirrored subjectivity is a rhetorical tropological exchange—there is a metonymic connection between an unformed subject who is not integrated into the Symbolic and an image of who the subject is supposed to be, but this exchange is also quintessentially dependent on the labor of enjoyment. Elevating metonymic connection to a metaphor that retroactively names subjectivity, the mirrored subject manages its gaps through a metaphorical misidentification with an image by *enjoying* its own subjectivity. Once again, this is a site of metaxis, where subjectivity is a daimon bridging a divide between image and experience: more precisely (in Boal's terms) between the autonomous registers of the "reality of the image" of the subject and the "image of the reality" of the subject.

This is a productively perverse incarnational move—an embodiment that might be rendered as a "corporizing" disembodiment. In *Seminar XX* Lacan frames the problem this way: "Consider 'enjoying a body' . . . that symbolizes the Other—it perhaps can help us focus on another form of substance, enjoying substance . . . the substance of a body . . . defined only as what enjoys itself. . . . [W]e don't know what it means to be alive except for the fact that a body is something that enjoys itself. It enjoys itself only by 'corporizing' the body in a signifying way."[37] Hence, enjoyment is not structure or free-floating sentiment but economy and substance: a tropologically produced material cause of the signifying body's affects and labor. Enjoyment is intimately related to the tropological and rhetorical production of subjects, so much so that jouissance and the subsequent embodiment of all the subject's functions are inseparable from, if not identical with, the subject of trope. The signifier is the material cause of jouissance, and jouissance is the material substrate within which the (dis)embodied subject negotiates gaps in language through trope.[38] The subject is produced as a secondary excess of more fundamental processes of figural exchange in an economy of enjoyment. The primary agency in "the signifier represents a subject for another subject" lies with the sign, which enmeshes the subject in a larger economy of tropological exchanges that serve as the structuring logic of the social field or, as Lacan puts it, as the "support" for the social life of discourse.[39]

The dual gaps between langue and parole and the subject's relation to the Other converge and extend outward in an economy of tropological exchange, where the subject makes and is made by speech. The letter, signification, and its concrete embodiment in speech are the "material support that concrete discourse borrows from language."[40] In *Seminar II* Lacan reaffirms this insight, arguing that what is at issue in speech is not the specific content of an utterance, nor the deliberative benefits of exchanging ideas, but rather the way that material function of speech serves as a site for the Symbolic's emergence: "But one communicates, one recognizes the modulation of the human voice, and as a result one has the appearance of understanding which comes with the fact that one recognizes words one already knows. It is a matter of knowing the most economical conditions which enable one to transmit words people recognize. No one cares about the meaning. Doesn't this underline rather well the point which I am emphasizing, which one always forgets, namely that language, this language which is the instrument of speech, is something material?"[41] The employment of language requires that a kind of demand be placed on the Other to "make sense" or to bracket the vertiginous possibilities opened by metonymic association. As Lacan frames this relationship, language "cannot be anything other than a demand, a demand that fails. It is not from its success . . . but from its repetition that something of another dimension is engendered, which I have described as a loss—a loss whereby surplus *jouissance* takes a body."[42] Put differently, the exchange of language is an event in which failure, misrecognition, and misfires are necessary outcomes, and the immanent inevitability of this failure must be suppressed to authorize the continuing function of exchange in speech. But this relationship produces excess: in centering the possibility of communication between subjects through the repetition of tropological exchange, the subject emerges a site of investment in the form of enjoyment and subsequently founds the basic affective conditions for the persistence, durability, and effect of discursive forms.

If Lacan's conception of rhetoric's materiality is defined by persistence and effect of signifying relations, wrought through the labor of enjoyment, then his commitment to the materiality of rhetoric is perhaps best embodied in the commonsense maxim that what is said cannot be taken back: "we enter into the . . . unconscious . . . [where] words . . . cannot be taken back, for that is the rule of the game. From that emerges a speaking that does not always go so far as to be able to 'ex-sist' with respect to the words spoken. That is because of what gets included in these words as a consequence thereof."[43]

To say that the unconscious is structured like a language demonstrates that the unconscious does not presume easy reference between signifier and signified, referent and representation, or image and reality. The unconscious is the labor that has been done by other subjects in sliding their signifieds under their signifiers. The unconscious is structured *like* a language because it is a result of the structural possibilities for polysemous meaning in any act of signification, but it is *not* a language because it does not obey concrete rules of reference. The exchange of signs between subjects always says both too much and not enough: too much in that it is saturated with a virtual infinity of possible metonymic connections, and not enough in that the vertiginous possibilities for meaning cannot be disciplined by acts of specification. Hence the exchange of signs between subjects must fail at achieving consummation, suspended in metaxical immediation between the sign and the concrete condition of signifying exchange, a relation of non-relation only sustained by enjoyment.

Provocation: The Return of the Repressed in Theory and Practice

How might critical practices best attend to the materiality of speech, the subject, and the unconscious? Taxis-centered approaches read against the immediation and excess that inform Lacan's material rhetoric. Excesses cannot be "too excessive" lest they lose the ability to be coded in the logic of a system or situation. The danger is that in relying on taxis, critical and cultural rhetorical theory often produces a reductive account of texts by reading exclusively through logics of form, articulation, or context at the expense of reading the ways that these logics fail. The danger of taxis is also its explanatory power: taxis presumes that every rhetorical phenomenon reproduces the logic of a theory of rhetorical function at the level of specific rhetorical practice, *without remainder.*

In articulating a materiality of rhetoric as taxis, materialists such as Stormer, McGee, and Greene often flirt with the temptation to see explicit reading protocols as either disfiguring ideal impositions on the material functions of rhetoric or as automatically derivable from observation of a context. This is an extension of the idea I forwarded earlier that rhetoric in its imaginary manifestations is ultimately reducible to a conception of propriety, read as the relation between speech and the context of articulation. An attempt to resist the explicit development of interpretive protocols employs a disavowed observational hermeneutic, paradoxically feigning critical neutrality under the guise of simply observing the movements and processes of everyday discourse. The simple observation of a site of material production is not in itself sufficient for spontaneously generating interpretive protocols, unless one can identify a taxical relationship between the materiality of rhetoric and specific rhetorical phenomena that seamlessly authorize interpretive protocols. But in asserting a taxical mode of attending to the materiality of rhetoric, materialists bracket metaxis, paradoxically exempting the act of interpretation from the very symbolic failings and principles of (im)mediation that produce the drive toward the material in the first place. Here, rhetoric surpasses the limit of the Real, becoming an all encompassing account of affect as affectus—as the global character of relations of affecting and being affected in turn, condensed in a doctrine of articulation without necessary reference to the structuring functions of the Symbolic as an interpretive principle.

This is a problem of reference. For instance, when McGee claims that rhetorical inquiry ought to focus on the symbolic constitution of everyday life in the persuasive and "coercive power of the symbols which unite society," he flirts with a call for a certain kind of science of reading such connections.[44] With this reading, the scientific character of rhetoric would not inhere in a conception of repeatable forms but rather in the possibility of giving an exhaustive rhetorical account of all the operations of the Real. Even though rhetoricians should eschew the "idealist" tendency to presume an ahistorical reality outside of discourse, the essential goal of rhetorical criticism is to work through moments of coordinated symbolic action bounded by a context. In other words, there is a presumed referential relationship between a representation of rhetoric as a "natural social phenomenon" or object in everyday discourse and the messy reality of rhetorical practices.[45]

Can one articulate the terms of mediation between a critic interpreting the materiality of rhetoric and the empirical "reality" that is the discursive function of rhetoric's materiality? The difference turns on a disavowed doctrine of interpretation in rhetorical materialism that claims non-interpretive status: taxis is a hidden reading protocol that authorizes interpretation of the world external to discourse, while metaxis explicitly asserts interpretation as a tragic impossibility. The opening gambit of *Seminar XX* is an exploration of the tension between the law, love, and sex: law and the ideology of love stand for two principles of taxis or modes of disciplining trope and enjoyment by reducing them either to formal rules for reference or to a communally produced conception of meaning. Lacan responds to a hypothetical lawyer who asks him about discourse by saying that "I felt I could respond . . . that language is not the speaking being."[46] Lacan tells the imaginary lawyer that at the level of form, language is based on a system of rules, of codes that govern its proper operation, but that the speaking being is an altogether different thing that can only be understood by assuming that one is "in bed, a bed employed to the fullest, there being two of you in it."[47] The function of the law is to read out or limit excess, to discipline surplus enjoyment so that it is channeled toward a productive end. Law is an interpretive principle of taxis: law serves to "divide up, distribute, or reattribute everything that counts as jouissance."[48] When applied to language, the problem of the "law" is that it relies on rules, structures, and programs as a way of accounting for the social world, and in doing so it ignores the central relationship between failure and enjoyment.

The alternative to the law is not love, or the sexual relation, since the presupposition of relationship and implicit unity suppresses the function of enjoyment, ignoring its own kind of failures. Love is a taxical interpretive strategy that assumes discourse is consensual, shared intercourse or coordinated symbolic effect, a blessed union of act and meaning. While love is often figured as a desire for unity between two irreducibly unique subjects, Lacan figures love as a narcissistic demand on the other. Love's demand is narcissistic in that it reduces the other to an object for the sake of achieving a subjective "oneness," of rendering subjects divided by lack and language as unified selves and able to be unified with others. In this instance Lacan's argument about love is really a critique of taxis, which presumes meaning can be reduced to an account of symbolic unities without remainder.

The ideology of love as union with one's beloved in their intrinsic uniqueness conceals the fact that love is a demand on the beloved, driven by enjoyment in figuring the beloved as an extension of one's imaginary apparatus. The ideologies of love, relationship, and reference forge an (un)natural connection between the ontology of rhetorical function and the act of interpretation, thereby occluding the question of disconnection and the enjoyment that feigns unicity for each of them: where love is taxis, enjoyment is metaxis. The ideology of love as attention to the other on its own terms highlights interpretation as a practice of intervention as opposed to a simple act of revelation or consensual meaning making.

There is an affinity between the labors of the lover and the lawyer that mirrors the place of taxis in rhetorical studies of materiality. For both the lover and the lawyer, what is at stake is really a conception of propriety—the lover seeks to be appropriate to the demands of the beloved and the lawyer to the law that governs any given case. But both the lover's and the lawyer's theories of language miss failed unicity and the modes of feigning unicity authorized by the function of trope and enjoyment. For example, the idea that a theory of articulation can exorcize the problem of interpretation is a lawyerly solution. There are affinities between Greene's framing of articulation and psychoanalysis: for example, both positions harbor suspicions about the hermeneutic reliance on unities and moments of commensurability between subjects and texts. But a psychoanalytic theory of rhetoric's materiality breaks ranks with articulation theory on the question of representation. For rhetorical materialists such as Greene, articulation strives to break free of the subject and representation by offering "a materialism based on how rhetoric traverses a governing apparatus. Instead of focusing on how rhetoric represents, we should focus on how rhetoric distributes different elements on a terrain of a governing apparatus."[49] This shift to questions of distribution and the problematic of governmentality is undoubtedly productive. But were the problem of representation to be abandoned in pursuit of this strand of rhetorical materialism, materialists would risk turning a blind eye to the tropological supplements and practices of enjoyment that grow out of attention to representation and its failure. Articulation theory displaces what is productively problematic about interpretation in the search for a solution to the problem of the subject: that the hermeneutic project is never fully consummated does not mean that one should adopt a "logic of articulation" that risks an implicit observational hermeneutic by framing the task of rhetoric as simply observing the operations of articulation in structuring the world.[50] Instead of throwing rhetorical practice too quickly at the feet of articulation, one might theorize the materiality of interpretation by detailing the constitutive failures of hermeneutics and the metaxical enjoyment that sustains them.[51]

Alternatively, reference to the context that generates a discourse, through consensus, identification, or coordinated symbolic action in everyday speech represents a rhetoric for lovers. For those inheriting the tradition of McGee's "A Materialist's Conception of Rhetoric," especially in the rhetorical study of ideology, there is a natural affinity between the articulation of rhetoric's materiality and the practice of observing everyday discourse, which represents a context as a shared history. This framing of rhetoric's materiality ignores both enjoyment in structure and the gap that generates it. It ignores enjoyment by assuming that meaning is generated on the fly, bound up in historically specific moments of process-based consensus instead of sedimented structures of enjoyment that produce the subject. This is why Lacan is fundamentally suspicious of the reference to communal practices of meaning making as a basis for an account of signification—because such a reference tends to privilege moments of shared symbolic action at the expense of articulating failures and gaps between the subject, the sign, and the Real. There is both a structure that dictates the possibilities for signification and a gap between the lived experiences of subjects and communities negotiating this gap. As Lacan argues, "reference to the experience of the community, or the substance of this discourse settles nothing. For this experience assumes its essential dimension in the tradition that discourse establishes . . . long before the drama of history is inscribed in it. . . . [T]hese structures reveal an ordering of possible exchanges . . . is inconceivable outside of the permutations authorized by language."[52] Reference to the substance of discourse does not serve, in Aristotle's terms, as an inartistic proof—that is, as a mode of interpretive practice that does not require attention to the conditions of its mediation. Critical protocols that engage the conditions under which discourses are formed and articulated are a precondition for reading a discourse.

But doesn't it stand to reason that a sufficient account of the materiality of rhetoric would automatically generate critical protocols informing criticism? Alternately, wouldn't an account of criticism that foregrounded material modes of interpretation naturally imply an accompanying (if implicit) account of the ontology of language? The difficulty lies in the presupposition that either mode of inquiry "naturally" generates the other. One is only able to claim primacy for practice by naturalizing the ontological status of language under the rubric of simply observing "everyday language." Despite McGee's rejoinder that one did not have to discuss ontology to do rhetorical criticism, a taxical mode of rhetoric's materiality relies on an irreducibly ontological claim to situate the reality of discourse in the Real of context.[53] A description of rhetoric's social and material function implicitly drives the modes of criticism. This ontological and referential claim is naturalized by inartistic proof: the materialist critic is just "observing the everyday function" of discourses.[54]

Materialists attempt to cast out the problem of theory and practice by establishing the relative priority of each term. "It is not enough," argues McGee, "to *distinguish* theory and practice. . . . One must also decide what *relationship* exists between theory and practice—which 'comes first' in . . . communicative behavior."[55] McGee avers that the "obvious alternative" to ignoring practice by making a fetish of theory is to believe "that practice 'comes first,' that the essential mission of rhetorical theory is not to *prescribe* technique but formally to account for what seems to be an essential part of the human social condition."[56] A theory of articulation is methodologically cognate with McGee's solution, that one should abandon fictions of the subject and interpretation in favor of simply tracking the productivity of points of articulation and struggle in culture.

To return to sex, perhaps one might discern romanticism in McGee's presumption that an exhaustive description of the relationship between theory and practice might be sufficiently articulated to allow for a rational prioritization of both registers. Such a prioritization, one in which practice comes first, would discipline modes of theorizing and interpretation by centering them on the Real of everyday discursive practice. Thus, a prurient Lacanian question to the problem of whether theory or practice, interpretation or the material realities of rhetoric, come first: what if in this "relationship" neither of them "comes" first, if at all?[57] What if the relation between theory and practice or between interpretation and the material rhetorical practices it interprets are bound up in an insufferable jouissance driven by a missed meeting or an impotent liaison? What if these relationships can never be consummated but must remain suspended in metaxis, in a productively failed unmediated encounter of autonomous registers? In the light of this unbridgeable gap, perhaps the best response is to track the productivity of our failures in closing it, casting rhetorical sutures as a supplement underwritten by enjoyment and materially situated interpretation as metaxy. What if there is no such thing as a rhetorical relationship? Even if this is the case, there is certainly rhetoric.

6
Lacan in Public

From the point of view of the public, my wish is to emit a sign of alarm.
—Jacques Lacan, "Interview, 1957"

So far, my task has been to locate the place of rhetoric in Lacan's work, primarily by mapping the diverse discursive functions entailed in a theory of rhetoric onto the the Symbolic, Imaginary, and Real Orders. My attempt to locate rhetoric has focused on articulating its suspension between the formal charge of the Symbolic, imaginary commitments and practices of relation, and the limit implied by the Real. In this chapter, I take the concept of location a bit more literally than I have so far, focusing on the public as the site in which the subject and its discourses unfold.

Whether in the guise of the public sphere or spheres (the public as an antithesis to the private), public address, or public culture, things public have become a significant site for locating and analyzing the circulation of discourse in contemporary life. While many segments of the contemporary humanities embrace a variety of concepts rooted in the traditions of public theorizing, there is little consensus on how one might understand the concept "public." The ways of theorizing it are as diverse as the tasks to which the concept can be applied. Has the concept suffered death by a thousand iterations? The plurality of public concepts may testify to the usefulness of the concept in a broad range of fora, each with distinctive needs. But plurality potentially comes at the expense of precision: Arthur Strum's history of the German term *Offentlichkeit*—from which the idea of the public and cognates such as publicness, publicity, or the public sphere derive—concludes that the theorizing around the concept of the public has become cacophonous, embodying "loudly competing but mutually incomprehensible disciplinary public spheres, each with its own practical presuppositions and theoretical-methodological languages."[1]

This confusion invites equivocation. The confusion surrounding the idea of the public stems from conceptual slippages between the varied elements that Offentlichkeit has harbored from its inception: between public spheres, specific publics, and the "public" qualities of social phenomena. Inspired by

Lacan, I propose a framework for parsing things public by defining three registers of publicness: public practices of address, specific identitarian publics, and finally, "the" public as a space of appearance. *Practices of publicness* name the habituated modes of imaginary affiliation and address that position subjects relative to others. When practices of publicness cohere around subjects who consume shared texts through common affinity to an economy of trope, enjoyment, and modes of relation to one another, a *specific public* emerges. *Public "space"* is the site where the practices that make up specific publics are mediated by exchange between the general and specific economies of trope and enjoyment that animate subjects and underwrite the production of their discourses.

This tripartite distinction has an analytic and an empirical component. Analytically, this distinction signals that public making relies on three locative functions: an addressive function, an identitarian function, and an ontological function. At the level of address, practices of publicness are constituted by the specific modes of relation to other subjects that invest practices of public talk with an imaginary sense of the public as a space of the mutual negotiation of meaning-making practices—thus, modes of address are the imaginary supplement that ensures speaking subjects of the possibility of relation to other public subjects in advance, covering over the failures in unicity that inhere in the sign. At the level of identitarian practices, the lifeblood of specific publics, a public is a mode of shared affinity between subjects that is both a site of tropological production and a site of investment, one that both ensures an identity that a subject might enjoy and that orders their modes of relation to the self, to other subjects, and to the world. Finally, at the ontological level, public space refers to the fact that entry into a publically shared language entails the labor of abstraction, which is the condition of possibility for establishing a shared language and simultaneously disfigures the subjects that enter into public discourse.

Empirically, each of these registers comes together in an economically interlocked set of practices of tropological exchange and affective labor that constitute the field of publicness within which empirical publics emerge and are reproduced. A public is a specific formation that functions as it does because it solves a problem for a subject. Because speaking subjects are both produced and disfigured by their entry into symbolic life, they seek publics, or imaginary modes of affiliation that are largely premised on practices of address that validate the fantasy of untroubled relation with others, and specific identitarian practices that give substance to the addressed relation by investing a subject in commitments that lend them a coherent individual identity and mark this identity via relations of commonality and difference.

Thus, the field of publicness is a social form that serves as the location of and site of production for the (dis)continuous rhetorical economy of tropological exchange that mediates the production of subjects and their discourses. Why the somewhat tired parenthetical "(dis)" before the continuous? This economy is continuous because each of the modes of labor implied in public making (ontological, addressive, and identitarian) refer to the other sites of exchange—for example, the addressive labor covers over the disfiguring effects of ontological abstraction, and identitarian labor populates the comparatively empty form of the addressed relation. But these sites of production are also discontinuous because the work of supplementing the various anxieties that subjects face at each of the three sites via deferral to another site conceals the failure of unicity at each site.

Put simply, a Lacanian reading of public making reveals the sites of tropological exchange where the subject is produced, places where subjects are situated in relations of address to other subjects and invest in a mode of enjoyment that lends durability to social formations. Similarly, it is possible to loosely map these functions over accounts of "the public," "the public sphere," and "publics." The idea of "the public" as a space distinguished from "the private" and as a space of appearance roughly maps over a conception of what I am framing as Lacan's Symbolic-ontological register. The global function of "the public," as distinguished from private life, signals a commitment to understand the ways that subjects are made and unraveled in relation to a larger space of discourse. Similarly, the concept of a "public sphere" often encompasses a number of functions that deal with the ways that speaking subjects take up a relation to others. Although this way of talking about the public as a sphere usually retains a latent or sometimes more explicit proceduralist bent, it loosely names what I am identifying as the "addressive function" in that the idea of a sphere usually defines the modes of address—that is, the modes of speech, reception, writing, reading, and media consumption—that constitute public space. And finally, the idea of "publics" maintains a strong affinity with what I am calling the "identitarian" function: if a public is a specific set of textually mediated practices that creates common points of attention for subjects who would otherwise be strangers to one another, then what is usually at stake in such an articulation is the practices of identification, misidentification, and disidentification that specify who exactly is a stranger with whom I have a relation based on common reading practices.

Part of the problem that theorists encounter in engaging specific publics is that an account, for example, of the texts or modes of affinity that organize a specific public often functions in isolation from the larger discursive economy that produces and organizes modes of affinity or textual consumption. The question incumbent on any claim to account for a public-making practice is: what work is the text or mode of affinity in question doing for the subjects that perform it? Whether pegged to a shared practice of speaking or a common set of texts, publics are neither "normative" as some Habermasians assert in dealing with procedures of public speech, nor "autotelic" or "self-organized" as Michael Warner has asserted in theorizing specific publics.[2] Practices of public making are not normative because different publics might employ distinctive modes of address as a way of accommodating to the lacks entailed by the Symbolic order. Similarly, a specific public cannot be autotelic because the circulation of texts that produce a community of attention is not an end in and of itself: one must ask why the attention of strangers comes together around one text or set of texts as opposed to another. Attention to a text does not only refer inward, by nature such practices also gesture or turn (tropos) outward toward the whole economy of trope and enjoyment that makes a text a site for the production of enjoyment. Practices of address and shared attention to a texts both function as a means of public making because they elicit investment from the subjects who practice them—otherwise the public as a social form would not attain the degree of durability, regularity, and reproducibility that it does. A specific public's practices of address, reading, or meaning making work because they are situated in a larger economy of subject production, discursive exchange, and enjoyment that is the precondition for a durable public practice.

Beyond simply attempting to rewrite existing theories of public making in Lacanian vernacular, I would also like to frame Lacan's rhetorical conception of public making as an antidote to a vision of his work as a self-executing structuralist poetics. In making this case I take up Frederic Jameson's prominent critique of the translatability of psychoanalysis to the larger sphere of culture. For Jameson, the question is whether a technology originally intended to analyze individual subjects can be appropriate to the task of unpacking the production of culture. Jameson discerns in psychoanalytic criticism a virtual "absence" of any sustained reflection on the means by which essentially "private" subjective practices become more durable "public" social formations.[3] In response to this criticism, I hope to show that a rhetorically configured conception of the public as an economy provides a translational principle for psychoanalysis by situating publics and, as I will argue later, "objects of public utility" as sites of exchange between the general and specific economies of tropes and affects.

I begin by framing the public as a "space of appearance" through an ontology of being-in-public pegged to Lacan's conceptions of the gaze and the "Corsican dialect." Speech, which both ensconces and dispossesses the speaking subject as one language user among others, is not reducible to the expression of private ideation nor simple intersubjective production. While speech is premised on a relation to an other, and rooted in the experience of inhabiting a language that is, in some ways, comfortingly common, the entry into speech is simultaneously alienating in that shared signification cannot communicate that which is radically unique to the individual. If the entry into the Symbolic dispossesses subjects via its abstracting qualities as much as it makes them at home, the implication is, as I will argue later, that permanent and even constitutive misunderstanding is an intrinsic part of the public exchange of signs. Put more succinctly, the condition of possibility for a shared public language also entails a fundamentally alienating relationship to the sign and, by extension, explains why the subject's communicative relationship with its others is so precarious.

Second, constitutive misunderstanding in the public exchange of signs forces a question about the nature of the public relation. If shared intersubjective meanings, which presumably hold public discourse together, are rendered problematic by constitutive misunderstanding, then a theory of the public would require attention to the modes of imagined relation and symbolic triangulation that supplement the failings of intersubjectively grounded public speech. When a subject speaks in public, it imagines a specific set of practices for relating to its addressees. The intrinsic difficulties in this relationship of address were already revealed in Schema L: although classical rhetorical theory is accustomed to thinking about public address as the work of a singular subject addressing a collection of others, in practice the condition of address is always multiple. Thus, I will take up Lacan's conception of the "navel" of public speech as a way of theorizing the idea that when one speaks in public, one primarily serves as both addressor and addressee, only engaging the others at speech that is presumably aimed by indirection or, in the register of tropology, by turning toward them.

Finally, I would like to address the identitarian practices that constitute specific publics against the backdrop of the ontological and addressive registers. "Publics" are specific tropologically organized sites of affinity where subjects who are otherwise strangers find imaginary points of commonality, define themselves, and demarcate the bounds of their identities relative to those who are presumed to be inside and/or those marked as outside of the bounds of a specific identitarian public. Public making's identitarian functions provide a site for engaging publics as a means of cultural production and, perhaps more importantly, for detailing the ways that an economy of trope and enjoyment is situated within a specific material context. Understanding publics as a site of exchange between the general symbolic economy and the specific economies that make up an identitarian public grants a decidedly rhetorical slant to the constitution and reproduction of publics, a claim that I will take up at two specific sites of public making in the next chapter. I conclude with a provocation on the nature of violence and stasis in public making.

The Public and Ontology

The last half century saw a number of projects taken on under the rubric of "Being" and something else. Prominent examples include Sartre's *Being and Nothingness,* Heidegger's *Being and Time,* and Alain Badiou's *Being and Event,* to name a few. Despite Lacan's hedging on the question of whether he offers an ontology proper, on the basis of the problem of naming the Real, his work theorizes a particular kind of "being in": Lacan is a theorist of being-in-public. What do I mean? The secondary literature on Lacan contains few references to the concept of the public.[4] This is understandable, given Lacan's sparing use of the word. But leaving this fact aside, it is quite clear that Lacan is addressing the idea that subjects come to be against the background of a public and that public space is crucial to the appearance and emergence of a subject.

The inextricable link between the public appearance and constitution of the subject is a central concern of Hannah Arendt's work. Though they make strange bedfellows, the connection between Lacan's and Arendt's conceptions of the public as the stage on which the subject appears has not escaped notice. For example, Frederick Dolan argues that there is a tight complementarity between Arendt's and Lacan's reflections on the public discursive production of the subject.[5] In *The Human Condition* Arendt argues that the public is the "space of appearance" for the human; that "the twilight which illuminates our private and intimate lives is ultimately derived from the much harsher light of the public realm"; that "the term public signifies the world itself"; and that "only the existence of a public realm and the world's subsequent transformation into a community . . . gathers men together and relates them to each other."[6] If the implication is that the human subject is produced by means of discursive and social exchange, the public is the space where subjects enter into these exchanges in the presence of others. The public names the place where the subject emerges from privation and is put in full view of other subjects.

This understanding of the role of the public provides a useful corrective to a commonsense reading of psychoanalysis as largely about intimate family relations. It is true that in many appropriations of the Freudian tradition relationships with mothers and fathers are a crucial site for understanding the development of a human subject. But if the virtue of Lacan's work is that it turns these categories into metaphors that describe the workings of the Symbolic—for example, in the shift from the Freudian conception of the father to Lacan's idea of the Name of the Father as a symbolic function—the implication is that the primary site where the subject is articulated is not in relation to the family but in relation to the whole economy of discourse that determines even the character of the family. Lacan argues in addressing the symbolic function of naming that: "Founding speech, which envelops the subject, is everything that has constituted him, his parents, his neighbors, the whole structure of his community, and not only constituted him as symbol, but constituted him in his being. The laws of nomenclature are what determine—at least up to a point—and channel the alliances from within which human beings copulate . . . and end up creating, not only . . . symbols, but also real beings, who . . . have that little tag which is their name, the essential symbol which will be their lot."[7] If founding speech constitutes the subject, the ways it relates to others, and plots the basic coordinates for the subject's existence, it does so not only in the act of naming the subject but in the subject's continual negotiation of common symbolic space. The most direct articulation of this facet of a Lacanian being-in-public is Lacan's infamous conception of the gaze, which represents the idea that subjects come into being and live out their lives in the presence of others.

Sartre, Lacan's predecessor in theorizing the gaze, provides a cue for understanding its function. In the play *No Exit* Sartre's character Garcin utters the famous line "l'enfer, c'est les autres," which is traditionally rendered "hell is other people" but might also be translated as "hell is the others."[8] Here, the other serves as the sometimes suffocating horizon of one's status as a subject. Extending this logic, Lacan's *Seminar XI* lays out a now famous distinction between the eye and the gaze, figuring the ways that subjectivity is dependent on *appearing* in public. Noting the ocularcentrism of the predominant Western conception of the subject, Lacan uses the idea of the eye as a metaphor for an understanding of subjectivity that "sees" the subject through the lens of phenomenology—where the subject is both given in advance and primarily engages the world by interpreting it as data. The eye is not necessarily reducible to the field of vision. Although vision is one significant site at which the subject emerges under the attention of others, the eye is a synecdoche for the ontological givenness of the subject of phenomenology. The eye, Lacan notes "is only the metaphor of something that [he] would prefer to call the seers 'shoot' (*pousse*)—something prior to his eye" that embodies a kind of "ontological status."[9] The metaphor of the eye stands in for a subject that seemingly precedes the act of sight: a pre-given, self-possessed, naturalized conception of the self. But the condition of the eye cannot be maintained in its pre-given ontological purity. For Lacan the eye/I of the subject stands in a difficult dialectical tension with the gaze of others.

The gaze encompasses the idea that the field of sight is constituted by the presence of another who also sees but is more generally a metaphor for the idea that the subject is neither pre-given nor self-possessed; being looked at is a marker of and metaphor for the co-presence of the subject and others in an imagined social field. The ocular accent of the gaze is less significant than the relationship of (mis)recognition between the subject and the other that the metaphor of the gaze demonstrates. The alienating character of the gaze overlaps the traumatic character of the Symbolic. One encounters the presence of the gaze in distilled form in the idea that others may not see the subject as it understands itself. But the possibility for misrecognition inheres as much in speech as it does in sight, in the idea that the other may not understand the subject. By the same token, if the gaze is threatening, it is because it reveals the contingency and the dependency of the eye/I on an other's attention in the same way that the Symbolic embodies an ambivalent relationship to the speech of the Other. As Lacan frames the gaze in reference to Merleau-Ponty, "we are beings who are looked at, in the spectacle of the world. That which makes us consciousness institutes by the same token as *speculum mundi*."[10] Paradoxically, being the mirror of the world (speculum mundi) is generative of a subject and simultaneously an intensely decentering experience reflecting the subject's contingent social situation, as opposed to the pousse of the eye, which presumes the subject's self-sufficient potency. Thus, in framing the pousse by posing it against the constitutive field of others, Lacan's conception of the gaze reveals that the subject is not the exclusive author of its own intentions or action and, when it comes to the social field, is affected as much as it exerts effects. The gaze thus embodies the moment of castration anxiety par excellence, which is less about the penis than the phallus, or the subject's conception of its own potency and self-sufficient intention: "The gaze is presented to us only in the form of a strange contingency, symbolic of what we find on the horizon, as the thrust of our experience, namely the lack that constitutes castration anxiety."[11] In saying that the gaze is an agent of castration, what Lacan means is that when a subject encounters the formative power of the Symbolic, it loses the imaginary certainty that it is the insular, self-possessed, and self-authoring agent of its own intentions and encounters itself as both a product and object of discourse.

Therefore, the eye, gaze, and appearance are metaphors for the imaginary genesis of the subject in relation to the Symbolic. As Malcolm Bowie frames it, the same dynamic inheres in the idea that the signifier is both a site for the articulation of the individual subject and its passions and a kind of "public property." The embodiment of the dispossessing function of the Other is not simply the gaze understood as an ocular function but rather the presence of others who also signify (in literature, for Bowie, but arguably the same holds true for speech):

> The signifier is the writer's domain, but it is everybody else's too. And if the signifier is subdivided according to local modes of action, and thought of as a competitive interplay between two "slopes" or rhetorical dispositions that Lacan, following Jakobson, names metaphor and metonymy, it becomes still more plainly a piece of public property. . . . Literature has the virtue of allowing us to inspect these and other rhetorical devices under laboratory conditions, and in unusually concentrated forms, but rhetoric itself has the corresponding virtue of allowing us to look beyond literature once more—and into the lingua franca of human passion as it might be heard . . . in the street.[12]

The specific other—"other" writers and speakers—is also a sign user, and the other's use of signs (as a necessary implication of the idea of the unconscious) prefigures the meaning of an addressee's sign usage along with the dialectic of the eye and gaze: in both instances, what is at stake is the constitutive function of a structurally determined misrecognition. In a function analogous to the gaze's relation to the eye, the big "O" Other is present as the condition of possibility for the idea that "the signifier is subdivided" between local modes of action and the more general purview of the symbolic functions of metaphor and metonymy, which also script a subject's usage of the sign in advance of any individualized intention. The sign is public property because it is made intelligible only through the language use of others, and the condition of this public property is the general symbolic logic that underwrites it. By extension, the public character of signs is inseparable from the alienating properties of entry into the Symbolic.

If this is too abstract an account of the "abstracting" functions of the Symbolic, consider an analogy that Lacan employs in explaining the public character of subjectivization and symbol use. In *The Psychoses,* Lacan recounts an experience with a Parisian analysand born into a Corsican family. In public settings the analysand spoke in a flawless Parisian accent; yet despite the fact that the family had lived in Paris from the time he was a boy, "nothing in the household was conceived in anything but the Corsican dialect." The analysand encountered "great difficulty" in recounting his childhood experiences, exclaiming "I can't get it out."[13] Even though the analysand could talk about the general structure of his symptoms in a perfectly lucid way, he found it impossible to recount his childhood without returning to the Corsican dialect. From the fact that "nothing in the household was conceived in anything but the Corsican dialect" Lacan infers that the analysand exists between "two worlds," one constituted by the Corsican dialect and another constituted by "that which went on outside."[14] Lacan's analysand serves as a paradigm for what Michael Warner frames as the dislocating experience of prosthetic public personhood in the radical disconnect between two ways of speaking that are, for him at least, inextricably tied to two fundamentally different registers of experience. Warner argues that the making of a public subject is dependent on a condition of abstraction, and this condition of abstraction exerts a form of violence on one's irreducible individuality because one cannot translate that which is unique about their experience into a public vernacular without cost.[15] If entry into public enables the possibility of relation with others, it also presupposes the impossibility of translating that which is radically specific to the individual into the language of the social without remainder.

But, in contradistinction to Warner, it is not simply the fact that language is a product of the "mass public" and "mass subject" that creates a dislocation for the subject of speech: "mass" dislocation is a symptom of the logic of the Symbolic, present even in the most intimate conditions of one-to-one address. For Lacan, the Corsican dialect stands in for a more fundamental problem in shared and, by extension, public discourses: "the establishment . . . of a public discourse I would say, is an important factor in the specific functioning of the mechanism of repression . . . [that] stems from the impossibility of granting discourse to a certain past of the subject's speech."[16] The establishment of a common discourse requires the suppression of the traumatic past of the subject's entry into speech, serving as a productive prohibition on the full entry of the individual qua individual into public speech. This repression is productive because it authorizes the fantasy that common discourses are a realm in which the subject can create meaning, transparently signal meanings, disclose intentions, and communicate. If the violence of entry into the Symbolic is the disavowed product of public speech, practices of public making manifest a difficult intertextual relation for the subject whose modes of speech are only precariously held together in a figurally determined gap between two mutually exclusive registers: one aiming at the articulation of common communicative ground, at forging imaginary communicative unicities, and another rooted in an only seemingly autochthonous experience of being an individual. Thus, the presupposition of shared speech is a general precondition for the social bonds that underwrite particular social affinities. The reaffirmation of shared speech shores up a subject's sense of coherence and the possibility of relations with others and therefore feigns unicity in the context of unicity's failure. Common speech implies the possibility of intersubjective relations, it authorizes the specific relations of affinity that invest a subject with identity, and finally, the cumulative effect of the preceding two functions is that shared speech retroactively implies the coherence of the subject and the social field that locates subjects in relation to its others.

If being-in-public names the process of acceding to an abstracted language for the sake of enabling social exchange, it is equally a process of making the signifier stupid. "Perhaps stupidity is not," as Lacan put it, what "people think, a semantic category, but rather a way of collectivizing the signifier."[17] In the empirical life of speech, signifiers seem to express individual intentions and ideations—in the classical rhetorical tradition speech, and especially political speech, was the index of a specifically human intelligence. Though acts of speaking originate with individuals, speech requires a collective signifying body wrought by collective repetition of signs, lodged in an economy beyond the control of any individual intellect, formed by the labor of collective investment, and sustained only by the stupidity of the sign. Thus, the signifier is stupid in a dual sense: it is both reduced to the lowest common denominator, and thus it becomes mute or unable to speak what is radically unique to an individual subject. Lacan's productive paradox of discourse appears in condensed form: language is the condition of possibility for a subject with identity investments and, simultaneously, the stupidity of signification prevents subjects from grounding or sharing these commitments via authentic intersubjective exchange.

Here the public relation between the signifier, trope, and the addressive preconditions of sociality also appears in condensed form. In public, the subject is made a stranger among other strangers. The idea of the stranger relies on the stupidity of the signifier, because a stranger is someone who the subject relates to primarily through the stupidity of the sign. If, as an addressee of discourse, a stranger is an addressee for whom a subject does not have an intimate sense of what defines or invests the stranger with a radically unique character, the means by which a subject relates to a stranger (as an addressee of a subjects address or as a fellow addressee of another discourse) can be nothing more than the empty form of stupid discourse, framed by practices of imagined relation. The practice of being a stranger among other strangers requires that publics act as stupid spaces of abstraction.

Abstraction is both a logic and a performance, or a situating practice of being a subject among other subjects. If the public is a kind of metatopical space, the character of this space cannot be separated from the concrete conditions that make it possible; namely, a subject loses something of its specificity in entering a public bond between strangers. Subjects in public are split between their status as unique individuals imbued with all the characteristics that subjects refer to in marking their own uniqueness from others (a specific history, identity, outlook, and emotional life) and their status as public subjects interpolated by the circulation of mediated texts that provide a point of common addressivity with other subjects. Warner frames this as a kind of prosthetic personhood that is as much a wrenching process of dislocation as it is a way of identifying with other strangers. This split status relies on the function of a trope: specifically, prosopopoeia, traditionally the term for the figure where an author addresses an audience by speaking as another person (for example, the chorus in a classical drama) or object. Prosopopoeia derives from the Greek terms *prosopon,* which means person but also a mask employed on the dramatic stage, and *poesis,* meaning production. In public, prosopopoeia signifies the prosthetic production of the self as the stranger among other strangers, speaking a public language to other prosthetic persons. The figural charge in abstraction as prosopopoeia cannot be separated from the fact that it is also a performance, a specific and concrete practice of selfhood. But what is the nature of the prosthetic person? It is a metaphor in Lacan's sense, a mode of subjectivization that causes subjects to speak "as if" they were already positioned in and related to the social field in advance. Thus, the ontological problem of the public as a space of appearance drives us toward an account of the conditions of address that underwrite public subjectivization. The question is how one might account for the transition between the general economy of exchange that produces the public as a space of appearance and the specific economies of tropological exchange that underwrite specific publics. To answer this question, it is necessary to turn to an analysis of the practices of address that serve as the hinge between the general and specific economies of tropological exchange.

Public Addressivity

Addressivity defines the fact that practices of public making cannot be reduced simply to the articulation of symbolic forms, requiring attention to concrete habits and modes of social relation implied in the public as a mode of performing a relation to others. Addressivity marks the ground of the second moment in Lacan's economy of trope where subjects substitute a signifier—

here a vision of the addressed social relation—for the original signifier of the subject. This conception of addressivity, which requires attention to the specificity of and differences inherent in plural modes of address, is a relatively underdeveloped theme in psychoanalytically influenced encounters with rhetoric. For instance, the concept of address does not meaningfully inform Laclau's tropological configuration of the demand, nor does it occupy the critical sensibilities of the structural poetic strand of theorizing the constitutive function of trope in comparative literature. For these schools of thought, address is reducible to a formal relationship between the subject of speech and the Symbolic order; the character of address is almost exclusively understood as a demand that the subject places on the Symbolic for recognition and that the Symbolic imposes on the subject's speech in the form of a demand for intelligibility. But address implies more than this in the rhetorical traditions, specifying not only a generalized relation to the system of discourse but also a set of practices of relation that inhere when one takes up the task of speaking to an other. Thus the insight of Lacan's work for understanding rhetoric's addressive functions: a relationship of address inheres both in the subject's imaginary relation to other subjects and in the subject's relation to the order of discourse more generally—thus, the addressive nature of rhetoric is present in the Imaginary register and in the Symbolic.

Lacan suggests that the imaginary components of public affiliation, which are ostensibly composed by the exchange of speech between an addressor and others, are ultimately a practice of navel gazing: "In public speech, one directs one's attention at subjects, touching what Freud calls the navel—*the navel of the dreams* Freud writes, to designate their ultimately unknown center—which is simply, like the anatomical navel that represents it, that gap of which I have already spoken. There is a danger in public discourse precisely insofar as it addresses those nearest—Nietzsche knew this, a certain type of discourse can be addressed only to those furthest away."[18] What is involved in this navel gazing? "Navel gazing" folds three distinct components of the act of public address into an overarching metaphor that highlights address's narcissistic quality. First, the navel suggest a point of focus at which address is aimed, but paradoxically the navel has the status of something that a subject might fix its eyes on and of a literal hole or space in the body of the other. While, for example, many of the metaphors for the intersubjective relation suggest that it ideally encounters the face of the other or "looks her in the eye," that the navel is the point of address's focus on the other suggests that the relationship with the other is conditioned more by the symbolic gap that constitutes it than by authentic intersubjective exchange. Second, and by extension, Lacan borrows the original Freudian conception of the "navel of dreams" to suggest that the addressees' relationship never quite achieves access to the one that it addresses. As Robert J. C. Young notes, Freud originally invoked the term when referring to a dream whose source was unknown to him, and as such it stood for "the navel of dreams, the point of contact with the unknown."[19] Finally, the connection with the colloquial idea of navel gazing recalls the insight of Schema L that in speech the subject receives its message in inverted form, and therefore that the greater part of "public" address is largely constituted narcissistically, despite what subjects might imagine to the contrary.

But the results of this narcissism are productive: gazing at the navel of the other is both the mode and condition of possibility of address, one that paradoxically invents (that is, discovers) the other in the act of looking at and addressing it.[20] Navel gazing represents both the imaginary aspiration of address as authentic intersubjective exchange but simultaneously marks, on the grounds of the symbolic gap that the navel represents, the impossibility of intersubjective consensual relations that are the condition of possibility for intersubjective address. Paradoxically, the eminently narcissistic act of navel gazing is the authorizing logic behind the idea that one can communicate with other subjects. The public is both a mode of relation and an affective investment in the social character of the space of public appearance, paradoxically by marking the conditions of an individual's address. Put in the register of the general and the specific economies that constitute the subject, in the specific economy the navel stands for the point of focus, or the mode of relation that retroactively figures the character of the addressee in speech, while as a hole or gap, the navel marks the presence of the general economy of tropological exchange. But the navel is not either of these: it is always both, and therefore it serves as one of the primary sites that suture the relationship between the general and specific economies of tropological exchange that constitute a subject. The public subject's acts of address are suspended between the formal symbolic preconditions for the relation of address and the imaginary instantiation of a relationship with others. Thus, the dangers of navel gazing are not exclusive with its productive functions: navel gazing is productive of an (a)social bond.

If navel gazing implies that the addressee in public address is as much the speaking subject as the external other, then the danger of the Imaginary register in public address is that the subject tends to forget that the navel is nothing more than a gap. This nearness has two effects. First, it implies that the other subject is accessible on its own terms and without the mediation of the Symbolic. Second, in cultivating a sense of nearness to other subjects the subject also cultivates a sense of nearness to the self and thus begins to hold ever more tightly to an Imagined conception of itself at the expense of addressing the symbolic gaps that are the precondition for the imaginary emergence of the self.

The solution to this dilemma is not to accede fully to the power of the Symbolic in determining the subject: privileging the formal charge in public speech, one risks eclipsing the imaginary commitments that give public life its tone and tenor. In privileging transcontextual forms and structural imperatives too strongly, total accession to the generative power of the Symbolic results in reading practice that would overdetermine the messiness of public social life. Alternatively, if one reads the relationship of address through seamless and intersubjectively constituted sociality, the symbolic gaps that mark public address are occluded, and the social descends into an arena of mutually shared consensual interaction. In holding steadfastly to the dual character of address, it is possible to reveal the core tension between a subject situated in a social field and the "non-relations" of immediation that requires affective labor to suture a public together as a collective identitarian practice.

This relationship might be approached through a second of de Man's famous aporias that mirrors the aporia between trope and persuasion introduced earlier: de Man claims a theory of discourse necessarily inhabits an aporia between the reduction of rhetoric to forms (what he calls a "grammatization of rhetoric") and the reduction of rhetoric to contingently situated acts of persuasion, which he calls the "rhetorization of grammar."[21] Lacan's reading of the public is a grammatization of public rhetoric in that it refers the operation of publics to the formal charge of an economy of trope. The introduction of trope allows Lacan to articulate the ways that figural economies materialize the Symbolic in speech. But this grammatization of public rhetoric needs to be knotted together with the ways that the public, as an expressive modality, also relies on a rhetorization of grammar or the articulation of symbolic form in a specific contingent setting.

As Lacan repeatedly notes in *Seminar XX,* "language is not the speaking subject."[22] Signification must pass through the gristmill of the speaking subject. As a result, speech is not the site of perfect reference where subjects transparently exchange signifiers. Speech is the site where subjects employ broken signification, an exchange that is not characterized by the perfect implementation of symbolic codes but a messy kind of intercourse to be read through reference to the bedroom as much as to Saussure. This is the point where the gaps between langue, parole, and the subject's relation to the Other converge: the act of speech is not a perfect transmission of langue, as speech is caught up in the subject's economy of enjoyment, in the messy particularities of a rhetorical situation. If a conception of the contingency of rhetorical situations represents a rhetorization of grammar and the particularity of speech as the act of a specific subject speaking from a specific location, rhetoric can never be grammatized without remainder. Conversely, rhetorized imaginary intersubjective commitments to the rational, ideational, or communitarian roots of the public language ought to be displaced by the "grammatical" charges of speech as a material manifestation of the Symbolic mediated by the affective functions of enjoyment.

Identitarian Publics

At this intersection between the public evocation of both structure and contingency in the imagined act of address, publics require specific texts and objects as specific nodes for organizing identity. The identitarian functions of the public stem largely from the fact that every relation with a small "o" other is an object relation. If what is at stake in a relation with an other is less the intrinsic uniqueness of the other than the ways that a subject figures the other as an object for its own purposes—as a point around which the subject's world is organized—then every practice of relation to an other is also a practice of identity production, albeit one that can be understood more through the politics of a narcissistic projection than through the idea of reciprocal intersubjective exchange. Lacan views others/objects as sites of sublimation with "public utility." Borrowing from a reframed Freudian vocabulary for defining enjoyment in *The Ethics of Psychoanalysis,* Lacan defines sublimation as the idea that the object of investment is "elevated to the dignity of a thing."[23] Sublimation is less a function of the individual psyche than a "socially validated" process whereby subjects organize collective identities around specific nodal sites: "sublimation is characterized by a . . . [libidinal] satisfaction in objects . . . as objects that are socially validated, objects of which the groups approves, insofar as they are object of public utility. That is how the possibility of sublimation is defined."[24] Here Lacan affirms the basic insight of even the most conservative elements of the rhetorical tradition in characterizing the public relation: the objects (whether they be texts or more abstract ideographic forms) that subjects attend to and invest in configure both publics and public identities. The point of difference with the more conservative elements of the rhetorical tradition is that although sublimation is about social sanction, the tenor of this relationship is primarily defined by almost accidental, formally organized, mutually overlapping narcissistic investments and not by the mutual negotiation of intersubjective meanings. Even though processes of sublimation are essentially narcissistic, the imaginary character of the social field implies that the function of the social ought to be folded into an account of processes of sublimation—not as a product of the intersubjective relation but rather as an extension of the symbolic ordering of imagined relations:

> At the level of sublimation, the object is inseparable from imaginary and especially cultural elaborations. It is not just that the collectivity recognizes in them useful objects; it finds rather a space of relaxation where it may delude itself on the subject of [the Thing] or, colonize the field of [the Thing] with imaginary schemes. That is how collective, socially accepted sublimations operate. . . . [S]ociety takes some comfort from the mirages that moralists, artists, artisans, designers of dresses and hats, and the creators of imaginary forms in general supply it with, but it is not simply in the approval of that society gladly affords that we must seek the power of sublimation. It is rather an imaginary function, and in particular, that for which we use the symbolization of fantasm ($ à a), which is the form on which the subject's desire depends.[25]

Whereas the space of shared meanings is a site of active negotiation or the mutual "recognition of a useful object," the space of the overlapping object is almost a shortcut: it is a space of "relaxation" where the negotiation of meaning between subjects is essentially evacuated and where the primary functions of labor refer to the subject's labor in relation to the object, as opposed to the object's mediation of the labor between subjects. Here, a vision of rhetoric as active intersubjective exchange and negotiation cedes to an interpassive conception of overlapping discursive nodes, producing the subject as an effect of discourse, as opposed to seeing it as the cause of insular discourses. If I may cite an expanded version of a quote from chapter 3, the idea of relaxation as opposed to actively negotiated meaning making is yet another way of saying that the rhetorical character of the object is primarily inventional (in that it is discovered or found) as opposed to sought (that is, constituted hermeneutically) and is "interpassive" as opposed to "intersubjective." One might read a different significance in the relationship between the object and the Thing: the object of public utility is another way of saying that the identitarian function of public making is properly inventional in the rhetorical tradition's sense of the term: "The object by nature is a refound object. That it was lost is a consequence of that, but only after the fact. It is thus refound without our knowing, except through refinding, that it was ever lost. . . . And that is the second characteristic of the Thing as veiled; it is by nature in the refinding of the object. . . . You cannot fail to see that in the celebrated expression of Picasso, 'I do not seek, I find,' that this finding (*trouver*), the *trobar* of the Provençal troubadours . . . and all the schools of rhetoric . . . takes precedence over the seeking."[26] Three implications flow from this realization. First, at the level of the specific economy, the objects of public life, often in the form of texts, are part and parcel of the whole economy of tropological exchange, which invests them with a set of identity-forming functions that figure both the contents of texts and the modes of social relation that they invoke. An economic conception of trope and investment accounts for why specific contents of texts are compelling for us. But this relationship is inseparable from an account of the modes of social relation that texts imply. This dynamic will take up a central portion of my treatment of *The Passion of the Christ* in the concluding chapter.

If the identitarian functions of the public are inextricable from the relationship to objects that both figures the place of the specific qualities of the object and the modes of social relation that it implies, by implication a public relation is one that is not universally extensible or inclusive but rather meaningfully bounded by commitments of inclusion and exclusion that follow the identitarian center of publics. Because of the tight complementarity between objects, the identity of subjects, and the modes of social relation that they imply, a public identity is always constituted by a relationship of inclusion and exclusion. Put differently, any theory of the public must attempt to come to grips with two questions: What is the character of public space, or how does it function as a social bond? What are the conditions for inclusion in a public space? Whether this question is rendered in a normative sense, in empirical study, or in systems theory, concepts of the public require articulating conditions of inclusion and exchange between subjects, whether they are theorized as fellow citizens, readers of a text, strangers, or speakers participating in a common sphere.

Articulating the conditions of possibility for the public as a social link requires specificity. Whether this specificity comes in the form of concrete conditions for stranger relationality, or as set of procedural norms that govern proper modes of participation in the public, these conditions of inclusion also create conditions of exclusion: for some procedures, social links, or modes of textual engagement to be meaningfully called public, they must logically exclude other procedures, social links, or modes of textual engagement. Exclusion is the disavowed supplement of the public, as the thing that is required but is productively barred in the formation of a public as a historically specific set of social coordinates and practices.

What the object/identity nexus demonstrates is that inclusion and exclusion are necessary for an effective affective identification with a public—a subject will cast its lot with participation in a public because the conditions of inclusion help to manage the problems of being a subject by providing a set of narrative practices about who the subject is. Here, investments at the level of the specific economy function as a suture for the failed unicity of the general economy. The conditions implied by the logics of exclusion in a public generate a mode of enjoyment that stems from embracing a violent dissymmetry against others as a proxy for the problems of the general economy. This dialectic is made maximally efficient if this violence is repressed: repressing the fact of exclusion works to bolster the fantasy of the social as a space of symmetrical relation without violence. As a result, accounts of the public as a social bond are caught in a difficult paradox between their political commitments and the affective basis for public participation. The more abstract the conditions of public inclusion, the less effective a public is in generating affective commitment. Conversely, as the conditions of inclusion in a public become more specific, and thus more effective in motivating continuing participation in a public, the degree of concrete exclusions embodied in a specific public escalates.

Finally, directing an economy of trope and investment through the object answers the concerns that some commentators have about the translatability of psychoanalysis to theorizing the social. The object is the site through which one can understand the ways that an economy of trope constitutes and by extension can meaningfully explicate the social. But there is a historical difficulty in making this argument: readings done in the name of the psychoanalytic tradition are often utterly decontextualized. This problem may lie in the presupposition that a universal set of precepts govern all acts of reading, speaking, and interpretation, or it may lie in the fact that often psychoanalytic readings are simply agnostic toward the context within which specific modes of reading and address are situated. Often, author and reader, even if influenced by a network of signifying associations and an economy of trope that exceeds them, are essentially imagined to be speaking, reading, and writing in private—that is, not imagined as emplotted in any particular context. In most cases, it makes no difference to whom the text is addressed, the form that address takes, in what context it is presented, among what others a speaker or author produces a discourse, and what readers or audiences consume it.

In some ways, it is understandable that psychoanalytic readings often elide considerations of context, address, and the irreducible specificity of social forms within which tropes circulate, because part of the goal of psychoanalytic criticism is to avoid a reduction of meaning to context. At the same time, in avoiding a reduction to context, one need not elide context entirely;

rather, an analytic protocol ought to engage the logic of trope and enjoyment, attending to the ways that such articulations organize and fail to organize a relationship to context and to how discourses are not only "addressed" in the abstract but also the specific forms of address that they take and the specific others to whom they are addressed. Put differently, address is always at least tripartite: it is split between a relationship to the Symbolic in the abstract (the Other), to a particular addressee (an other), and the self to subject (which is other in relation to the unorganized body). The wager of a rhetorical conception of Lacan's work is that the presence of each of these addressees figures the character of an act of address in ways that are crucially influenced by but not ultimately reducible to the formal charge of language. In ignoring this fact, one also elides the presence of the social field in figuring address, a dynamic that prompted Frederic Jameson to write that:

> What is so often problematical about psychoanalytic criticism is therefore not its insistence on the subterranean relationships between the literary text on the one hand and the "obsessive metaphor" or the distant and inaccessible childhood on the other: it is rather the absence of any reflection on the transformational process whereby such private materials become public—a transformation which is often, to be sure, so undramatic and inconspicuous as the very act of speech itself. Yet insofar as speech is pre-eminently social, . . . we will do well to keep Durkheim's stern warning constantly before us as a standard against which to assess the various models psychoanalytic criticism has provided: "Whenever a social phenomenon is directly explained by a psychological phenomenon, we may be sure that the explanation is false."[27]

A rhetorically inflected account of Lacan's work that focuses on the work of trope and enjoyment in figuring objects of "public utility" provides a crucial link between "subterranean" psychoanalysis and cultural mediation. If the object has public utility, it is precisely because it is the site of this translational process, and because it serves as a site for articulating practices of public making with the economy of tropes and investments that knits together the sign, subject, and social as nodal articulations of an underlying process of tropological exchange.

Provocation: Eros and the Static Public

Fascination with the public as a social form is rooted in the political possibilities of the public as a space for social relation. The turn to public reason or reasons heralds the possibility of a mode of political organization that supplants the turn to violence or coercion in constituting a social order. This is the dream of the public relation envisioned by so many prophets of the public as a new political order: Immanuel Kant calls for the exercise of public reason to counteract the prejudices of "immaturity," the dangers of tyrants, and the threat of revolution;[28] John Dewey envisions public practices of "common will" formation and "creative intelligence" as an alternative to coercion;[29] for Jürgen Habermas, the public is an alternative to violence because "a communicative practice of power of this kind can develop only in undeformed public spheres; it can issue only from structures of undamaged intersubjectivity found in nondistorted communication."[30]

But for Lacan, these claims ring hollow because dialogue, the basis for a non-coercive public relation, fails to meaningfully exorcise violence: "Dialogue in itself seems to involve a renunciation of aggressiveness; from Socrates onward, philosophy has always placed its hope in dialogue to make reason triumph. And yet ever since Thrasymachus made his mad outburst in the beginning of . . . *The Republic,* verbal dialectic has all too often proved a failure."[31] The reasons for this failure ought not be surprising given the claims made in the preceding chapters: communication and intersubjectivity are constitutively broken, the self and social relation are only wrought by a framing of the self and the other as objects of competition and aggression, and unicity does not inhere in the social any more than it does in any other register of human experience.[32]

One of the earliest organizing principles for rhetoric, repeated in various iterations throughout the rhetorical traditions, is the opposition between *peitho,* or persuasion, and *bia*—force, compulsion, or violence.[33] In one reading, this dyad represents perhaps both the condition of possibility for and founding exclusion of rhetoric. Here, rhetoric's domain is defined by persuasion, and persuasion is defined, as Vincent Farenga argues, in relation to what it is not, namely the application of violence to achieve a given end.[34] As Lacan puts it, "the mirror stage . . . manufactures for the subject . . . the armor of an alienating identity."[35] Lacan explicitly connects the aggressive functions of the Imaginary with the concealment that makes the Imaginary as a mode of social relation possible. Put in the light of the mirror, while "in itself dialogue seems to involve a renunciation of aggressivity," the Imaginary is only constituted through the exercise of aggression.[36]

At issue is not only the violence latent in the public social bond but the character of the social bond as a specific kind of affinity, one perhaps best characterized by the idea of love as uninterrupted union. The question is whether love in public is premised on union and agapic mutuality or on the erotic reduction of the other to an object of desire. The second option is an extension of the impossibility of the sexual relation: if the sexual relation is impossible, a rhetorical relation founded on intersubjectivity or identity is also impossible.

What if there is no such thing as a rhetorical relationship? Pursuing this question, one might figure eros as a synecdoche within a synecdoche: eros condenses one of love's modalities, and love condenses, in a particularly stark manner, the conditions of possibility for the social relation. It is precisely at the messy intersections of eros and the possibility of union between subjects that Herbert Marcuse and Erich Fromm opened a heated debate over Freud's conception of eros.[37] The exchange revolves around the following question: does the principle of eros require its own frustration, that is, does it contain within itself the fundamental impossibility of its satisfaction (Marcuse's understanding of Freud) or, alternately, is the primary blockage in eros external to it—for example, in civilization (Fromm)? Fromm and Marcuse's debate over the nature of eros pits two views of erotic prohibition against each other. In locating eros's prohibitions differently, Marcuse and Fromm produce substantially different versions of the relationship between the subject and its erotic impulse. If there are prohibitions internal to eros, the very logic of eros requires its frustration; but if the prohibition of eros is external to it, eros must precede its suppression by an external force. Thus, if the primary site of eros's inhibition is external to it, then perhaps it is possible to bring erotic union to consummation, provided one can navigate the structures that impinge upon the erotic drive. Fromm's framing of Freud figures eros as something akin to an innate impulse or desire. Eros is an affect generated by a subject that aims at union with others. This conception of eros does not stray too far from one prominent understanding of eros in Greek antiquity, mirroring a Platonic conception of eros as a kind of affectively saturated madness that moves the soul toward unity with the divine (toward "communion with being," as Harvey Yunis puts it).[38]

Against eros as an internally unfettered positivity frustrated by an external force and the promise of unmediated union between subjects such a view implies, a Freudian and (later) Lacanian conception of eros foregrounds the constitutive unachievability of erotic union. Marcuse suggests such a reading of Freud in his rebuttal to Fromm: "Far from identifying happiness with the 'unrestricted satisfaction' of the sexual instinct, Freud held that 'unrestricted sexual liberty from the beginning' results in lack of full satisfaction, and that the 'value' of erotic needs 'instantly sinks as satisfaction becomes readily obtainable . . . something in the *nature* of the sexual instinct is unfavorable to the achievement of absolute satisfaction'" (emphasis added).[39]

For Lacan, this picture of eros as union omits an important player: the object. Despite our ethical and political pretensions to the contrary, when other subjects appear to us, they almost invariably appear to us as objects. Subjects do not desire others; they desire objects, and objects are always in some significant way not only a representation of another but also a reduction of the other. If eros requires an "object" of desire, this object is also a bar to full communion with the other: the object is both a point of access to the other and a barrier to ever receiving the other on its own terms. The object serves as a bar in two distinct ways: first, eros dictates that a subject hold the object of their desire at a certain distance, and this distance is one of the things that motivates an affective logic of impossible union; second, the object is a reduction of the other in that it serves as a partial and interested (that is, narcissistic) representation of the other in the economy of the subject's representational practices. If there is distance both between a subject and its object and simultaneously between an object and the other for which it stands in, one might unpack this dynamic from the perspective of eros as love and, more specifically, from the maxims that "there is no such thing as a sexual relationship" and "enjoyment of the other is not the sign of love."[40]

There is enjoyment in this relationship that exceeds the ostensible embrace of the beloved in their intrinsic uniqueness: the vision of love not only implies access to the lover on their own terms, it also implies the unity of the subject who loves, retroactively producing a sense of oneness for the lover, rendering a subject who is divided by lack and language as a unified subject. To love in this sense is to identify (or rather misidentify) with the beloved on one's own terms, to identify with one's image of the other. To love is to render the other an object, an "*objet petit a,*" or as an object around which a subject organizes its enjoyment and from which desire flows. The enjoyment that is derived from love is not an enjoyment of the other on the other's term, but a mode of enjoyment that the demand on the other (or at least the image of the other) produces. This "remainder" in the desire of the other (the enjoyment that the demand and frustration of the demand create) is the enabling condition for an image of the other, ultimately sustaining desire for the little "a" object "through the lack of satisfaction."[41]

Here the basic logic of Fromm's eros is reversed: according to Lacan, eros is not an innate desire for unity with the other; rather, eros is produced by its object or, more appropriately, the object cause of desire. But perhaps the most important implication of this reversal is that erotic union is by definition prohibited. One does not enjoy the other as much as one organizes one's enjoyment around an objectal reduction of the other. In this sense, union with the other is impossible, but it is the constitutive impossibility of union with the other that makes the object the site of affective investment in the form of enjoyment.

Consider the rhetorical relationship between love and its object in Lacan's account of courtly love, which serves as a synecdoche for the broader relationship between love, the object, and the practice of "objection" or enstasis. In the February 20, 1973, session of *On Feminine Sexuality,* "God and Woman's Jouissance," Lacan defines "courtly love" as "a highly refined way of making up for . . . the absence of the sexual relationship, by feigning that we are the ones who erect an obstacle thereto. . . . It is along this pathway that I shall deal . . . with the notion of the obstacle, with what in Aristotle's work . . . is called the obstacle, *enstasis.* . . . Consult Aristotle and you will know everything when I at last come to this business of enstasis. You can read, one after the other, the passage in the *Rhetoric* and the two sections of the *Topics* that allow you to truly know what I mean when I try to integrate my four formulas [about the impossibility of the sexual relationship] into Aristotle's work."[42] This is no minor point for readers of Lacan's work. Fink, who translated *On Feminine Sexuality,* sees the concept of stasis as a central Lacanian concept, noting that the concept of stasis as "an obstacle one raises to an adversary's argument [and] the exception to a universal predicate . . . [or] an instance or counter instance that refutes a general claim" is intimately connected with Lacan's consistent use of the concept of "instance," usually translated as "agency" in most English versions of Lacan's work.[43] For Fink, "this is but one example of the inappropriateness of translating Lacan's 'Instance de la Lettre' as 'Agency of the Letter.'"[44] Although Fink opts for the "instance" of the letter in his translation, it would be equally legitimate to render the title as "The Stasis of the Letter in the Unconscious." The rhetorical sensibility imparted by the idea of the "stasis" of the letter figures the functioning of trope in a field of contingent contestation in opposition to a more structuralist reading of Lacan that sees the formal qualities of trope as prefiguring all discourse.

Enstasis, as rhetoricians well know, is a rich term meaning to "step in," to "object," and to situate one's self. Stasis (at least in book 2 of the *Rhetoric*) presumes that one "steps in" in the context of an ongoing dialectical exchange. Raising an objection is as much a contingently situated act of address as it is an abstract logical form. Lacan's citation of Aristotle's stasis moves the idea of the object in Lacanian thought from a structurally determined apparatus for organizing enjoyment (an object) to a contingently produced function of the exchange of signs—that is, from object to *objection.* For Aristotle, an objection (enstasis) is a form of refutation (*luseos*). *Lysis,* as George Kennedy notes, literally means to "unloose" or "untie" the logic of the other.

Both senses of "object" are present here: to object is both to render the speech of the other an object and to take issue with it. "Objection" presumes a given characterization of the other and simultaneously refuses or unlooses it in the name of maintaining stasis or the point of objection. What better analogy for the productive non-union of the subject and the other at the site of the object than to highlight that our objections often become the point at which the subject and the other are made static or, rather, made not amenable to being changed by the encounter between the two? The ultimate terms of the big "O" Other's nonexistence are made plain in Aristotle's enstasis: the Other is a stasis point in the function of the sign that situates a subject's relation to the law of signification but, as stasis, the Other is also vulnerable to a loosing or undoing by revealing that it exists only as the product of the signifying labor of stasis.

Aristotle's conception of stasis is an important component of Lacan's attempt to outline the plurality of different subject positions in relation to the sign. Both in the *Rhetoric* and the *Topics,* one of the most significant modes for "lodging an objection" figures enstasis as an exception to a universal predicate. The concept of stasis as exception to a universal predicate allows Lacan the luxury of defining a subject position that is subject to castration and the exception to it—the jouissance of the woman (with the standard caveat that these positions do not describe biological sex as much as two positions relative to the other and the sign). Put differently, if Lacan's later work envisions the possibility of a mode of enjoying the other that is not reducible simply to the object relation but that enjoys the otherness of the other as pure alterity, this possibility is the logical extension of the idea that the other is a site of stasis—and thus is amenable to the exception to the universal predicate.[45]

Joan Copjec's reading of Lacan's conception of alterity stakes its claim at precisely this point. For example, in *Imagine There's No Woman: Ethics and Sublimation,* Copjec argues on the basis of the exception to the universal predicate that orthodox Lacanian thought overstates the inaccessibility of the other. Citing a debate around the reception of Leo Bersani's work, she notes that the "French Ecole Lacanienne . . . was delighted to see in it confirmation of Lacan's aphorism, 'There is no sexual relation.' This only goes to show that being French does not automatically entitle one to understand Lacan."[46] Copjec claims that "Lacan did not maintain . . . that 'the sexual [is] an absence of relations, a failure to connect'" but that Lacan "says only that there is no sexual ratio or . . . predefined aim of the sexual drive."[47] As evidence of this Copjec argues that Lacan "fully acknowledges that sexual encounters happen," and "that the drive, working blind, without guide or goal, does occasionally stumble on a satisfying object."[48] Copjec is correct in saying that the sexual relation is productive, and that it can constitute a satisfying relation toward an object. Of course, her reading of the claim of the Ecole Lacanienne is a bit overstated: what is at issue in the sexual relation is not whether or not sex can be satisfying, or productive, but whether or not it implies authentic intersubjective communion with the Other. The impossibility of intersubjectivity, as opposed to sex, is, in fact, a direct result of the lack of a "sexual ratio": as Copjec herself argues in *Read My Desire: Lacan against the Historicists* the sexual relation fails to produce the conditions for "authentic" intersubjectivity because it fails from both the perspective of the two symbolic positions: the "male" and the "female" position. These positions do not represent biological sexuation as much as they are a metaphor for two ways of missing communion with the Other, where the "male" position represents the reduction of the Other to an object for the sake of phallic jouissance, and the "female" position represents the impossibility of communion because of a metonymically inflected refusal to foreclose the Other by defining or reducing it to an object relation.[49] The point of this paradox is that to encounter another, to render it intelligible, subjects must engage via the mediation of the sign; therefore, because a subject cannot engage an other in its absolute alterity, the subject must engage it as an object. If, from one position, direct relation with the other is impossible because the subject reduces the other to an object, the alternative position, which refuses to reduce the other to an object, also prohibits access to the other by denying the subject the ability to encounter it in the stable, coherent, and intelligible form that an object implies.

Thus, it is no surprise that Copjec affirms, despite reservations about reading "there is no sexual relation" as an argument for the unproductivity of the sexual relation, the communicative implications of the lack of a sexual relation. Despite the productivity of the sexual non-relation that Copjec defends, from the perspective of communication, sex as communion, and the terms of the intersubjective relation: "Sex . . . becomes that which does not communicate itself, that which marks the subject as unknowable. . . . *Sex serves no other function than to limit reason, to remove the subject from the realm of possible experience or pure understanding.* This is the meaning, when all is said and done, of Lacan's notorious assertion that 'there is no sexual relation': sex . . . is also, by definition, opposed to relation, to communication."[50]

What Copjec intends, then, is a conception of sex that is in line with a reading of the productive nature of stasis. Here, as an argument about the possibilities for relationship, or more accurately the undoubtedly productive terms of non-relationship to the other, stasis affords an account of the variety of subject positions that one takes in relation to the other. Versions of the self are invariably understood as forms of exception to union with the other: what it is that defines me in relation to the other is that I am not the other, and this exception becomes the core moment in the specifically rhetorical production of the self. The "I," which is formed in relation to others, is also the exception to the rule of the other as an all encompassing field of intersubjective production. So, the idea of stasis as exception becomes an important device for theorizing the productive impossibility of the intersubjective union and the subject's ambivalence toward the other.

Accounts of public talk and public bonds can be reconfigured in light of Lacan's account of stasis, an account that reframes rhetoric's presuppositions about the public as a space of mutual, reciprocal, intersubjective, ideational exchange. The ideology of publics holds that public speech is an act of lovemaking or a productive union where mutually satisfactory exchange takes place. But the force of Lacan's argument dictates that in the vast majority of communicative relationships, the erotic relation to the other produces a bar to accessing such mutual, reciprocal, and transparent relationships with the other. Put differently, what if most public speech is less consummated union than mutual masturbation? What if in public subjects enjoy the objection, the production of stasis, more than they take pleasure in communicative exchange of the communion of signs?

The violent impossibility of the rhetorical relationship should change the texture of our accounts of rhetoric, especially when considered from the perspective of persuasion as a mode of mobilizing and organizing hypothetically shared affects. This account of eros refigures the idea that ideas and arguments matter for properly communicative reasons by highlighting the economy of enjoyment that figures subjects in relation to themselves, to others, and to the forms of "shared" life that underwrite public talk and textual consumption. This refiguring of the impossibility and enjoyment of blocked eros helps to explain the proliferation of public subject positions that are premised less on principled ideational stands or classically defined political interest and simply on the public pleasures of refusing to see the basic intelligibility of the other's public claims—in an age where ideologues on the Right and Left assert the abject stupidity and incoherence of the arguments of their respective counterparts, it behooves rhetoric to pay attention to the ways that public subjects often enjoy the blockages of eros more than the agapic possibility of consensual meaning making.

7
Trope, Affect, and Public Subjectivity

> It is in the realm of experience inaugurated by psychoanalysis that we may grasp along what imaginary lines the human organism, in the most intimate recesses of its being, manifests its capture in a symbolic dimension.
>
> —Jacques Lacan, "The Seminar on the Purloined Letter"

In this chapter, I demonstrate two strategies for reading public economies of tropological exchange. I undertake these readings under the presumption that the general and specific economies of tropological exchange and affective investment are mutually constitutive, and my goal is to embody a form of critical practice that takes seriously the Symbolic and Imaginary charges in rhetoric without reducing one to the other. Thus, I hope to demonstrate the productivity of a rhetorical theory that engages two specific economies of tropological exchange in the light of failed unicity and that, by extension, attends to the productivity of feigned unicity.

The first reading, which focuses on Mel Gibson's *The Passion of the Christ,* takes up the economic exchange between identitarian practices and the ontological register of public making by tracing the metaleptic exchanges that constitute an evangelical Christian public around the metaphor of constitutive violence. I engage in a close reading of *The Passion* and the tropological exchanges it performs in constituting an evangelical public through, around, and beyond the film. The second reading focuses less on a close reading than on characterizing the logic of investment and formal rhetorical processes that animate a specific kind of demand: in this case, the demands of radical antiglobalization protestors to be recognized as dangerous. Thus, my reading of radical antiglobalization protest takes up the political possibilities of the democratic demand, arguing that a purely formal account of the demand eschews attention to the rhetorical production of enjoyment and therefore overstates the political potential both of the democratic demand and a politics of resistance. Here I would like to show how a rhetorically inflected reading of Lacan's work provides an analytic prescription for public politics that moves beyond enjoyment and aims at the articulation of collective political desire. If the first reading is focused on the relationship between the specific imaginary contents that underwrite a public bond, the second is engaged in understanding the ways that symbolically constituted practices of address and investment imply determinate political consequences.

Both of these readings imply critiques of conventional rhetorical practices of interpretation, suggesting an alternative analytic practice of engaging the nexus between trope and affective investment. Thus, these readings form a critical-interpretive couplet: in reading *The Passion,* I would like to demonstrate the shortcomings of fetishizing the Imaginary in isolation from the broader symbolic economy that underwrites it; conversely, in reading the demands of radical antiglobalization protest, I would like to show the shortcomings of a purely formal account of the demand that operates in isolation from the practices of enjoyment and the imaginary relations of address underwriting radical demands.[1]

Evangelicals in Public

As I characterized it in the preceding chapter, Michael Warner defines publics as social forms that exist "by virtue of being addressed," "organized by nothing other than discourse itself" and "constituted through mere attention" to specific texts.[2] Warner's publics come into being when strangers forge affinities to one another based on shared attention to texts. Although Warner provides a powerful account of how textual circulation organizes publics, he provides a comparatively thin theory for figuring why strangers are paying attention to a text in the first place. Warner's account, which privileges the act of paying attention to a text, draws focus away from both the general economy of signifying exchange that organizes the specific economy that comes together around a text and, by extension, from the modes of investment that constitute the durability of specific publics. Attention to a singular text does not create a public ex nihilio: members of a public pay attention to a text because it solicits them, trading on investments that, although manifest in a text, precede and organize a public's attention to it.[3] Implicit, although not fully explicated, in Warner's model of a public is a process not unlike an *economy,* a process of exchange where preexisting discourses and identity investments are presumed and remade in a public's encounter with a text. Were this model of economy to be made explicit, we might define particular publics *as* a mobile assemblage of associations and relationships of address mediated by common attention to a text; *through* a specific economy that integrates regularized exchanges of preexisting discourses, investments, and identitarian commitments; and simultaneously *in* the act of paying attention to a text.

An economic theory of the constitution of specific publics focuses on the articulation of different elements of the specific economy of exchange as manifest in a social field, but it also reads these articulations as part and parcel of practices that negotiate a relationship to the general economy of tropological exchange. As one example, I offer an account of the specific and general rhetorical logics, both figural and affective, that animate an evangelical Christian public around Mel Gibson's *The Passion of the Christ,* thereby figuring both the contours of evangelical public identity and affinity and the logics underwriting an evangelical public's attention to *The Passion.* The evangelical public's enthusiastic embrace of *The Passion* stems from the film's status as a nodal point in an economy of trope that articulates evangelical identity.[4] *The Passion* reaffirms and reformulates tropes of evangelical marginality, an identity commitment that a number of scholars see as a core component of American evangelicalism—one unique both in its intensity and in its reliance on metaphors of culture war that configure evangelical identity in opposition to a hostile public sphere.[5] Thus, in highlighting that affinity and affective investment are lodged within an economy of tropes that precede, operate in, and point beyond *The Passion* as a public-making text, I argue that the film demonstrates the inextricable link between public affinities and affects.

Unpacking this connection requires more than a formal account of trope: the evangelical public's response to *The Passion* virtually mandates attention to affective investment, forcing critics to distinguish between emotion as phenomenon constituted by the subjective experience of meaning and enjoyment as a formal practice organizing one's relationship to the world through objects. Otherwise, one cannot account for the overwhelming popularity of *The Passion* among evangelicals despite the fact that the film "sickened" many pious viewers, and that it stages a brutal violence against Jesus meant to inspire "revulsion" in its most committed audience.[6] An evangelical audience's palpable discomfort and equally intense attraction to *The Passion* is paradoxically productive: although the emotional reaction to the violence of *The Passion* repulses evangelical viewers, it inspires affective investment in an evangelical identity organized around a metaphor of victimhood. Thus, the evangelical viewer "enjoys" *The Passion* because it reinforces an identity-forming commitment to imagining evangelicalism under siege, thereby activating a core element in the identitarian economy of evangelical publicness. Ultimately, the point of this reading is to demonstrate that the link between public affinity and public affects is not exactly a question of a theory of "the public" as a sphere, set of structures, or normative procedures. Instead, affinity and affects pose the question of the *practices* and *investments* that underwrite identitarian relations between strangers in specific publics.

Screening Jesus

The prerelease strategy for Gibson's *The Passion* invoked the specter of Christian marginality, figuring opposition to *The Passion* as antagonism toward Christianity, a theme that resonates particularly strongly with evangelical Christians. Framing Hollywood studios' refusal to work with him as evidence of Hollywood's anti-Christian bias, Gibson argued that no studio in Hollywood was willing to produce the film, forcing Gibson's Icon Productions to shoot and release *The Passion*. Icon Productions' prerelease marketing emphasized that many theater chains would be unwilling to carry *The Passion,* highlighting the refusal of Twentieth Century Fox to distribute the film.[7] Compared to films with similar earnings, the initial release of *The Passion* showed at a relatively small number of theaters, a fact that Icon's promotional efforts persistently referred to in pitching the film to individuals and churches. This campaign was wildly successful, grossing a record-breaking ten million dollars in prerelease sales, primarily among evangelical churches.[8]

Though Gibson's claims to an "anti-Christian bias" did not invoke a specific strand of Christianity, this framing of the relationship between the culture industry and Christians has a unique resonance with evangelical Christians, a subset of American Christianity that often understands itself to be the losing party in a war for American culture and under the assault of a configuration of secular humanist interests, including the so-called liberal media and the entertainment industry. Gibson's prerelease strategy took advantage of this fact, visibly vetting the film in front of prominent evangelical leaders, most significantly at a special prerelease showing in front of the leadership of the National Association of Evangelicals in Colorado Springs, Colorado, the spiritual home of the evangelical movement. This marketing strategy achieved its intended effect. Although attended by a broad range of non-evangelical viewers, an intensely committed evangelical audience coalesced around the film. A Barna Group survey of viewers found that roughly half (53 percent) of the viewers of *The Passion* self-identified as "born again Christians," a percentage significantly higher than the incidence of self-identified "born again Christians" in the adult population (38 percent).[9] "Not surprisingly," noted the Barna survey, "evangelicals were the most enthusiastic about the movie," registering significantly higher quality ratings for *The Passion* among evangelical Protestants, even when compared to Catholics.[10] A similar poll reported that self-identified evangelicals constituted the primary viewership of *The Passion,* and that such viewers reported a substantially favorable response to the film and of the film's fidelity to the biblical narrative.[11]

While evangelicals lauded the film, resistance to it grew in non-evangelical communities, especially in those that feared its anti-Semitic overtones and graphic violence. This opposition was recoded in evangelical circles as a fundamental antagonism toward Christianity—here the film served as a synecdoche for Christianity and specifically for an evangelically coded version of Christianity that affirms the centrality of the Bible, of the work of evangelism as the core of Christian belief, and as a religious commitment under threat from a broader secular culture. Perhaps unsurprisingly then, resistance to and criticism of the film by "secular culture" became one of the best modes of advertising the film to evangelicals, and arguments about the possible dangers of *The Passion* were refigured through the metaphor of constitutive marginality as a grander scheme by secular and evil powers to wage spiritual warfare in the public sphere. Obviously, there is a self-perpetuating quality in evangelical dispositions toward *The Passion:* "secular" resistance to the film prompted intense investment in and politicization of *The Passion,* and the intensity of such investments prompted more "secular" resistance. This dynamic of investment and resistance, which recapitulates the logic of evangelical identity, is not only present in the discourses surrounding the marketing of the film, it is also at the heart of the economy of trope that the film text establishes.[12]

Scourging as Synecdoche

Gibson's avowed motivation for producing *The Passion* was a lack of realism in earlier treatments of the passion narrative. On his account, earlier films were too "ethereal" and tended to downplay the brutality of the violence of Jesus's last days, presenting Jesus as "effeminate" and a "weak" figure.[13] For Gibson, a brutal version of the scourging of Jesus serves as an antidote to a weak, effeminate Christ. The scourging scene takes place in the middle of the film, occupying a full fifteen minutes of the screen time. The length of the scene, its central position in the narrative of the film, and the unparalleled intensity of its violence demonstrate the importance of scourging to Gibson's *The Passion.* The scourging is also the point at which Gibson takes the greatest degree of artistic license, implying an attempt to punctuate it with the careful application of cinematic artifice. A comparison between the biblical account of the scourging and Gibson's cinematic amplification of it provides the evidence for this strategy. The scriptural account of the scourging is relatively sparse. The gospels of Matthew and Luke fail to mention it. The gospel of John gives it only seven words: "Then Pilate therefore took Jesus, and scourged him."[14] Mark gives it even a more cursory treatment, commenting almost in passing that Pilate delivered Jesus to be crucified "after he had scourged him."[15]

Gibson's amplified scourging scene begins with a high-perspective shot of a crowd of Roman guards, officials, and other onlookers standing at attention around a small tiled outdoor court. An overseer sits at a small desk with instruments of torture displayed on a table next to him, including switches, cat o' nine tails, and chains. A three-foot tall pillar with iron manacles chained to its top sits in the center of the court. Soldiers drag a limping and bloodied Jesus into the court while bearish Roman guards laugh and mock him. The guards approach the table of weapons as if it were a buffet, excitedly picking up switches, testing their pliability, and smiling. Jesus is passive, led easily to the pillar; yet close ups of his bloodied face reveal a look of steely resolve. There is a brief moment of silence and the camera cuts to a close-up of the Jewish high priest Caiaphas, who strains forward for a better view. The official at the desk gives the command; the guards let out monstrous grunts and drive the switches at Jesus's bare back, swinging with every fiber of their strength. A loud crack of wood on flesh peals as the camera cuts to Jesus's face.

During the first ten lashings the camera focuses on Jesus's back. With each blow the audience sees skin flayed off, bloody welts, and tremors of pain in Jesus's hands and legs. Each of the blows is counted aloud by a Roman guard. The camera cuts between faces in the crowd and a now writhing Jesus, while the sound of lashes against flesh and insistent counting of blows drones on in Latin, broken only by cries for the guards to whip harder. This part of the scene seems to be structured to give the audience the feeling that it will go on forever: there is no music, and the only sounds are the whizzing of the switch in the air, the smack of pliable wood on flesh, the seemingly interminable whipping accompanied by counting, accented by the rhythmic, repetitive changes of the camera's viewpoint.

Around the twenty-fifth blow, the sense of temporality in the scene changes significantly, and a new character is added to the scene. The sounds of whipping and counting become more distant, providing the viewer with a sense of detachment. A mournful sounding chant backed by a drawn out low note on a cello fades in over the distant but still audible sounds of the scourging. Satan emerges from behind Caiaphas. Cuts between Jesus and the various members of the audience are replaced by a series of cuts between the exquisitely pained face of Jesus and the hooded but oddly beautiful gender indeterminate face of Satan. Although the crowd surrounding the scourging is dense, Satan moves through it effortlessly, circling around a collapsed Jesus whose hands tremble involuntarily in excruciating pain.

The sounds of the scourging return, the music stops, and the camera pans to the guards, who are bent over in exhaustion. Still tethered to the pillar, Jesus has collapsed, his body covered in blood. He glances at Mary and, gaining strength from the sight of his mother, picks himself up, standing as erect as the manacles will allow, and glares at the guards. The guards are shocked and enraged by this show of resolve and pick up cat o' nine tails made of leather straps with sharp pieces of metal and glass tied to the end of each. With the first eight blows the viewer sees skin, fat, and muscle torn apart, spattering blood on the faces of the guards. If one detects an element of pornography in this unparalleled and graphic spectacle of violence, the ninth blow can only be termed the "money shot"—a penetration shot staged with the vivid and exacting detail of the most explicit pornography. The camera cuts to Jesus in the foreground. Since his hands are fastened securely to the pillar, his naked side is exposed from the shoulder to the waist, occupying the majority of the screen. In the background over Jesus's shoulder, the guard swings the cat o' nine tails in a backhanded arching motion. The viewer sees, in the most graphic detail possible, four of the metal and glass studded straps dig into Jesus's side. The force of the blow has lodged the metal and glass heads of the straps into his ribs. The guard pulls the whip out by jerking his arms and turning his torso in the reverse of the striking motion, ripping away as much flesh as possible. Fragments of flesh and blood spatter the crowd and the faces of the guards, and the white of exposed bone shows through the gaping wounds. With another blow of the whip, the viewer sees glass and metal lodge in Jesus's face and eyes, marring him to the point of unrecognizability.

What is the evangelical viewer to take from this scene besides the visceral trauma of the violence done to the body of Jesus? Given the intensity of the evangelical commitment to marginality, the scene is structured to promote a metaphorical identification of the evangelical viewing public and the beaten body of Jesus. While other viewers might also receive the scene through an articulation of the body of Jesus and the church, this connection has particular salience for those steeped in the American evangelical articulation of the church and "Christian" way of life as under constant threat in the culture wars. *The Passion* activates a readily available association between piety and threat for the evangelical viewer, promoting identification between violence done to the historical person Jesus and the contemporary threats to the evangelical church.

This identification of the evangelical viewer with Jesus as the subject of violence is accomplished by drawing on the phenomenological experience of witnessing the violence, the employment of Christian metaphors of the "body of Christ," and the intricate staging of lines of sight in the scene. The primary tropological substitution invites the viewer to read the person of Jesus as synecdoche, as a metaphor for Christian community formed and reformed under conditions of violence and victimhood. One of the clever cinematic devices of *The Passion,* most brutally demonstrated in the scourging scene, is that it is structured to not only invite this identification by the play of viewpoints, shots, and gazes but also by the brute force of the violent images. In an interview with the Catholic news service EWTN's Raymond Arroyo, Gibson hints at the logic of suffering structuring the scene:

> Arroyo: Some would say why does it have to be so graphic . . . that it removes the art, it kills the imagination we could all apply to this by being so on the nose.
>
> Gibson: No, it's a puzzle that I have, I think what I have to do is to be truthful, to take you through suffering with it. The audience has to suffer to understand it more, what I am seeking here is a deeper understanding of this event.[16]

The overwhelming representations of graphic violence induce and perform the trauma that the film works to establish as a constitutive pole of evangelical identity. *The Passion* aims at more than a deeper ideational understanding of the brutality of the scourging by showing a particularly shocking version of it; the viewer is literally called to suffer *with* Jesus in viewing the intensely painful violence done to his body. This use of representations of violence against Jesus is specifically effective for audiences steeped in the Christian tradition, taking advantage of the tropologically saturated incarnational theology of the Christian Church. Viewers within Christian traditions might tend to connect trauma to the human body of Jesus with violence done to the corporate body of believers. This mediation is accomplished by a central Christian metaphor, namely the theological concept of the "body of Christ," which takes advantage of tropes of incarnation to connect the body of the person Jesus with the church as a whole through the idea of the participation of all believers in the imagined body of Christ. But this is specifically effective for the evangelical viewer, who, unlike other Christian viewers, is highly sensitized to framings of the Christian body defined by a position of marginality and under a condition of threat.

As opposed to the "Passion of Jesus," the title of *The Passion of the Christ* is telling: one of the basic insights of systematic theology regarding Christology is that "Christ" is not Jesus's last name. In most Christian theologies, Christ is the second person of the Godhead, uncaused and existing eternally, both before the incarnation in the human body of Jesus and after the assumption of Jesus's body. Jesus is the name of a specific historically existing person, in whom Christ is incarnated. Jesus is granted the title of *christos* (Χριστός, from the Greek for anointed or messiah) by virtue of the incarnation of the eternal Christ in his body. Pauline theology extends this logic of incarnation, claiming that as Christ was incarnated in the person of Jesus, Christ is also continually present in the Christian community as the animating principle of corporate life: "So we, being many, are one body in Christ, and every one members one of another."[17] Framing the movie specifically as a passion story of "the Christ" as opposed to the person of Jesus or as "*The Passion* of Jesus" invites an unavoidable metonymic connection between the body of Jesus and the "body of Christ" elevated to a metaphorical equation of the body of Christ and the Christian Church.

Employing the metaphor of Christ, Gibson frames Jesus's body as a site of imagination, specifically framing the tortured body of Jesus as a site of Christian affiliation premised on marginality. In the EWTN interview, Gibson reiterates his claim that earlier treatments of the passion story were not historically true to the extent of the torture done to Jesus.[18] Gibson's antidote to this problem draws on images, activating a link between imagery and imagination:

> Arroyo: Where did this "Passion" passion develop—where did it originate? . . .
>
> Gibson: I was starting to look into things that I had knowledge of but really hadn't explored. . . . I read all the gospels. . . . One of my gifts is that I have a gift for imagery so that I would imagine it like that, what was that like?[19]

The Passion specifically invites an act of imagination; the purpose of this act of imagination is to counteract perceived tendencies to diminish the violence done to Jesus in previous films. But imagination implies more than the ability to consume an image: imagination, as I have argued, is also a mode of practicing a relation to another, a prerequisite for public affinity, and is the primary means by which social relationships are envisioned, sustained, and reproduced. Thus, Gibson's cultivation of the imagination as a faculty for receiving the brutality done to Jesus does more than display the violence of the passion narrative. It articulates conditions of public affinity in figuring evangelical sociality through the metaphor of the victim. Read against the organizing metaphor of the "body of Christ," Gibson's *The Passion* is an intervention into the heart of the battle over the cultural imagination, organizing evangelical affinities through a relation to "secular" culture as a source of injury, thereby reaffirming conservative Christian discourses about the culture war.

As implied in the previous chapter, the connection between image and imagination in practices of public affinity invokes conditions of identification and exclusion. Imagination is the faculty that both frames the conditions for recognizing another as a fellow member of a public and simultaneously determines which others are counted out of affiliation with a specific public. But cementing the connection between the trauma induced by watching one's god being beaten and a politics of public affiliation requires deft cinematography to (mis)identify the viewer with a scourged Jesus and against the powers that persecute him. The scourging scene stages a careful manipulation of the politics of seeing and representing, which exchanges the general trauma induced by the film's violence for a specific claim for identification with Jesus and by extension with a persecuted evangelical community. The viewer is invited first to see the torture done to Jesus from a distance, from the perspective of Roman guards and officials, the Jews, and other onlookers in the crowd. As the scene progresses and the violence intensifies, the controlling point of view switches from multiple angles of the lacerated body of Jesus interspersed with wider angle cutaways to various members of the crowd to a more regular switching between the perspective of Jesus and a progression of closer angles on the faces of significant characters such as Satan and Mary. With the intensification of the violence in the scene, Gibson includes ever closer and more intimate shots of the face and wounds of Jesus and focuses more directly on the eyes and faces of the onlookers. The viewer is drawn from the position of a passive observer to a participant in the scene, identifying with the pain of Jesus, the maternal gaze of Mary, and with the subject position of a man under the persecuting gaze of evil.

The conclusion of the scene consummates the metaphoric equation of a scourged Jesus and the scourged collective body of Christ. The viewer has moved from an observer in the scene to an intimate participant as the violence against Jesus escalates. This identification intensifies to the point of feigned consubstantiation: with the final blows of the whip the camera switches, for the first time, to a first-person subjective shot from the eyes of Jesus. Since he is on his back, the viewer sees the world upside down; the bloodied feet of the guards occupy the screen. The calculated use of a first-person perspective shot unites the eyes of the viewer and Jesus. This viewpoint is held for a few brief seconds, creating a climax in terms of (mis) identification—the viewer is now Jesus, receiving blow after blow from the guards.

If the viewer is only viscerally aware of the progression of shots and intensification of violence that serve to identify them more closely with the person and the viewpoint of Jesus as the blows multiply, Gibson provides an explicit framing device to fully cement the relationship between imagination and affinity. Immediately after the first-person subjective shot from the eyes of Jesus and the viewer, the film cuts from an extreme close-up of the mangled face of Jesus to a flashback of the foot washing as recounted in the gospel of John. The flashback begins with Jesus standing in a simple room made to seem simultaneously dreamlike and intimate by the gentle hues of a Mediterranean evening sun. The orangish hue of the light kisses the brown earth tones of the room's wooden table and adobe walls, creating a feeling of a soft and easy intimacy—a stark contrast with the sound of grunts, screams of pain, of leather, glass, and metal biting into flesh, and the hard grey and bloodied stone hues of the scourging court.

By the end of the scourging Jesus's eyes are somewhat vacant, swollen shut, obscured by his own blood. By contrast, in the flashback Jesus stares directly into the camera, speaking with a kind but impassioned voice, interpellating the audience with inviting eyes and imploring his addressees to receive his words with the gentle pastoral manner of a person speaking edifying spiritual truth. The Jesus of Gibson's flashback utters the words of John 15:18, 13:16, and 15:20: "if the world hates you, remember that it hated me first [15:18]. Remember also that no servant is greater than his master [13:16]. If they persecuted me, they will persecute you [15:20]. You must not be afraid." The inventional choice to cite scripture directly is significant for evangelical members of the audience who privilege a literalist understanding of the Bible. Citing what are understood to be the direct and unadulterated words of Jesus, tropological substitutions invited by the intricate interplay of speech, viewpoint, perspective, and the rhythm of the scene are condensed in a pastoral framing mechanism. "If the world hates you, remember that it hated me first": the conditional "if" is not offered to open the question of whether the world hates the Christian community; instead the reality of the world's hatred is enacted in the invited metaphorical substitution of the community of Christians for the brutally scourged person of Jesus. In this context, the egalitarian impulse of the "no servant is greater than his master" is redeployed, moving from a vision of ethical relationships within Christian community toward an argument for the inevitability of violence against it, enthymematically linking the violence done to Jesus to the inevitability of violence against the "body of Christ." Since Jesus was unable to escape violence of the most extreme nature, those who recognize themselves as followers of Jesus ought not expect to be exempted from such violence. Piety requires that the individual believer accept the reality of violence against the Christian community if they are to avoid vainly presuming their superiority to God: "If they persecuted me, they will persecute you."[20] Since the premise for the flashback is the persecution of Jesus, the viewer is led to the unavoidable conclusion that the Christian community will also be persecuted and that this persecution defines the Christian's relation to secular culture.

The implication of inevitable persecution fits seamlessly with Gibson's inventional choice to frame the scourging through the flashback to the foot washing, a choice that is not immediately obvious from the biblical narrative. In John 13, the one scriptural citation that ties the flashback to the foot washing with the biblical narrative, Jesus proclaims and performs a model for Christian community that Gibson employs in imagining a community formed under duress. The narrative of John 13 pairs Jesus's statement that "no servant is greater than his master" with a performance of mutual and intimate submission embodied is his kneeling to wash the feet of his disciples. Collectively, this scene presents a vision of the idealized Christian community, where believers activate intimate associations (caring for each other, washing each other's dirty feet) as a mode of community building premised on love and mutual service. Gibson's inventional choice to collapse the foot washing and the politics of persecution metonymically connects persecution by the outside world with intimate submission within Christian community, rendered as the experience of intimate touch in a warm setting. The contrast of the loving and gentle touch of a fellow believer kneeling to wash another's feet visualized in the flashback forms a stark phenomenological contrast with the imagined feeling of the cold steel of a cat o' nine tails wielded by a hostile stranger violently penetrating the body of Christ, which is continually present in the diegetic reality of the scene, even as Jesus has his flashback. As Jesus imaginatively recalls the ideal moment of Christian community, the viewer cannot but be aware that he is also being viciously scourged, even in this moment of internal respite. Gibson's metonymic connection between the intimate inner imaginative act of Jesus and the implied presence of continual torture to his body becomes a metaphor for Christian affiliation writ large and specifically for those invested in the evangelical articulation of speaking the literal truth of the Scripture under threat of violence.

By this metaphor, in its most intimate moments, Christian communities are imagined through the presence of continual, if sometimes imperceptible, scourging by the non-Christian world. This metaphor activates an antithesis between violence and intimacy as a kind of organizing metaphorical unity or a cinematic conceptual chiasmus: Christians are to love and serve each other because they are persecuted, and they are persecuted because they love and serve each other. In juxtaposing foot washing and the scourging, the film organizes love as communal intimacy over and against the hostility of secular society. This juxtaposition authorizes a politics of public affinity based on an inclusionary exclusion, figuring who is counted as a member of a supposedly marginalized Christian public by excluding a secular other who is figured as hostile. This scene might be usefully read as a "disciplining of the disciples," as a structure of investment that controls theological tendencies to claim that the Christian obligation to love the other is unqualified. In this model of affiliation, the obligation to love is not unconditional but is framed by an obligation to members of a community of victims, where the outsider, far from being worthy of love, is an object of threat or suspicion. Gibson's representation of the scourging articulates the economy of Evangelicalism through a metaphor articulating the simultaneity of communal intimacy and victimhood and thereby teaches an evangelical audience how to frame and interact with the non-evangelical world in an organization of intimate affect for the sake of constituting a structure of simultaneous inclusion and exclusion.

But this inclusionary exclusion produces a paradox for adherents to Christian theology: how can a believer hold to a radical conception of love of the neighbor and the enemy alike while simultaneously holding to a conception of community premised on exclusion? The answer lies in enjoyment as a structure of affect that organizes subject and public affinities through trope, specifically in organizing evangelical public affinities around the enjoyment of constitutive victimhood.

Thus, widely reported feelings of revulsion, guilt, or visceral bodily sickness by evangelicals viewing the violence of *The Passion* extend the logic of enjoyment that invests an evangelical public in violence, producing an economy of affinity and identity organized around an imaginary relation between *The Passion*'s evangelical public and explicitly posed against the secular threat that constitutes it. This dynamic comports with Lacan's insistence that enjoyment is often experienced as the unbearable. Despite evangelical narratives of being sickened or overwhelmed by the film, Gibson's committed evangelical viewers enjoy the violence done to Jesus because it provides a central node of exchange in the specific economy that constitutes an evangelical public. The experience of revulsion both conceals and makes acceptable the evangelical community's cathectic investment in the grotesque violence—a textbook case of a practice of enjoyment despite manifest emotional signals to the contrary. This relationship, in turn, is premised on a reading of secular powers as agents of evil who conspire against not only the savior, or the film that memorializes him, but the body of Christ as a whole.

But what is signified by evil? In Christian theological traditions, evil tends to be a kind of final end point that anchors all the various manifestations of pain, suffering, and sin in a binary opposition to God's goodness. In the evangelical dispensation, evil often moves beyond an abstract account of moral intentions toward its embodiment in institutions that represent a threat to evangelical belief, for instance in the form of the culture industry's promotion of secular values and antifamily lifestyles. Under a Lacanian dispensation, evil represents something more, albeit something that is reflected in the embodiment of evil. As argued previously, in the ontological register of the public the gaze of the other is disconcerting (recall Sartre's "hell is other people"). This gaze is threatening because it reveals the subject's dependency on the others who look at it, thereby revealing that the subject is not self-sufficiently the author of its own intentions, modes of being, or forms of enjoyment. The dynamics of the gaze explain why the mythology of so many cultures articulates the image of the eye and evil: "The evil eye is the *fascium* . . . that . . . has the effect of arresting movement and, literally, of killing life. . . . [T]he eye . . . is maleficent."[21] The concept of the evil eye of the other in evangelical discourses is the subject of a triple act of public address: it refers to the ontological register of the public in locating a generalized anxiety about being a subject among other subjects, it refers to an identitarian configuration that frames the evangelical public as an object of evil intentions by secular others, and it operationalizes the addressive register by figuring the terms of relation between evangelicals and the broader culture. The gaze that embodies the other represents the other who threatens, who wishes to consume the subject. In the case of *The Passion,* this evil gaze is metaphorically condensed in the Satan figure, who takes pleasure in watching Jesus and, by extension, the Christian community suffer. Satan's pleasure in watching the body of Christ suffer is subsequently posed against the intimate, injured, identificatory eye of Jesus.

As a pedagogy of seeing and a mode of public togetherness, *The Passion* stages a logic of sight that resolves the problem of the eye and the gaze by specifying the other as the non-evangelical other embodied in the Satan figure and, further, by retroactively defining evangelical sociality as a community of eyes/"I"s connected by the bond of shared victimhood. In specifying the anxiety surrounding the gaze by reducing it to a problem of public affinities, the general anxiety surrounding a generalized other is reduced to a specific anxiety over non-evangelical others, and this reduction is effective in creating a community defined by its relation to the other as a threat. Creating a community of suffering, the gaze manifest in *The Passion* figures the other as an enemy who enjoys watching the injured community suffer.

Although paradoxical under any dispensation other than the Lacanian gaze, the other's enjoyment in watching a community suffer organizes the suffering community and its modes of enjoyment. The conclusion of this logic is that the other's enjoyment in the community's suffering is constitutive but also that the community is impelled toward regulating the enjoyment of this maleficent other if it is to survive. What makes the condensation of the logic of the eye and the gaze in *The Passion* so striking is the way that it articulates with an evangelical framing of the social field that holds that the other's pleasure is dangerous and that it needs to be ruthlessly regulated to ensure not only the safety but the practices of enjoyment and affinity that constitute an evangelical public.

This logic explains, in part, why the same evangelical communities that are significantly invested in regulating the enjoyment of others (in terms of family values, reproductive rights, school curricula, and so on) comprised the most numerous and enthusiastic audience for Gibson's *The Passion*. But perhaps, more importantly, this reading of *The Passion* offers insight into what is perhaps the most puzzling question of evangelical politics: given that evangelicals exert substantial influence in the public sphere, how is it that a public that exerts a significant degree of hegemony can sustain itself around an identity premised on its marginality?[22] The answer lies in the texts and tropes that constitute evangelical publics, specifically in the work these texts and tropes do in negotiating a precarious balance between a position of relative hegemony and an identity premised on marginality: a balance that *The Passion* strikes via careful staging of representations of violence and lines of sight that, in turn, articulate new modes of public intimacy and new ways of understanding the politics of identity, public affinity, and inclusion.

The Formal Politics of the Demand, or, On Being Bound to Equivalential Chains

In "The Ego-Function of the Rhetoric of Protest," Richard Gregg noted that when viewed as a rhetorical transaction, the "ego-function" of protest often works at cross-purposes with the political goals that motivate protest.[23] Gregg's analysis is pegged to an understanding of Freud aligned with ego psychology. As a result, Gregg's insight comes at the cost of an account of the productive political effects of political struggle premised on collective identifications, primarily by presuming such identifications are self-serving and therefore antithetical to a democratic politics. Still, there is something seductive about the claim that protest often makes a fetish of oppositional stagings of collective political sentiment and therefore tactically privileges antagonism at the expense of strategic goals. For Lacan, this paradox of radical politics stems from the nature of the demand as a mode of address. That the demanding subject might achieve satisfaction in the tactical performance rather than strategic satisfaction of its demands comprises the danger of radical political demands and therefore of the forms of populist politics that see the demand as the privileged mode for political agency.

Engaging Ernesto Laclau's work on popular demands, I focus on the imagined politics of address, specifically by arguing that the demand often constrains political subjects by alienating them from their desire, promoting a dependency on the intransigence of the political institutions that demands reform. This analysis extends the treatment of enjoyment in chapter 5 by applying it to two exemplars of demand as a political practice drawn from antiglobalization activism. I treat the political effects of these demands by posing them against Lacan's framing of the relationship between demands and enjoyment. Finally, I turn to the politics of demand as an everyday political practice. This analysis does not imply an argument for abandoning demands as a political strategy. In the Lacanian vocabulary "demand" is central to processes of signification generally. This is also not an argument for consigning radical political demands to futility. To the contrary, evaluating the relationship between enjoyment, demand, and desire is a prerequisite for a form of radical politics that takes the collective political potential of desire seriously.

Demanding Your Own Repression

In the run up to the 2003 World Trade Organization (WTO) talks in Cancun, the Mexican Government composed a list of the sixty most "globalophobic" leaders of antiglobalization groups. The document, subsequently leaked to the Mexican newspaper *La Reforma,* was met with predictable criticisms regarding the relationship between state security apparatuses, the institutions of global economic governance, and democratic protest. But there were less predictable responses: in addition to criticisms that the list chilled democratic dissent, some antiglobalization groups criticized the list for not being *comprehensive* enough, demanding its expansion. Activist Josef Schneider wrote: "What do we have to do to get a little credit? . . . In a not-very secret document . . . the Mexican government compiled a list of 'globalophobic leaders' who will be singled out for special scrutiny by the Mexican police. Despite the role that Portland activists played in the collapse of the WTO Ministerial meeting in Seattle, *none* of us made the list!"[24] More than a passing lament, the remainder of the article analyzes the reasons why the Mexican government neglected to include any Portlanders, arguing that the Mexican state's class bias prompted them to ignore the true threat that ordinary citizens posed to the WTO: "They can't accept that a bunch of ordinary citizens are the ones who are the biggest threat to shut down the WTO. . . . How typical."[25] By this diagnosis, the Mexican response typifies institutional attempts to downplay protest. Here, the lack of recognition does not make the protest ineffective, instead the fact that the Mexican government and the WTO underestimate the danger posed by ordinary citizens animates this critique.

Not to be outdone, the Mexico Solidarity Network created an online form letter for self-identified "dangerous antiglobalization groups":

> Dear Government Agents Bent on Restricting Civil Liberties,
> I recently found out about the "watch list" prepared by Mexican authorities, purportedly to quell the voice of civil society at the upcoming WTO Ministerial in Cancun. . . . Please add my name to your "watch list" immediately!! Nothing less is acceptable.[26]

One might read such demands as parodic critiques of globalization and security, as ironic calls for mobilization, as a strategy of overidentification, or as any combination of these. Even though these demands represent a call for inclusion as a means of democratizing global governance, these demands are not simply for inclusion: they are also demands to be recognized as dangerous and in solidarity with other similarly dangerous global citizens.

How is it possible to ground a reading of the rhetorical functions of the demand to be recognized as dangerous? For Laclau, such demands ought be read through their potential to activate relations of solidarity: the individual call to be recognized as dangerous and excluded opens the possibility for equivalential linkages between the subjects who lodge such demands and others who are similarly situated in relation to the hegemonic order. Here, all demands entail a split between the concrete particular conditions of their articulation and the more universal political possibility that they potentially ground. This split implies that demands are caught up in a formal logic of trope: metonymic connections between disparate demands are condensed in metaphors that figure a relation to and make claims on a political order.

But in a Lacanian reading another split is at work in and underwrites the split identified by Laclau between the particular content and universal possibilities for affinity implied in the demand. This supplementary split inheres between the subject who enjoys the mere fact of affinity with a group as a mode of (mis)identification and the set of identitarian equivalences inaugurated by investing in the specific content of the demand. Specific political demands contain a universal commitment that authorizes equivalential linkages and are simultaneously sites of enjoyment that create ritually repeated relationships to a hegemonic order. Based on this Lacanian reading, it is not the change that the demand anticipates, nor the political potential of forging equivalential links that is significant, but the role demand plays for the one who utters it and the modes of interpassive political affinity entailed that are of primary analytical importance. Working through the complexity of demands requires reading the demand for recognition as a practice of enjoyment—as an affectively invested call for sanction and love by the governing order. Demands also entail a perverse dialectic of political agency as resistance and simultaneous interpassive political constraint. Demands empower forms of political agency by generating an oppositional relationship to hegemonic structures and by providing the equivalential preconditions for identity. As Žižek might have it, there is always the risk that the demands of protestors are the supplement that authorizes the functioning of capital.[27]

Enjoyment provides one particularly difficult stumbling block for a dedicated formal account, a dynamic that stands out in particularly stark relief in Laclau's work. Although Laclau owes a significant debt to Freud and Lacan, his theory of demand is not explicitly crafted from psychoanalytic categories. As Glynos and Stavrakakis have argued, there is a "complete and conspicuous absence in Laclau's work of Lacanian categories such as fantasy, and, perhaps more importantly, jouissance."[28] Glynos and Stavrakakis claim that there is "to [their] knowledge no reference in Laclau's work to the concept of jouissance."[29] *On Populist Reason* contains a brief discussion of the concept of jouissance in Copjec's work, which Laclau summarizes by saying: "There is no achievable jouissance except through radical investment in an *objet petit a*. But the *same* discovery (not merely an *analogous* one) is made if we start from the angle of political theory. No social fullness except through hegemony; and hegemony is nothing more than the investment in a partial object, of a fullness which will always evade us. The logic of the *objet petit a* and the hegemonic logic are not just similar, they are simply identical."[30] There is an elegance to Laclau's point about enjoyment, provided that enjoyment is reducible to a set of logical forms. This presupposition makes the lack of talk about jouissance in Laclau's work understandable. If jouissance and hegemony are identical, one does not need Lacan to say something that might be said more elegantly with Gramsci.

But with Laclau's insight on the formal similarities of enjoyment and hegemony come certain blind spots. To start with, enjoyment is never quite as "achievable" as the preceding quotation might suggest. Far from being the consummation of a logic of structure and investment, enjoyment is a supplement to a *failing* in a structure: for example, Lacan frames jouissance as a useless enjoyment of one's own subjectivity that supplements the fundamental failings of a subject in either finding grounding or consummating an authoritative account of its coherence. This "uselessness" defines the operation of jouissance. When Lacan suggests that "language is not the speaking subject" in the seminar *On Feminine Sexuality,* lodging a critique of structural linguistics as a law governing speech, jouissance is understood as something excessive that is born of the failure of structures of signification. Language is not the speaking subject precisely because what is passed through the gristmill of speech is the result of a misfiring of structure as much as it is prefigured by logics of structure, meaning, and utility. Therefore the interpretive difficulty for a structuralist account of enjoyment: the moment that the fact of enjoyment is recoded in the language of structure, the moment that it is made *useful* in a logic of subjectivization, is precisely the moment where it stops being jouissance.

Framing enjoyment as equivalent with hegemony, Laclau identifies the fundamental "split" in psychoanalytic theory between the universal and the particular demands of a group. Posing the split in this way, and as the privileged site of the political, Laclau occludes attention to another split: namely, the split within a subject, between the one who enters an equivalential relationship and the identitarian claim that sutures this subject into a set of linkages. This too is a site of enjoyment, where a subject identifies with an external image of itself for the sake of providing its practices of subjectivity with a kind of enjoyable retroactive coherence. The demand is relevant here but not simply because it represents and anticipates a change in the social order or because it identifies a point of commonality. The demand is also a demand to be recognized as a subject among other subjects and to be given the sanction and love of the Symbolic order. The implication of this argument about the nature of enjoyment is that the perverse dialectic of misfirings, failure, and surpluses in identity reveals something politically dangerous in not moving beyond demand. Put another way: not all equivalences are equally equivalent. Some equivalences become fetishes or points of identification that eclipse the ostensible political goal of the demand. To extend the line of questioning to its logical conclusion: can we be bound to our equivalential chains?

Freud, Lacan, and the Demand

Despite the tendency of some commentators to naturalize Freud's tripartite schema of the human psyche, Freud's account of the ego does not characterize the ego as preexistent or automatically given. The ego is not inevitably present in every human subject: the ego is a compensatory formation that arises in the usual course of human development as a subject negotiates the articulation and refusal of its needs as filtered through demand. Hypothetically a "subject" whose every need is fulfilled by another is never quite a subject: this entity would never find occasion to differentiate itself from the other who fulfills its every need.

As a mode of individuation and subjectivization, egos are economies of frustration and compensation. This economy relies on a split in the Freudian demand, which is both a demand to satiate a specific need and a demand for the addressee to provide an automatic fulfillment of a need. The generative power of the demand relies on two things: the split between the demand and the need that it attempts to redress, and the fact that some demands will be refused. This economy of need and frustration works because the refusal of a specific need articulated as a demand on another is also a refusal of the idea that the addressee of the demand can fulfill all the subject's needs, requiring a set of compensatory economic functions to negotiate the refusal of specific demands.

"Ego," then, names the economy of compensatory subjectivization driven by the repetition and refusal of demands. The nascent subject presents wants and needs in the form of the demand, but the role of the demand is not the simple fulfillment of these wants and needs. The demand and its refusal are the fulcrum on which the identity and insularity of the subject are produced: an unformed amalgam of needs and articulated demands is transformed into a subject that negotiates the vicissitudes of life with others. Put in the metaphor of developmental psychology, an infant lodges the instinctual demands of the id on others but these demands cannot be, and for the sake of development, must not be fulfilled. Thus, pop psychology observations that the incessant demands of children for impermissible objects ("may I have a fourth helping of dessert") or meanings that culminate in ungroundable authoritative pronouncements (the game of asking never ending "whys") are less about satisfaction of a request than the identity-producing effects of the parental "no." In "The Question of Lay Analysis," Freud argues that "if . . . demands meet with no satisfaction, intolerable conditions arise . . . [and] . . . the ego begins to function. . . . [T]he driving force that sets the vehicle in motion is derived from the id, the ego . . . undertakes the steering. . . . The task of the ego [is] . . . to mediate between the claims of the id and the objections of the external world."[31] Later, in *Group Psychology and the Analysis of the Ego,* and *Civilization and Its Discontents,* Freud relocates the site of the ego's genesis beyond the parent/child relationship and in the broader social relationships that animate it. Life with others inevitably produces blockages in the individual's attempts to fulfill certain desires, since some demands for the fulfillment of desires must be frustrated. This blockage produces feelings of guilt, which in turn are sublimated as a general social morality. The frustration of demand is both productive in that it authorizes social moral codes and, by extension, civilization writ large, although it does so at the cost of imposing a contested relationship between desire and social mores.[32]

Confronted by student calls to join the movement of 1968 Lacan famously quipped: "as hysterics you demand a new master: you will get it!" Understanding the meaning of his response requires a treatment of Lacan's theory of the demand and its relationship to hysteria as an enabling and constraining political subject position. Lacan's theory of the demand picks up at Freud's movement outward from the paradigmatic relationships between the parent/child and individual/civilization toward a more general account of the subject, sociality, and signification. The infrastructure supporting this theoretical movement transposes Freud's comparatively natural and genetic account of development to a set of metaphors for dealing with the subject's entry into signification.

As already noted, the Lacanian aphorism that "the signifier represents a subject for another signifier inverts the conventional wisdom that a pre-given subject uses language as an instrument to communicate its subjective intentions."[33] The paradoxical implication of this reversal is that the subject is simultaneously produced and disfigured by its unavoidable insertion into the space of the Symbolic. An *Es* assumes an identity as a subject as a way of accommodating to the Symbolic's demands and as a node for producing demands on its others or of being recognized as a subject.[34] As I have already argued, the demand demonstrates that the enjoyment of one's own subjectivity is useless surplus produced in the gap between the Es (or it) and the ideal I. As a result, there is excess jouissance that remains even after its reduction to hegemony. This remainder may even be logically prior to hegemony, in that it is a useless but ritually repeated retroactive act of naming the self that produces the subject and therefore conditions possibility for investment in an identitarian configuration.

The site of this excess, where the subject negotiates the terms of a nonrelationship with the Symbolic, is also the primary site differentiating need, demand, and desire. Need approximates the position of the Freudian id, in that it is a precursor to demand. Demand is the filtering of the need through signification, but as Sheridan notes, "there is no adequation between need and demand."[35] The same type of split that inheres in the Freudian demand inheres in the Lacanian demand, although in Lacan's case it is crucial to notice that the split does not derive from the empirical impossibility of fulfilling demands as much as it stems from the impossibility of articulating needs to or receiving a satisfactory response from the Other. Thus, the specificity of the demand becomes less relevant than the structural fact that demand presupposes the ability of the addressee to fulfill the demand. This impossibility points to the paradoxical nature of demand: the demand is less a way of addressing need to the other than a call for love and recognition by it. "In this way," writes Lacan, "demand annuls the particularity of everything that can be granted by transmuting it into a proof of love, and the very satisfactions that it obtains for need are reduced to the level of being no more than the crushing of the demand for love."[36] The Other cannot, by definition, ever give this gift: the starting presupposition of the mirror stage is the constitutive impossibility of comfortably inhabiting the Symbolic. The structural impossibility of fulfilling demands resonates with the Freudian demand in that the frustration of demand produces the articulation of desire. Thus, Lacan argues that "desire is neither the appetite for satisfaction, nor the demand for love, but the difference that results from the subtraction of the first from the second."[37] This sentiment animates the crucial Lacanian claim for the impossibility of the other giving a gift that it does not have, namely the gift of love: "all demand implies . . . a request for love. . . . Desire begins to take shape in the margin in which demand becomes separated from need: this margin being that which is opened up by demand, the appeal of which can be unconditional only in regards to the Other . . . having no universal satisfaction. . . . It is this whim that introduces the phantom of omnipotence, not of the subject, but of the other in which his demand is installed."[38] This framing of demand reverses the classically liberal presupposition regarding demand and agency. Contemporary and classical liberal democratic theories presume that the demand is a way of exerting agency and, further, that the more firmly the demand is lodged, the greater the production of an agential effect. The Lacanian framing of the demand sees the relationship as exactly the opposite: the more firmly one lodges a demand, the more desperately one clings to the legitimate ability of an institution to fulfill it. Hypothetically, demands ought reach a kind of breaking point where the inability of an institution or order to proffer a response should produce a reevaluation of the economy of demand and desire. In analytic terms, this is the moment of subtraction, where the manifest content of the demand is stripped away and the desire that underwrites it is laid bare. The result of this "subtraction" is that the subject is in a position to relate to its desire, not as a set of deferrals, avoidances, or transposition but rather as an owned political disposition.

As Lacan frames it, demanding subjects are either learning to reassert the centrality of their demand or coming to terms with the impotence of the Other as a satisfier of demands: "But it is in the dialectic of the demand for love and the test of desire that development is ordered. . . . [T]his test of the desire of the Other is decisive not in the sense that the subject learns by it whether or not he has a phallus, but in the sense that he learns that the mother does not have it."[39] The point of this disposition is to bring the subject to a point where they might "recognize and name" their own desire and, as a result, become a political subject in the sense of being able to truly argue for something without being dependent on the other as a support for or organizing principle for political identity. Thus, desire has both a general status and a specific status for each subject. It is not just the mirror that produces the subject and its investments but the desire and sets of proxy objects that cover over this original gap. As Easthope puts it: "Lacan is sure that everyone's desire is somehow different and their own—lack is nevertheless *my* lack. How can this be if each of us is just lost in language . . . passing through demand into desire, something from the Real, from the individual's being before language, is retained as a trace enough to determine that I desire here and there, not anywhere and everywhere. Lacan terms this *objet petit a* . . . *petit a* is different for everyone; and it can never be in substitutes for it in which I try to refind it."[40] Though individuated, this naming is not about discovering a latently held but hidden interiority, rather it is about naming a practice of thinking the uniqueness of individual subjects as a product of discourses that produce them. Thus, this is an account of political subjectivization that is not solely oriented toward or determined by the locus of the demand but that is also determined by the contingent sets of coping strategies that orient a subject toward others and a political order and serve as the condition of possibility for demands. As Lacan argues, this is the point where a subject becomes a kind of new presence or a new political possibility: "That the subject should come to recognize and to name his desire; that is the efficacious action of analysis. But it isn't a question of recognizing something which would be entirely given. . . . In naming it, the subject creates, brings forth, a new presence in the world."[41] Alternatively, subjects can stay fixated on the demand, but in doing so they forfeit their desire, or as Fink argues, "an analysis . . . that . . . does not go far enough in constituting the subject as desire leaves him or her stranded at the level of demand . . . unable to truly desire."[42]

A politics defined by and exhausted in demands is by definition a hysterical politics. The hysteric is defined by incessant demands on the other at the expense of ever articulating a desire that is theirs. In the *Ethics of Psychoanalysis,* Lacan argues that the hysteric's demand that the Other produce an object is the support of an aversion toward one's desire: "the behavior of the hysteric, for example, has as its aim to recreate a state centered on the object, insofar as this object . . . is . . . the support of an aversion."[43] This economy of aversion explains the ambivalent relationship between hysterics and their demands. On one hand, the hysteric asserts their agency, even authority, over the Other. Yet, what appears as unfettered agency from the perspective of a discourse of authority is also simultaneously a surrender of desire by enjoying the act of figuring the other as the one with the exclusive capability to satisfy the demand.

Thus, "as hysterics you demand a new master: you will get it!" At the register of manifest content, demands are claims for action and seemingly powerful, but at the level of the rhetorical form of the demand or in the register of enjoyment, demand is a kind of surrender. As a *relation of address* the hysterical demand is more a demand for recognition and love from an ostensibly repressive order than a claim for change. The limitation of the students' call on Lacan does not lie in the end they sought but in the fact that the hysterical address never quite breaks free from its framing of the master. The fundamental problem of democracy is not articulating resistance over and against hegemony but rather the practices of enjoyment that sustain an addiction to mastery and a deferral of desire.

Hysteria is a politically effective subject position in some ways, but it is politically constraining from the perspective of organized political dissent. If not a unidirectional practice of resistance, hysteria is at best a politics of interruption. Imagine a world where the state was the perfect and complete embodiment of a hegemonic order, without interruption or remainder, and the discursive system was hermetically closed. Politics would be an impossibility: with no site for contest or reappropriation, politics would simply be the automatic extension of structure. Hysteria is a site of interruption, in that hysteria represents a challenge to our hypothetical system, refusing straightforward incorporation by its symbolic logic. But, stepping outside this hypothetical non-polity, on balance, hysteria is politically constraining because the form of the demand, as a way of organizing the field of political enjoyment, requires that the system continue to act in certain ways to sustain its logic. Though on the surface it is an act of symbolic dissent, hysteria represents an affirmation of a hegemonic order and is therefore a particularly fraught form of political subjectivization.

The case of the hysteric produces an additional problem in defining jouissance as equivalent with hegemony. One way of defining hysteria is to say that it is a form of enjoyment that is defined by its very disorganization. As Gérard Wajcman frames it, the fundamental analytical problem in defining hysteria is precisely that it is a paradoxical refusal of organized enjoyment by a constant act of deferral. This deferral functions by asserting a form of agency over the Other while simultaneously demanding that the Other provide an organizing principle for hysterical enjoyment, something the Other cannot provide. Hysteria never moves beyond the question or the riddle, as Wajcman argues: the "hysteric . . . cannot be mastered by knowledge and therefore remains outside of history, even outside its own. . . . [I]f hysteria is a set of statements about the hysteric, then the hysteric is what eludes those statements, escapes this knowledge. . . . [T]he history of hysteria bears witness to something fundamental in the human condition—being put under pressure to answer a question."[44] Thus, a difficulty for a relatively formal/structural account of hegemony as a substitute for jouissance without reduction: where is the place for a practice of enjoyment that by its nature eludes naming in the order of knowledge? This account of hysteria provides a significant test case for the equation between jouissance and hegemony, for the political promise and peril of demands and ultimately for the efficacy of a hysterical politics. But the results of such a test can only be born out in the realm of everyday politics.

On Resistance: The Dangers of Enjoying One's Demands

The demands of student revolutionaries and antiglobalization protestors provide a set of opportunities for interrogating hysteria as a political practice. For the antiglobalization protestors cited earlier, demands to be added to a list of dangerous globophobes uncannily condense a dynamic inherent to all demands for recognition. But the demands of the Mexico Solidarity Network and the Seattle Independent Media project demand more than recognition: they also demand danger as a specific mode of representation. "Danger" functions as a sign of something more than inclusion, a way of reaffirming the protestors' imaginary agency over processes of globalization. If danger represents an assertion of agency, and the assertion of agency is proportional to the deferral of desire to the master upon whom the demand is placed, then demands to be recognized as dangerous are doubly hysterical. Such demands are also demands for a certain kind of love, namely, the state might extend its love by recognizing the dangerousness of the one who makes the demand. At the level the demand's rhetorical function, dangerousness is metonymically connected with the idea that average citizens can effect change in the prevailing order, or that they might be recognized as agents who, in the instance of the list of globalophobic leaders, can command the Mexican state to reaffirm their agency by recognizing their dangerousness. The rhetorical structure of danger implies the continuing existence of the state or governing apparatus's interests, and these interests become a nodal point at which the hysterical demand is discharged. This structure generates enjoyment of the existence of oppressive state policies as a point for the articulation of identity. The addiction to the state and the demands for the state's love is also bound up with a fundamental dependency on the oppression of the state: otherwise the identity would collapse. Such demands constitute a reaffirmation of a hysterical subject position: they reaffirm not only the subject's marginality in the global system but the danger that protestors present to the global system. There are three practical implications for this formation.

First, for the hysteric the simple discharge of the demand is both the beginning and satisfaction of the political project. Although there is always a nascent political potential in performance, in this case the performance of demand comes to fully eclipse the desires that animate content of the demand. Second, demand allows institutions that stand in for the global order to dictate the direction of politics. This is not to say that engaging such institutions is a bad thing; rather, it is to say that when antagonistic engagement with certain institutions is read as the end point of politics, the field of political options is relatively constrained. Demands to be recognized as dangerous by the Mexican government or as a powerful antiglobalization force by the WTO often function at the cost of addressing how practices of globalization are reaffirmed at the level of consumption, of identity, and so on or in thinking through alternative political strategies for engaging globalization that do not hinge on the state and the state's actions.

Paradoxically, the third danger is that an addiction to the refusal of demands creates a paralyzing disposition toward institutional politics. Grossberg has identified a tendency in left politics to retreat from the "politics of policy and public debate."[45] Although Grossberg identifies the problem as a specific coordination of "theory" and its relation to left politics, perhaps a hysterical commitment to marginality informs the impulse in some sectors to eschew engagements with institutions and institutional debate. An addiction to the state's refusal often makes the perfect the enemy of the good, implying a stifling commitment to political purity as a pretext for sustaining a structure of enjoyment dependent on refusal, dependent on a kind of paternal "no." Instead of seeing institutions and policy making as one part of the political field that might be pressured for contingent or relative goods, a hysterical politics is in the incredibly difficult position of taking an addressee (such as the state) that it assumes represents the totality of the political field; simultaneously it understands its addressee as constitutively and necessarily only a locus of prohibition.

These paradoxes become nearly insufferable when one makes an analytical cut between the content of a demand and its rhetorical functionality. At the level of the content of the demand, the state or institutions that represent globalization are figured as illegitimate, as morally and politically compromised because of their misdeeds. Here there is an assertion of agency, but because the assertion of agency is simultaneously a deferral of desire, the identity produced in the hysterical demand is not only intimately tied to but is ultimately dependent on the continuing existence of the state, hegemonic order, or institution. At the level of affective investment, the state or institution is automatically figured as the legitimate authority over its domain. As Lacan puts it: "demand in itself . . . is demand of a presence or of an absence . . . pregnant with that Other to be situated *within* the needs that it can satisfy. Demand constitutes the Other as already possessing the 'privilege' of satisfying needs, that it is to say, the power of depriving them of that alone by which they are satisfied."[46]

One outcome of framing demand as an affective and symbolic process tied to a set of determinate rhetorical functions enjoins against the simple celebration of demands as either exclusively liberatory, as unproblematic modes of resistance, as exhausting the political, or as nodes for the production of political identity along the lines of equivalence. Alternatively, a politics of desire requires that the place of the demand in a political toolbox ought to be relativized: demands are useful as a precursor to articulating desire; they are important when moored to a broader political strategy; but they are dangerous if seen as the summum bonum of political life. A politics of desire thus functions simply as a negative constraint on the efficacy of a politics of demand, and as a practice a politics of desire asks that political subjects constantly test their demands against the measure of desire or against an explicitly owned set of political investments that envision an alternative world. It is the presence of this alternative, explicitly owned as a desired end state of the political, that might become the prerequisite for desire-based solidarities instead of demand-driven affinities, and as such, a politics of desire recognizes the inevitability and productivity of frustrated demand as part and parcel of antagonistic democratic struggle.

Postscript

Recovering Rhetoric's Ornamental, Prophetic, and Protreptic Strands

> Just as we are satisfied with plausible reasoning from an orator, so it is necessary to demand from the mathematician demonstrations that are necessary.
>
> —Aristotle, *Protrepticus*

To conclude, I would like to return to an opening theme: there exists a collective indecision in rhetorical studies regarding the precise nature of rhetoric. This indecision, and the subsequent squeamishness toward defining rhetoric that accompanies it, stems less from a paucity of ideas about rhetoric than from the copious abundance of the term. Rhetoric overflows, as Nancy Streuver argues, with concepts inherited from the "disheveled rhetorical tradition . . . and theoretical expositions, containing a . . . ramshackle collection of discursive problems and solutions."[1] There are so many strands of rhetorical theorizing, practices of rhetorical interpretation, and conceptions of rhetoric's proper objects and domains that it has become nearly impossible to invoke rhetoric with any degree of confidence in a shared meaning function.

Although one might dismiss the messy plurality of meanings that have cohered around rhetoric as "mere" history, Lacan's conception of the unconscious reminds us that rhetoric cannot so easily eschew this past: what has been said, after all, cannot be taken back. Collective indecision about the nature of rhetoric is neither a simple theoretical failing nor a consequence of a lack of conceptual facility on the part of rhetoricians. This indecision is at the heart of rhetoric's unconscious status as a signifier whose conceptual centripetal charge has yielded to seemingly inexorable centrifugal forces. The proliferative character of the latent metonymic connections harbored by rhetoric has outstripped the condensing metaphors that would lend rhetoric a determinate identity.

Proliferative "rhetoric" conflates a number of discrete functions that, although crucial to any rhetorical account of discourse, are too quickly lumped together in an undifferentiated overarching account of rhetoric. When the traditions of rhetorical studies invoke rhetoric, the term invokes not only, for example, a theory of persuasion, but it also calls forth a doctrine of what counts as a rhetorical object; an implicit picture of the subject as addressee and addressor; a theory of context; conceptions of motivation, emotion, and cognition; an imagined audience; a theory of social affinity that constitutes audiences; an account of the formal properties of discourse; a theory of language's relation to the social and material worlds; a framing of contingency; and the history of the varied traditions that have theorized rhetoric. Proliferative rhetoric invokes to a range of concepts that extends ad infinitum.

In forwarding Lacan's conception of rhetoric as a means of reading rhetoric analytically, and thereby both locating and delimiting rhetoric, I have argued for mapping the various functions contained within rhetoric on to Lacan's three orders: the Symbolic, Imaginary, and Real. Specifically, I have argued for locating the varied offices of rhetoric in relation to their Symbolic and Imaginary functions and for delimiting rhetoric by posing the Real as its limit. Thus, I have located the Symbolic as the site of the economically configured, quasi-structuring functions of language and the Imaginary as the site that contemporary rhetorical criticism primarily attends to (including theories of persuasion, propriety, context, and audience), encompassing both the imagined modes whereby a subject relates to itself, to others, and through which the subject populates the formal properties of signs and representational forms with determinate contents. Finally, against the taken-for-granted character of the referential pretension, I have argued that the Real functions as the limit of rhetoric, comprising a field of effects that exceed the grasp of the Symbolic and Imaginary registers.

In both locating and delimiting rhetoric in the context of Lacan's three orders, I have also claimed that the relationship between these orders is only comprehensible against the backdrop of an account of rhetoric as failed and feigned unicity. The failure of unicity represents the fact that the sign intervenes or, better yet, prohibits a transcendent whole that unites signifier and signified, the subject and the social, or even speech and speaker in effortless communion. Although unicity fails, the labor of feigned unicity affords the subject the possibility of contingent, localized unicities, wrought only through the rhetorical labor of form and sustained by the subject's investment in imagined unicities. From the perspective of unicity then, rhetoric is pharmakon: it is both the poison and the cure. Rhetoric names the site at which the essential lacks in the subject, sign, and social relation are produced and made manifest and is simultaneously the means through which subjects are produced, signifiers are made to refer to the world, and by which social relations are imagined.

The relationship between failed and feigned unicity is an extension of and, more specifically, the means by which Lacan's three orders are tied into a Borromean knot. Unicity fails in the relationship between the Symbolic and Real at the site of failed reference: although the Symbolic order holds out hope for an automatic relationship of reference between discourse and the world external to it, signs and representations fail in achieving effortless and efficient adequation with the Real. But the site of reference's failure is also a site for the production of feigned unicity, specifically by eliciting the subject's labor, via investment in or, more precisely, enjoyment of the referential pretension. Similarly, unicity fails in the relationship between the Imaginary and the Real. This failure comes into stark relief in the distinction between reality and the Real. While reality "does not meet" the Real, the reality provides the subject with a socially effective feigned account of the subject's world. Finally, unicity fails in the relationship between the Symbolic and Imaginary, as detailed in my account of Lacan's Schema L in chapter 3. Though the Imaginary is figured by and relies on the quasi-structuring functions of the Symbolic, the subject's tendency to make a fetish of the Imaginary register, both in terms of subjective modes of self-constitution (as, for example, in the mirror) and in terms of the imaginary figuring of others (as in the case of the ideology of communication as a reciprocal, bilateral correspondence between addressor and addressee), occludes attention to the function of the Symbolic order.

What does this set of relationships mean for rhetoric and, by extension, for the theoretically oriented humanities in understanding discourse? Despite its centrifugal disorganization, theories of rhetoric authorize a series of regularizing unconscious effects that have crucial implications for practices of interpreting discourse. Practically, owing to privilege afforded the Aristotelian roots of rhetoric, the one thing that is consistent about rhetorical studies' uses of rhetoric (despite the impulse to not define rhetoric) is the presupposition that rhetoric names the exchange of meanings between subjects in a context. Whether context is understood narrowly, as in the case of a specific speech in front of a specific audience, or understood more broadly, as a field of contingent articulations, the idea of context exerts a regulatory function for practices of rhetorical interpretation. It would seem on first glance that so locating rhetoric would arrest its proliferative character, drawing rhetoric toward its true intersubjective center. I have argued that this attempt to locate rhetoric fails. Locating rhetoric around an intersubjective center defers what I have framed as the "ontological" constituents of rhetoric—of trope, affective investment, and the imagined modes of affinity that constitute an audience—and all the difficult questions that arise from this tangle of concepts regarding the proper objects and methods of rhetoric by subsuming them under the banner of an undertheorized conception of intersubjectively mediated "betweenness." As a result, such a configuration remains largely agnostic on the "context" of the various "contexts" of rhetorical action because it eschews any commitment to the formal properties that explain how discourses come into being, why they function as they do and, most crucially, why subjects invest in discourses in the first place.

Against this tendency, I have argued that it is necessary to wring rhetoric's neck by subjecting rhetoric's intersubjective fantasies to a rigorous symbolic analysis. What would this mean? A rhetorical theory worthy of the name ought to refuse fetishizing the Imaginary in the name of establishing rhetoric as a symbolic science. Specifically, I have argued that rhetoric ought to refuse a prevalent confusion between cause and effect by reading the Imaginary and the subjects inhabiting imaginary relations as an effect of a symbolic economy rather than seeing an imagined intersubjectively constituted communicative field as the cause of symbolic action. Here, an emphasis on the mathematical character of Symbolic economies of trope and investment serves as a counterpoint to the idea that imagined intersubjective relations are the efficient cause of rhetorical effectivity: the Imaginary is an effect of the Symbolic and is therefore derivative of a set of rhetorical effects as opposed to being constitutive of rhetorical effect writ large.

Such an analysis does not require abandoning the imaginary components of rhetoric. Rather, the goal of locating an imaginary rhetoric's Symbolic precursors is to more effectively situate an imaginary rhetoric by accounting for the force of the formal investments that prefigure imaginary commitments. By extension, I have attempted to not only locate the conceptual loci around which rhetoric might be organized but I have also attempted to define the empirical location of rhetoric by defining three registers of publicness as a complex relation between "being-in-public," practices of publicness, and the identitarian commitments of individual publics. My goal in reading publics in this way has been to argue that even the public can be fruitfully understood as both a product of, situated firmly within, and as the primary field of action for an economy of trope and investment.

Rhetorics Ornamental/Rhetorics Prophetic

In asserting the primacy of a tropologically constituted Symbolic, Lacan's conception of rhetoric aligns with an unlikely ally: Ernesto Grassi. This alliance is paradoxical because Grassi is one of the most vociferous critics of a reduction of rhetoric to formalism and to conceptions of a science of human discourse as a movement from objective first principles, asserting at one point that "rhetorical speech cannot be a scientific language."[2] But Grassi's critique of formalism, science, and philosophy all orbit around an essential core: any attempt to posit a foundation for rhetoric that is not in and of itself rhetorically constituted must fail, because the very nature of humans is to engage the world through tropes, a realization that is also at the heart of Lacan's defense of psychoanalysis as a specific kind of science. Thus, although Grassi and Lacan seem to stand at cross-purposes on the question of science, their conceptions of rhetoric unite around two functions: the radicalization of an ornamental conception of trope and the prophetic character of rhetoric.

Trope, as I argued in chapter 4, has largely been relegated to the status of an accessory or "outer dressing" adorning a more fundamental underlying communicative practice.[3] In a strand of argument extending from Plato through Ramus and Locke, trope has been subject to a series of attempts to discipline it as a mere ornament. "We should recall," enjoins Grassi, "that *ornatus* originally came from the Greek term *Kosmos,* which refers in an ontological perspective to the 'relationship' between particular parts and a whole and names the particular order that holds among them. The *ornatus,* therefore, is never something that belongs to particulars in isolation; only in relation to something else, a whole, does the particular receive its essential meaning and become part of an interconnected arrangement."[4] As it is for Grassi, so it is for Lacan: trope is ornamental in the original sense of the term, in that it names the principles of relation, distinction, and interconnection that produce subjects and their discourses. If the goal of Grassi's work is to highlight the generative character of the trope, the goal of Lacan's work is to define, in exacting detail, the operations of an economy of ornament that, on first glance, seems only to supplement or "add-on" to an account of human discourse but, on further analysis, serves as the constitutive principle for it.

Grassi notes that human being and insight into the human's modes of being are "only possible" by means of "an original *in*-sight as invention and discovery," emphasizing the primacy of *inventio* over "critical . . . purely rational thought."[5] Grassi's explanation of the human comports closely with Lacan's understanding of the subject and the economy of its discourses: the inventional act of insight that constitutes the human allows "things to appear (*phainesthai*) . . . in a way that is human. Such a capacity is characteristic of fantasy, . . . which lets the human world appear . . . in metaphors."[6] For Grassi, as for Lacan, the trope serves as the primary organizing principle for the subject's relationship to and comportment of the world, and the result of this mode of organization is appearance, in that the trope is the precondition for the appearance of the subject, the relation between subjects, and the imagined (or fantasized) commitments that sustain the discourse between subjects.

Thus, a conception of human appearance as an effect of the labor of trope unites Grassi and Lacan around what I have called a "science of rhetoric." As a result of the generative power of figuration, "we are also obliged to recognize," claims Grassi, "that every . . . original, former, 'archaic' speech (archaic in the sense of dominant, *arche*) cannot have a rational but only a rhetorical character."[7] Grassi's implication for this claim parallels Lacan's reading of rhetoric almost to the letter: "the term 'rhetoric' assumes a fundamentally new significance; 'rhetoric' is not, nor can it be the art, the technique of an exterior persuasion; it is rather the speech which is the basis of . . . thought. . . . [R]hetorical speech 'comes before' . . . [specific acts of] speech, i.e., it has a 'prophetic' (*pro-phainesthai*) character."[8] For Grassi, there is a rhetoric that comes before or in advance of the specific texts and practices that we usually treat under the banner of the art of rhetoric.

This is, in the end, the most important implication that I draw from Lacan's work. Contemporary rhetoric's attempts to develop an ever richer vocabulary and set of concepts for understanding the imaginary functions of rhetoric have focused too intently on that which appears in the rhetorical situation—the subject, its speech, and the effects that this speech has on an audience—at the cost of thinking that which is in advance of the situation, the context of the rhetorical context or the prophetic Symbolic. There is nothing wrong a priori with attending to appearances, provided that such a theory of rhetoric does not neglect one crucial factor: "rhetoric" is also at work before, or in advance of, the appearance and in fact exerts a determinative role in constituting the means by which and modes through which appearances function. If Grassi's prophetic rhetoric defines a relationship of priority between rhetorics scientific and artistic, Lacan specifies the means by which this transposition is wrought and the implications that it has for the practice of the rhetorical art.

Nowhere is this transposition more apparent than in a theory of the public. A tripartite theory of public-making functions that understands publics as a product of a symbolic economy, and through which subjects come into being and relate with other subjects, affords rhetoric an account of the site of and concrete means by which human discourses are constituted. The public is the space of appearance par excellence, and it therefore is not only a space within which a subject makes claims and consumes texts but through which the subject and its modes of relation to others are constituted. "Since the essence of *res* (things) is revealed only in their ingenious utilization [*usus*] in the context of social and political community," argues Grassi, "*res* proves to be *res publica*."[9] This claim too has a Lacanian analogue: the public, for Lacan, does not primarily name either a sphere or set of discursive procedures, nor does it only name an insular realm of human affairs situated among other potential for human action. The public is the site at which subjects come into being and through which the economy of tropes and investments that constitutes the subject achieves determinate form.

Recovering the Protreptic Strand

In the prevailing imagination of rhetoric, it seems that as soon as one invokes the idea of the public, one necessarily implies the question of persuasion. This is part and parcel of a commitment to seeing publics as constituted by shared meanings, given that persuasion offers the rhetorician unique access to the means by which meanings come to be shared. But what role does persuasion play in a science of rhetoric? I have made a number of claims here about the nature of persuasion, some direct and some indirect: persuasion is largely a function of the Imaginary register; it is bound to logics of intersubjectivity and identification and therefore is an effect of the symbolic logic that precedes it; finally, I have claimed that fetishizing persuasion as the primary means of rhetoric's effectivity draws rhetoric's attention away from the functions of trope and investment that constitute the subject and its discourses.

Of course, the most significant implication of a science of rhetoric is that a rhetorical theory ought to attend to the effects of privileging persuasion as an intersubjectively mediated means of rhetorical action, specifically by accounting for what a commitment to persuasion as the dominant mode of rhetorical action displaces or causes us to ignore. But there is also an argument about the very nature of imaginary persuasion contained in a science of rhetoric: persuasion cannot be separated from an account of the symbolic, an account of enjoyment, or an account of misidentification. The imaginary functions of persuasion are largely prefigured by a symbolic economy that invests specific tropological configurations with the power to move and organize the enjoyment of the subjects who encounter them. Similarly, a theory of persuasion needs to attend to the fact that the conceptions of identity that underwrite a conception of persuasion as propriety (embodied in many interpretations of the "available means") are not given in advance but are produced in the field of prophetic rhetoric and subject to the series of misidentifications that I identified in Schema L. Thus, the question posed by a science of rhetoric is not whether we should abandon persuasion as a rhetorical concept but rather the question is how we might retheorize persuasion as a kind of "interpassive relaxation" along the lines I suggested in chapter 6. Others have already begun this work: this is part of the thrust behind Diane Davis's claim that suggestion might function as an alternative to persuasion and

Joshua Gunn's suggestion that the labor and lack embodied in love are necessary supplements to a theory of persuasion and identification.[10]

But to conclude, I would like to ask a different question: how ought we to think about the relation between persuasion and the Symbolic? Here, I would like Aristotle to have the last word. Specifically, I would like to engage in a strategic reading of a lost Aristotelian text that might upset the conventional wisdom regarding Aristotle in rhetorical studies. The starting point of this reading is Streuver's observation that "Aristotle did not succeed in disentangling himself . . . from an unresolved tension between philosophy's necessitarian theses, and rhetoric's anti-necessitarian practices."[11] Nowhere is this tangle more apparent than in Aristotle's argument for the study of philosophy. In 2005, D. S. Hutchinson and Monte Ransome Johnson announced that they had reconstituted an almost complete version of a lost Aristotelian dialogue, *Protrepticus.*[12] Although portions of the *Protrepticus* were extant in fragmentary form, the full text was presumed to be lost until Hutchinson and Johnson reconstructed it from a third-century text by Iamblichus. The *Protrepticus* represents Aristotle's primary exemplar of a protreptic address. A protreptic is form of speech that seeks to sway its listeners toward an end (usually philosophy or religious practice) sometimes classified generically as a subspecies of epideictic rhetoric. In the case of *Protrepticus,* Aristotle's stated goal is to inspire students to turn toward the study of philosophy.

I have chosen the phrase "turn toward" quite carefully. The term "protreptic" has sometimes been translated as a synonym for persuasion, and with such a reading, there is not a meaningful distinction between the more general Greek term for persuasion, *peitho,* and protreptic speech. But the Greek term "protreptic" derives from *pro-trepein,* meaning not only to "exhort" but, more precisely, "to turn toward." The obvious resonance with the conception of trope as tropos or a turn lies at the core of the distinction that I would like to make: instead of seeing protreptic as a synonym for persuasion as peitho (with all the attendant investments in context, probability, propriety, and meaning that the term implies in Aristotle's *Rhetoric*), a reading of Aristotle's *Protrepticus* provides us with an alternative possibility for framing the tropological means by which discourse exerts effects. As opposed to persuasion as peitho, protreptic names not only a genre but also the means by which the *formal* properties of discourse (as a mode of turning) exert an effect on the subject of discourse via an economy of trope and enjoyment without the mediating functions of context, probability, propriety, and practical judgment.

Space does not permit me to recount how Hutchison and Johnson reconstructed the *Protrepticus,* nor does it allow me the luxury of a careful treatment of the text. But I would like to meditate on a handful of select passages for the sake of demonstrating an uncanny affinity between Lacan's science of rhetoric and the model of protreptic discourse that Aristotle performs in the *Protrepticus.* In Hutchison and Johnson's reconstruction of the *Protrepticus,* Aristotle engages in a dialogue with Isocrates (who presumably represents the Athenian rhetorician of the same name) and Heraclitus, who stands in as a representative for a mathematically based, geometrical understanding of philosophy. The dialogue begins, as Hutchison and Johnson frame it, with a "hostile challenge to philosophy," where an unidentified critic "sputters" that even things that seem self-evident are up for dispute in deliberation.[13] During the course of the dialogue, Isocrates defends a classical understanding of rhetoric as both a mode of philosophy and a means of living ethically, largely by emphasizing the ways that rhetorical practice can attend to contextually bounded prudential wisdom by cultivating a practice of imitation. Alternatively, Heraclitus defends a Pythagorean conception of philosophy as a true knowledge of mathematically derivable forms against Isocrates's contextualism.

What is most interesting about the dialogue, for my purposes at least, is that Aristotle rejects both the Isocratean and the Heraclitean framings of philosophy. Aristotle agrees in part with Heraclitus, but he does so only on the grounds that what Pythagoras's mathematical philosophy really suggests is a particular way of doing philosophy not reducible to meditation on abstract forms. In claiming that "Pythagoras transformed the philosophy of geometry into a scheme of liberal education," Aristotle is arguing for a vision of philosophy that individuals ought pursue not because of its effects but rather because it is a philo-sophia, a love for knowledge prized in and of itself and not as a result of any practical effect that derives from it: "and if it is necessary to attribute to this person too the name that is proper to his passion . . . the 'philosopher' seems to have a drive for a certain science that is prized for itself, and not on account of anything else resulting from it."[14]

Here Aristotle is implicitly arguing for at least two kinds of knowledge. The first kind of knowledge, rooted in Aristotle's conception of techne, is defined primarily by the fact that it is useful in specific kinds of human endeavors, namely those that deal in probability and that make judgments about particular cases. The second kind of knowledge is inartistic, in that it functions by necessity and by demonstration, which proceeds not by swaying opinion but by "observing the good as a whole" and thereby "delivering orders": "there is a difference between the kinds of knowledge that produce each of the things of which we want to have more and more in our way of life, and the kinds of knowledge that make use of these kinds of knowledge, and the ones that give service are different from the others that issue orders. . . . [O]nly that kind of knowledge which . . . [uses] reason, and observes the good as a whole—that is to say, philosophy—is naturally capable of using all of them and issuing orders, by all means one ought to do philosophy, since only philosophy includes within itself this correct judgment and this intelligence to issue orders without errors."[15] Thus, inspired by the rigor of math, a claim to philosophy functions inartistically, as if by demonstration, as opposed to artistically, by persuasion or probability: "taking the principles of the demonstrations to be cognizable and in themselves trustworthy, they use them . . . as to be a paradigm for those who wish to infer the demonstrations in any precise way, which is why it would seem to be fitting for those who think that the profession of doing philosophy is in itself valuable, and that mathematical theory is proper and akin to philosophy."[16]

Of course, for those of us who are invested in the traditions of rhetoric that emerge from a reading Aristotle's *Rhetoric* (often regrettably undertaken in isolation from Aristotle's other works), this claim borders on being an anathema: here Aristotle is making a case for the philosophical life in front of a specific audience and with the specific goal of moving them toward the study of philosophy. Why is it then that in the *Protrepticus,* a document that one might easily read as persuasive attempt to entice students toward the study of philosophy, Aristotle makes the case for inartistic proof and, further, implies that artistic proof would be inappropriate to making the case for philosophy? The explanation lies in the fact that while artistic proof relies on probability, prudence, and the mediating presence of a community of auditors, the demonstrative proof of philosophy, which is the expression of a prior good, speaks directly to the soul:

> For prior things are always more familiar than posterior things, and what is better in nature than what is worse, for there is more knowledge of what is determinate and orderly than of their opposites, and again of the causes than of the effects. . . . Hence since soul is better than body (being more of a natural ruler), and the kinds of skill and intelligence concerned with the body are medical science and athletic training (for we regard these as being kinds of knowledge and say that some people possess them), clearly for the soul too and the psychic virtues there is a certain discipline . . . and we are capable of acquiring it.[17]

The implication of this argument is that the mathematizable qualities of demonstrative form move the subject by "issuing orders," that is, protreptically, and not by means of persuasion as peitho, nor by any of the associated qualities of probability, contextual mediation, or practical judgment. Thus, though both discourses rooted in mathematical demonstration and in plausibility or persuasion can move humans, the means by which they move us and the claims to knowledge that they contain are radically distinct: this is the thrust of the claim in the *Nicomachean Ethics* that "it is the mark of an educated man to look for precision in each class of things just so far as the nature of the subject admits; it is evidently equally foolish to accept probable reasoning from a mathematician and to demand from a rhetorician scientific proofs."[18] Aristotle echoes this sentiment in the *Protrepticus,* though he does so as a means of theorizing the force of mathematical demonstration as logically prior to the rhetorician's demonstration through probability, claiming that there is a mode of demonstrative proof proper to making the case for philosophy: "Thus just as we are satisfied with plausible reasoning from an orator, so it is necessary to demand from the mathematician demonstrations that are necessary. . . . This kind of observation could contribute not only to judging but also to how research should be done, for having determined the causes of each thing, it will make the proper arguments, which, without being used to it, is not easy to do. For nature itself by itself is able to guide us to the principles. . . . For the mathematically educated man can both scrutinize the causes that have been supplied and observe their order."[19] Here, the priority of mathematics makes a prophetic claim: if artistic techne are reliant on manipulating appearances and perceptions, mathematics functions as a metaphor for an organizing principle that exists in advance of and determines the contents of perception—the mathematically educated person can observe both the causes and their orders. Therefore, argues Aristotle, we ought to turn toward a conception of intelligence, which names the very movements of the soul, and is more authoritative than even "true opinion": "if living is valuable because of the perception, and the perception is a kind of cognition, and we choose it because the soul is able to have familiarity by means of it; and we've been saying for a long time, just as of two things the more valuable one is always the one which has more of that same thing . . . and intelligence is more valuable than it and all the others, and more valuable than living, then intelligence is more authoritative than true opinion; hence the main pursuit of all humans is to be intelligent."[20]

It is at this point that Aristotle makes his most aggressive argument against the Isocratean tradition. Because Isocrates's conception of rhetoric, as much of the tradition, is premised on commerce in appearances and imitations, the techne of rhetoric is an inappropriate mechanism to make the case for philosophy. By extension, a protreptic discourse functions, if not by persuasion, by cultivating the intellect via means other than artistic proof. While in the realm of techne or "skills" one works within the realm of appearance and derives principles for action "second or third hand" from experience, the philosopher, inspired by mathematical demonstration, should seek to produce the experience of the demonstrative form directly, presumably bypassing the realm of collective judgments and addressing the soul directly: in regard to "skills people do not generally know their tools and their most accurate reasoning's by taking them from the primary things; they take them from what is second or third hand or at a distant remove, and get their reasonings from experience, whereas the imitation is of the precise things themselves only for the philosopher, for the philosopher's vision is of these things themselves, not of imitations."[21] Thus, a demonstrative discourse of philosophy functions beyond the realm of mimesis but aims directly at producing "laws and secure actions that are right and noble" without reference to the field of collective human practices:

> So just as no one is a good builder who does not use a ruler or any other such tool, but approximates them to other buildings, so too presumably if someone either lays down laws for cities or performs actions by looking at and imitating other human actions . . . is neither . . . good . . . nor . . . excellent . . . for an imitation of what is not noble cannot be noble, nor can an imitation of what is not divine and secure in nature be immortal and secure. But it is clear that the philosopher is the only producer to have both laws that are secure and actions that are right and noble. For he alone lives looking at nature and at the divine, and, just as if he were some good helmsman who hitches the first principles of his life onto things which are eternal and steadfast, gets anchored and lives on his own terms.[22]

Thus the paradox that Streuver identifies: in making a case for philosophy, Aristotle is caught between performing a necessitarian claim for philosophy while relying on the anti-necessitarian and quintessentially rhetorical goal of wooing an audience toward its study. Aristotle is of course cognizant of this paradox: it motivates the distinctions that he continually makes in the *Protrepticus* between math and rhetoric, inartistic demonstration and artistic proof, and between necessity and plausibility. But, making the case for philosophy, Aristotle adds one more significant distinction as a means of negotiating the necessitarian/anti-necessitarian paradox. Persuasion as peitho works by activating the available means in any given situation. In this configuration, the means change according to a context, and the epistemic conditions of a rhetorically persuasive argument rely on plausibility, the sensus communis, and on soliciting a mode of mediated agreement regarding probability and practical judgment between orator and audience. But the means of persuasion in the protreptic strand are quite different. A properly protreptic discourse works because it produces *enjoyment* in the form of demonstration itself, which is the result of philosophy eliciting intelligence to directly encounter the form. Aristotle begins this argument by making claim to the character of enjoyment that mirrors Lacan's conception of enjoyment as useless: what a subject enjoys is not simply the pleasure of undertaking a pleasing action but rather the performance of its status as a subject who is able to undertake such actions. Aristotle makes this distinction by arguing that

> there is a difference between enjoying oneself while drinking and enjoying drinking; for nothing prevents someone who is not thirsty, nor has been brought the drink he enjoys, from enjoying himself while drinking, not because he is drinking but because he happens at the same time to be seeing or being seen as he sits there. Thus we will say that this fellow enjoys himself, and enjoys himself while drinking, but not because he is drinking, and not because he enjoys drinking. . . . [T]hey live pleasantly whose presence is pleasant to those who have it, and that not all to whom it happens that they enjoy themselves while living are living pleasantly, only those to whom living itself is pleasant and who enjoy the pleasure that comes from life.[23]

This distinction allows Aristotle to make his final claim for how a protreptic discourse ought to function. A demonstrative claim to philosophy works because it produces enjoyment in the exercise of intelligence. This, then, for Aristotle, explains why the mathematically inspired conception of demonstration might woo an audience, not because it produces a probable claim but rather because it speaks directly to the intelligence, and therefore to the means by which one might realize the philosophical life, simply by means of observation:

> we attribute living more to the one who is awake rather than to the one who is asleep, and to the one who is being intelligent more than to the one who is unintelligent; and we say the pleasure that comes from life is the one that comes from the uses of the soul, for this is being truly alive. Further, even if there are many uses of the soul, still the most authoritative one of all, certainly, is the use of intelligence to the highest degree. Further, it is clear that the pleasure that arises from being intelligent and observant must be the pleasure that comes from living, either

alone or most of all. Therefore living pleasantly and feeling true enjoyment belong only to philosophers, or to them most of all.[24]

David Metzger's compelling *The Lost Cause of Rhetoric: The Relation of Rhetoric and Geometry in Aristotle and Lacan* argues that both Lacan and Aristotle relied on a certain "geometricization" of thought and discourse as an antidote to the philosophical dismissal of rhetoric. But what I would like to emphasize about this geometricization is not just that it might allow us to "move beyond a discourse of opinion concerning rhetoric" nor to establish a rhetorical conception of "discourse as a social link."[25] Rather, I would like to argue that the connection between Lacan's and Aristotle's conceptions of the power of demonstrative, mathematically configured forms to produce enjoyment is evocative for thinking about the protreptic-persuasive functions of symbolic address as a mode of turning rhetoric toward the trope. Both thinkers privilege the mathematical functions of form as a prior or prophetic form of discourse, and both understand the work of form to be primarily about enjoyment as opposed to intersubjectively mediated practical judgments. One might choose to read the *Protrepticus* for its more traditionally conceived persuasive functions: one could ask how *Protrepticus* functioned for its audience or how it activated the available means of persuasion for the situation that it addressed, as, for example, Mark Jordan's treatment of the protreptic genre does.[26] But to read in this way, folding protreptic discourse as a genre into the larger artistic category of epideictic, would be to deny the force of Aristotle's claim to read different kinds of knowledge practices differently. The point of the *Protrepticus,* after all, is to make a claim for the ways that mathematizable, demonstrative forms induce a kind of enjoyment that is not reducible to artistic interpretation but rather that relies on eliciting enjoyment in turning intelligence toward the philosophical life. Thus, the evocative nature of the connection between Lacan and Aristotle: a discourse of forms and enjoyment requires a science that is up to the task of accounting for it.

This connection is evocative, but it is not rigorously analogous. Undoubtedly, Lacan would part ways with Aristotle on a number of points, largely eschewing Aristotle's conception of the soul, argument for math as a liberal art, and on the idea of cultivating a conception of the good. Still, the *Protrepticus* presents us with a possibility that has heretofore lurked just below the surface of rhetorical studies: the prophetic function of trope, and the means by which it organizes and elicits enjoyment, offer an account of a species of persuasion that is not reducible to practical judgment, context, or probabilistic reasoning. Paradoxically then, a conception of rhetoric as a science, and as a mode of mathematizing and theorizing the enjoyment contained in discourse, has been an element of the rhetorical tradition from its very inception. In suggesting that protreptic identifies not only a genre of speech but a mode of theorizing the function of a rhetoric not reducible to context, I am even tempted to claim that the protreptic strand presents an uncannily Lacanian counterfactual strand in the evolution of the rhetorical tradition from its roots in Aristotle's *Rhetoric.* If for Aristotle, an account of the enjoyment a subject takes in demonstration underwrites the suasory effects of protreptic discourse, for Lacan, a mathematically figured conception of trope and enjoyment underwrites the affective force of symbolic address. Thus, a mathematical account of the sign forms the basis in Lacan's science of oratory for an account of the emergence of the subject, the production of its discourses, and its imaginary commerce with others. Here, a science of rhetoric rooted in the enjoyment of signs requires rejecting both an arid structuralism and the banal reduction of rhetoric to its imaginary coordinates. Grassi elegantly frames the task that Lacan's conception of rhetoric calls rhetorical theory to cultivate, uniting the public appearance of the subject with the prophetic, ornamental, and protreptic charges of rhetoric: "Everywhere today semiotics is mentioned. It is supposed to be a doctrine of the signs (*semata*) that open the meaning of sensory appearances; we find it in linguistics, rhetoric, and the history of literature. If such a doctrine is not to denigrate into pure formalism, it must be able to rise to the level of . . . [a] doctrine of signs on the basis of which specifically human work (*ergon anthropinon*) appears. . . . It means a principal rejection of formal semiotics, strict linguistics, and rhetoric understood only as an art of persuasion."[27]

Under this dispensation, rhetoric might once again flower, providing rhetorical theory with a means of engaging the field of failed and feigned unicity that constitutes the warp and woof of the human, interhuman relations, and human discourses. In so doing, the rhetorical tradition can claim the full force of Lacan's claim that the "psychoanalyst is a rhetor," not by borrowing a perfected interpretive framework from psychoanalysis, nor by finding a conceptual basis for rhetoric outside of the rhetorical tradition; rather, by asserting Lacanian psychoanalysis's inextricable commitment to and dependence on rhetoric, the rhetorical traditions might find a theory of discourse, the subject, and the public work of world making that places rhetoric at the core of the science of human discourse.

Notes

Introduction

1. Jacques Lacan, "Une Pratique de Bavardage," *Ornicar? Bulletin Périodique du Champ Freudien* 19 (1977): 7.

Chapter 1

1. Jacques Lacan, *The Psychoses (The Seminar of Jacques Lacan, Book III),* ed. Jacques Alain Miller, trans. Russell Grigg (New York: W. W. Norton, 1997), 167.

2. Jacques Lacan, *On Feminine Sexuality: The Limits of Love and Knowledge; Encore (The Seminar of Jacques Lacan, Book XX),* ed. Jacques Alain Miller, trans. Bruce Fink (New York: W. W. Norton, 1999), 56.

3. Sean Homer, *Jacques Lacan* (New York: Routledge, 2005), 34.

4. Jacques Lacan, "The Function and Field of Speech and Language in Psychoanalysis," in *Écrits,* trans. Bruce Fink (New York: W. W. Norton, 2006), 237–38.

5. For a treatment of Lacan as a structuralist poet, see Ellie Ragland-Sullivan's *Jacques Lacan and the Philosophy of Psychonalysis* (Illinois, Champaign-Urbana: University of Illinois Press, 1986), 104.

6. Ernesto Laclau, *On Populist Reason* (London: Verso, 2005), 224.

7. Jacques Lacan, "Of Structure as the Inmixing of an Otherness Prerequisite to Any Subject Whatever," in *The Languages of Criticism and the Sciences of Man: The Structuralist Controversy,* ed. Richard Macksey (Baltimore: Johns Hopkins Press, 1970), 191.

8. Bruce Fink, *Lacan to the Letter: Reading Écrits Closely* (Minneapolis: University of Minnesota Press, 2004), 75.

9. The idea of the "context of the context" is inspired by Lawrence Grossberg's *Cultural Studies in the Future Tense* (Durham, NC: Duke University Press, 2010).

10. A *New York Review of Books* essay identified Lacan as one of structuralism's defining "gang of four," along with Michel Foucault, Claude Lévi-Strauss, and Louis Althusser. See Thomas Sheehan, "Paris: Moses and Monotheism," *New York Review of Books* 26, nos. 21 and 22 (January 24, 1980).

11. Lacan, *On Feminine Sexuality,* 2.

12. Fink, *Lacan to the Letter,* 75.

13. Ibid., 72.

14. Loyd S. Pettegrew, "Psychoanalytic Theory: A Neglected Rhetorical Dimension," *Philosophy and Rhetoric* 10 (1977): 46–59.

15. Michael Hyde, "Jacques Lacan's Psychoanalytic Theory of Speech and Language," *Quarterly Journal of Speech* 66, no. 1 (1980): 96–118.

16. Hyde, "Jacques Lacan's Psychoanalytic Theory," 108.

17. Henry Krips, *Fetish: An Erotics of Culture* (Ithaca: Cornell Univeristy Press, 1999).

18. Krips, *Fetish,* 12.

19. See, for example, James P. McDaniel, "Fantasm: The Triumph of Form (an Essay on the Democratic Sublime)," *Quarterly Journal of Speech* 86, no. 1 (2000): 48–56; "Figures of Evil: A Triad of Rhetorical Strategies for Theo-Politics" *Rhetoric & Public Affairs* 6, no. 3 (2003): 539–50; and finally, "Speaking Like a State: Listening to Benjamin Franklin in Times of Terror," *Communication and Critical/Cultural Studies* 2, no. 4 (2005): 324–50.

20. See Joshua Gunn, "Mourning Speech: Haunting and the Spectral Voices of Nine-Eleven," *Text and Performance Quarterly* 24, no. 2 (2004): 91–114; and "For the Love of Rhetoric, with Continual Reference to Kenny and Dolly," *Quarterly Journal of Speech* 94, no. 2 (2008): 131–55.

21. Barbara Biesecker, "Rhetorical Studies and the 'New' Psychoanalysis: What's the Real Problem? or Framing the Problem of the Real," *Quarterly Journal of Speech* 84, no. 2 (1998): 222–39.

22. Biesecker, "Rhetorical Studies and the 'New' Psychoanalysis," 222.

23. See Barbara Biesecker, "No Time for Mourning: The Rhetorical Production of the Melancholic Citizen-Subject in the War on Terror," *Philosophy and Rhetoric* 40, no. 1 (2007): 147–69.

24. Barbara Biesecker, "Whither Ideology? Toward a Different Take on Enjoyment as a Political Factor," *Western Journal of Communication* 75, no. 4 (2011): 449.

25. Victor J. Vitanza, "Critical Sub/Versions of the History of Philosophical Rhetoric," *Rhetoric Review* 6, no. 1 (1987): 41–66.

26. David Metzger, *The Lost Cause of Rhetoric: The Relation of Rhetoric and Geometry in Aristotle and Lacan* (Carbondale: Southern Illinois University Press, 1995).

27. Susan Wells, *Sweet Reason: Rhetoric and the Discourses of Modernity* (Chicago: Univeristy of Chicago Press, 1996).

28. Diane Davis, "Identification: Burke and Freud on Who You Are," *Rhetoric Society Quarterly* 38, no. 2 (2008): 123–47; and "Addressing Alterity: Rhetoric, Hermeneutics, and the Nonappropriative Relation," *Philosophy and Rhetoric* 38, no. 3 (2005): 191–212.

29. For an incisive treatment of this approach, see Gilbert Chatian's *Rhetoric and Culture in Lacan* (Cambridge: Cambridge University Press, 1996).

30. See, Roman Jakobson's "The Metaphoric and Metonymic Poles," in *Metaphor and Metonymy in Comparison and Contrast,* ed. and trans. Rene Dirven and Ralf Porings (Berlin: Mouton de Gruyter, 2002).

31. Sharon Crowley, "Rhetoric, Literature, and the Dissociation of Invention," *Journal of Advanced Composition* 6, no. 1 (1985–86): 22–23.

32. Crowley, "Rhetoric, Literature, and the Dissociation," 22.

33. Steven M. Weiss, "Rhetoric and Poetics: A Re-Evaluation of the Aristotelian Distinction," *Rhetoric Society Quarterly* 12, no. 1 (1982): 27.

34. Jacques Lacan, *Freud's Papers on Technique (The Seminar of Jacques Lacan, Book I)*, ed. Jacques Alain Miller, trans. John Forrester (New York: W. W. Norton, 1991), 87.

35. See, for example, Juliet Flower MacCannell's *Figuring Lacan: Criticism and the Cultural Unconscious* (Lincoln: University of Nebraska Press, 1986); Jane Gallop's *Reading Lacan* (Ithaca: Cornell University Press, 1985); and Chatian's *Rhetoric and Culture in Lacan.*

36. See, for example, Ben Stoltzfus's attempt to graft a Lacanian theory of trope onto reader-response criticism in *Lacan and Literature: Purloined Pretexts* (New York: SUNY Press, 1996). Stolzfus's approach to trope and reader response is condensed in the closing reflection of his introduction: "Despite the differences in vision and narration, the materiality of language and the reality of the unconscious provide the warp and the woof with which the reader weaves a common figural motif" (17).

37. For example, see Jane Gallop's "Lacan and Literature: A Case for Transference," *Poetics* 13 (1989): 307; and Sean Homer's *Jacques Lacan* (New York: Routledge, 2001), esp. 123–30.

38. For a treatment of this theme based on a homology between mind and literature, focusing on the ways that reading constitutes an "I," see Peter Brooks's "The Idea of a Psychoanalytic Literary Criticism," *Critical Inquiry* 13, no. 2 (1987): 334–48.

39. Jean-Michel Rabate, *Jacques Lacan: Psychoanalysis and the Subject of Literature* (New York: Palgrave Press, 2001), 28.

40. Todd McGowan, "Looking for the Gaze: Lacanian Film Theory and Its Vicissitudes," *Cinema Journal* 42, no. 3 (Spring 2003): 28.

41. McGowan, "Looking for the Gaze," 28.

42. Christian Metz, *The Imaginary Signifier: Psychoanalysis and Cinema,* trans. Celia Britton, Annwyl Williams, Ben Brewster, and Alfred Guzzetti (Bloomington: Indiana University Press, 1982), 54; cited in McGowan, "Looking for the Gaze," 28.

43. Krips, *Fetish,* 98.

44. Martin Hall, "Time and the Fragmented Subject in *Minority Report,*" *Rhizomes* 8 (Spring 2004), http://www.rhizomes.net/issue8/hall.htm (date accessed, 12 August 2011).

45. Laura Mulvey, "Visual Pleasure and Narrative Cinema," in *Movies and Methods,* vol. 2, ed. Bill Nichols (Berkeley: University of California Press, 1985), 310; cited in McGowan, "Looking for the Gaze," 30.

46. McGowan, "Looking for the Gaze," 27.

47. Krips, *Fetish,* 99.

48. Laclau, *On Populist Reason,* 68.

49. Ernesto Laclau and Chantal Mouffe, *Hegemony and Socialist Strategy* (London: Verso, 1985). Three pivotal essays in the strand of critical/cultural rhetoric rely on

Laclau's *Hegemony and Socialist Strategy:* Raymie McKerrow's germinal essay on critical rhetoric, "Critical Rhetoric: Theory and Praxis," *Communication Monographs* 56, no. 2 (1989): 91–111; Barbara Biesecker's "Rethinking the Rhetorical Situation from Within the Thematic of *Différance,*" *Philosophy and Rhetoric* 22, no. 2 (1989): 110–30; and Ronald Walter Greene's "Another Materialist Rhetoric," *Critical Studies in Mass Communication* 15, no. 1 (1998): 21–41.

50. Michael Kaplan, "The Rhetoric of Hegemony: Laclau, Radical Democracy, and the Rule of Tropes," *Philosopy and Rhetoric* 43, no. 3 (2010): 254.

51. Laclau, *On Populist Reason,* xi.

52. Ibid., x.

53. Kaplan, "Rhetoric of Hegemony," 258.

54. Slavoj Žižek, "Our Daily Fantasies and Fetishes," *JAC* 21, no. 3 (2001): 648.

55. Slavoj Žižek, "The Limits of the Semiotic Approach to Psychoanalysis," in *Interrogating the Real* (New York: Contimuum, 2005), 123.

56. Jeffery T. Nealon, "The Cash Value of Paradox: Žižek's Rhetoric," *JAC* 21, no. 3 (2001): 599.

57. Žižek, "Limits of a Semiotic Approach," 142.

58. Alain Badiou, *Being and Event* (New York: Continuum, 2007).

59. Rabate, *Jacque Lacan,* 18.

60. Chaitin, *Rhetoric and Culture in Lacan,* 8.

61. Lacan, *On Feminine Sexuality,* 91, 130–131.

Chapter 2

1. Robert Scott, "On *Not* Defining 'Rhetoric,'" *Philosophy and Rhetoric* 6, no. 2 (1973): 81–96.

2. Herbert Wichelns, "The Literary Criticism of Oratory," in *Landmark Essays on Rhetorical Criticism,* ed. Thomas Benson (Davis, CA: Hermagoras Press, 1993), 1–32.

3. Wichelns, "Literary Criticism of Oratory," 26.

4. Lloyd Bitzer, "The Rhetorical Situation," *Philosophy and Rhetoric* 1, no. 1 (1968): 1–11.

5. James Kinneavy, *A Theory of Discourse: The Aims of Discourse* (New York: Norton Publishers, 1980).

6. McKerrow, "Critical Rhetoric," 101, 92, 94.

7. Ibid., 96.

8. Ibid., 105.

9. Ibid., 109, 106.

10. For an extended treatment of the concept of propriety, see Victoria Kahn's *Rhetoric, Prudence and Skepticism in the Renaissance* (Ithaca: Cornell University Press, 1985), esp. chapter 2.

11. Aristotle, *On Rhetoric: A Theory of Civil Discourse,* 2nd ed., trans. George Kennedy (New York: Oxford University Press, 2007), 37.

12. Dilip Parameshwar Gaonkar, "Object and Method in Rhetorical Criticism:

From Wichelns to Leff and McGee," *Western Journal of Speech Communication* 54, no. 2 (1990): 290–316.

13. Jacques Lacan, *The Four Fundamental Concepts of Psychoanalysis (The Seminar of Jacques Lacan, Book XI),* ed. Jacques Alain Miller, trans. Alan Sheridan (New York: W. W. Norton, 1998), 49.

14. Lacan, *Four Fundamental Concepts,* 49.

15. Ibid., 60.

16. This distinction parallels Kant's distinction between the noumenon and the phenomenon, but it also argues that what is relevant is not simply the difference between the two but the split or space between them: "it is not in this dialectic between the surface and that which is beyond [the thing and the thing itself, the phenomenon and the noumenon] that things are suspended. . . . [T]here is something that establishes a fracture, a bipartition, a splitting of . . . being" (Lacan, *Four Fundamental Concepts,* 108).

17. Lacan, *Four Fundamental Concepts,* 53.

18. Ibid., 60, 53, 167.

19. Charles Shepherdson, *Lacan and the Limits of Language* (Philadelphia: Fordham University Press, 2008), 17.

20. Interestingly, in *On Feminine Sexuality,* Lacan claims that one mode of symbolization can "reach a Real": mathematization (131). Lacan suggests that mathematization provides one mode of accessing the "Real" of form (which is only "a" or an aspect of the Real), though the whole of "the Real" still remains "the mystery of the speaking body." Thus, if mathematization describes a real, it only does so by emptying it of any specific contents. This possibility for addressing the Real has recently become salient for object-oriented ontology, as exemplified in Quentin Meillassoux's *After Finitude: An Essay on the Necessity of Contingency* (New York: Continuum, 2010).

21. Martin Heidegger, *What is Philosophy?,* trans. Jean T. Wilde and William Kluback (New York: Rowman and Littlefield, 1956), 69.

22. Jacques Lacan, "The Instance of the Letter in the Unconscious, or Reason since Freud," in *Écrits,* trans. Bruce Fink (New York: W. W. Norton, 2006), 421.

23. Aristotle, *De Anima,* trans. R. D. Hicks (New York: Cosimo Books, 2008), 91.

24. Immanuel Kant, *The Critique of Pure Reason,* trans. J. M. D. Meiklejohn (London, 1855), 93.

25. Jacques Lacan, "The Mirror Stage as Formative of the *I* Function as Revealed in Psychoanalytic Experience," in *Écrits,* trans. Bruce Fink (New York: W. W. Norton, 2006).

26. Lacan, "The Mirror Stage," 76.

27. Maurice Charland, "Constitutive Rhetoric: The Case of the Peuple Quebecois," *Quarterly Journal of Speech* 73, no. 2 (1987): 133–34.

28. Charland, "Constitutive Rhetoric," 138.

29. Lacan, *On Feminine Sexuality,* 118–31.

30. Stuart Schneiderman, *Jacques Lacan: The Death of an Intellectual Hero* (Boston: Harvard University Press, 1983), 172.

31. Jacques Lacan, "A Theoretical Introduction to the Functions of Psychoanalysis in Criminology," in *Écrits,* trans. Bruce Fink (New York: W. W. Norton, 2006), 104–5.

32. Lacan, "Theoretical Introduction," 105.

33. Jacques Lacan, "Variations on the Standard Treatment," in *Écrits,* trans. Bruce Fink (New York: W. W. Norton, 2006), 299.

34. Jacques Lacan, "Variations," 299.

35. Lacan, "Instance of the Letter," 433.

36. Jacques Lacan, "The Subversion of the Subject and the Dialectic of Desire," in *Écrits,* trans. by Bruce Fink, (New York: W. W. Norton, 2006), 676.

37. Jacques Lacan, "Psychoanalysis and Its Teaching," in *Écrits,* trans. Bruce Fink (New York: W. W. Norton, 2006), 366.

38. Jacques Lacan, "Appendix II: Metaphor of the Subject," in *Écrits,* trans. Bruce Fink (New York: W. W. Norton, 2006), 755.

39. Lacan, *On Feminine Sexuality,* 12.

40. Lacan, "Une Pratique de Bavardage," 6.

41. For a treatment of the relation of non-relation, see Philippe Lacoue-Labarthe and Jean-Luc Nancy's *Retreating the Political* (London: Routledge, 1997), 10–11, 19.

42. Lacan, "Une Pratique de Bavardage," 7.

43. Ibid., 8.

44. Marcelle Marini, *Jacques Lacan: The French Tradition,* trans. Anne Tomiche (New Brunswick, NJ: Rutgers University Press, 1992), 89–90.

45. Sacvan Bercovitch and Cyrus R. K. Patell, *The Cambridge History of American Literature: Poetry and Criticism, 1940–1955* (London: Cambridge University Press, 1996), 322.

46. Michael C. Leff, "Lincoln at Cooper Union: Neo-Classical Criticism Revisited," *Western Journal of Communication* 65, no. 3 (2001): 239. The original text is Michael C. Leff and Gerald P. Mohrmann, "Lincoln at Cooper Union: A Rhetorical Analysis of the Text," *Quarterly Journal of Speech* 60, no. 3 (1974): 346–58.

47. Leff, "Lincoln at Cooper Union," 239–40.

48. See Ceccarelli's "Polysemy: Multiple Meanings in Rhetorical Criticism," *Quarterly Jounral of Speech* 84 (1998): 395–415.

49. Gaonkar, "Object and Method,"291.

50. Aristotle, *On Rhetoric,* 200.

51. Ibid., 14.

52. Ibid., 200.

53. Ibid.

Chapter 3

1. Lacan, *Psychoses,* 37.

2. Ibid.

3. For Lacan, the concept of a "node" represents both a point of condensa-

tion and "knots" in the interweaving of discourse. Nodes are intersections of verbal forms (see "Function and Field of Speech," 223) and words are "nodal [points] of signification." Lacan, "Presentation on Psychical Causality" in *Écrits,* trans. Bruce Fink (New York: W. W. Norton, 2006), 136.

4. Lacan, "Function and Field of Speech," 220.

5. Lacan, "Purloined Letter," 12.

6. Lacan, *On Feminine Sexuality,* 142.

7. David Lewis, "General Semantics," *Synthese* 22 (1970): 18–19.

8. Lewis, "General Semantics," 19.

9. Lacan, "Purloined Letter," 6.

10. Jacques Lacan, *The Ego in Freud's Theory and in the Technique of Psychoanalysis (The Seminar of Jacques Lacan, Book II),* ed. Jacques Alain Miller, trans. Sylvana Thomaselli (New York: W. W. Norton, 1988), 307.

11. Lacan, "Purloined Letter," 6.

12. Lacan, *Psychoses,* 32.

13. Lacan, "Instance of the Letter," 741.

14. Ibid., 743

15. Lacan, *On Feminine Sexuality,* 37.

16. Lacan, *Four Fundamental Concepts,* 20–21.

17. Lacan, "Purloined Letter," 31.

18. Jacques Lacan, "On a Question Preliminary to Any Possible Treatment of Psychosis," in *Écrits: A Selection,* trans. Alan Sheridan (New York: W. W. Norton, 1982), section III.

19. This account of repression refers to Heidegger's maxim that every act of revealing is simultaneously and productively an act of concealing. See Martin Heidegger, "On the Essence of Truth" in *Basic Writings,* 2nd ed., revised and expanded, ed. David Farrell Krell (San Francisco: Harper Books, 1993), 111–39.

20. Lacan, *On Feminine Sexuality,* 48 (emphasis added).

21. For a treatment of the concept of *glissement,* or sliding, see Lacan, *Four Fundamental Concepts,* 129.

22. Ibid., 20.

23. Sigmund Freud, "Notes Upon a Case of Obsessional Neurosis" [1909], in *Three Case Histories,* ed. Philip Rieff (New York: Scribner Paper Fiction, 1963), 1–82.

24. Jacques Lacan, "Aggressiveness in Psychoanalysis," in *Écrits,* trans. Bruce Fink (New York: W. W. Norton, 2006) 85.

25. Lacan, *Psychoses,* 9.

26. Ibid., 6.

27. Ibid.

28. Ibid., 7.

29. Lacan, *Four Fundamental Concepts,* 18.

30. Lacan, "Function and Field of Speech," 33.

31. Lacan, *On Feminine Sexuality,* 15.

32. Lacan, *Psychoses,* 36.

33. Jacques Lacan, *Freud's Papers on Technique (The Seminar of Jacques Lacan, Book I),* ed. Jacques Alain Miller, trans. John Forrester (New York: W. W. Norton, 1988), 48–49.

34. Lacan, *Freud's Papers,* 48–49.

35. Ibid.

36. Jacques Lacan, *The Ethics of Psychoanalysis (1959–60): The Seminar of Jacques Lacan, Book VII,* ed. Jacques-Alain Miller, trans. Dennis Porter (New York: W. W. Norton, 1997), 118.

37. Lacan, *Freud's Papers,* 242.

38. Dylan Evans, *An Introductory Dictionary of Lacanian Psychoanalysis* (London: Routledge, 1996), 133.

39. Jacques-Alain Miller, "Extimacy," *Symptom* 9 (2008), http://www.lacan.com/symptom/?p=36 (date accessed 7 February 2010).

40. Miller, "Extimacy."

41. Lacan, *Psychoses,* 24

42. Lacan, *Ego in Freud,* 243.

43. Lacan, *Psychoses,* 55–56.

44. Lacan, *On Feminine Sexuality,* 83.

45. Lacan, cited in Anthony Wilden's *Speech and Language in Psychoanalysis* (Baltimore: Johns Hopkins University Press, 1968), 106.

46. Lacan, *Freud's Papers,* 49–50.

47. Lacan, *Ego in Freud,* 244.

48. Lacan, *Psychoses,* 36.

49. Ibid., 37.

50. Ibid., 39.

51. Lacan, *Ego in Freud,* 244.

52. Ibid.

53. Ibid., 248.

54. Ibid., 244.

55. Ibid.

56. Lacan, "Function and Field of Speech," 209.

57. Ibid.

58. Jacques Lacan, "Response to Jean Hyppolite's Commentary on Freud's *Verneinung,*" in *Écrits,* trans. Bruce Fink (New York: W. W. Norton, 2006), 327.

59. Kittler's work is strongly Lacanian. For the account of the relation between hardware and software that inspired this analogy, see Kittler, "There is No Software," http://www.ctheory.net/articles.aspx?id=74 (last modified 18 October 1995; date accessed 12 January 2011).

60. This is the moment where the possibility of an "evental" rhetoric identified by Biesecker comes into sharpest relief (Biesecker, "Whither Ideology," 449). A rhetoric is "evental" in her sense if it refuses reduction to or interrupts the function of communication as an interface: a given speech act is evental, insofar as it gestures toward "full speech" (where the Symbolic determination of speech is "owned"); it

would function as an "exorbitant" demand that exceeds the possibility of an Imaginary coding without reduction; and it would exert effects not reducible to timeliness or propriety but would instead stage a form of performed sublimation. Such a reading mandates that rhetoric becomes evental not as a quality of a speech itself but rather as a result of the conditions of its circulation: thus the "event" must be an immanent possibility in all speech, as opposed to the interruptive quality of a specific speech act.

61. Schneiderman, *Jacques Lacan,* 169.

62. Alain Vanier, *Lacan* (New York: Other Press, 2000), 7.

63. Schneiderman, *Jacques Lacan,* 169.

64. Sigmund Freud, *The Interpretation of Dreams,* ed. and trans. James Strachey (New York: Avon Books, 1998), 311.

65. For example, Yannis Stavrakakis argues that: "Lacan's strategy is to use modern linguistics in order to 'recover' the truth of the Freudian enterprise. . . . [T]he strategic genius of Lacan's move is that while interpreting Freud according to his view of modern linguistic theory, he can also claim to recover the lost meaning of Freud." Yannis Stavrakakis, *Lacan and the Political* (New York: Routledge, 2000).

66. Lacan, *Psychoses,* 238.

67. Lacan, *Four Fundamental Concepts,* 22.

68. Ibid.

69. Lacan, *Freud's Papers,* 21.

70. Lacan, *Psychoses,* 221.

71. Ibid.

72. Lacan, "Function and Field of Speech," 31.

73. Lacan, *Psychoses,* 238.

74. Lacan, *Ego in Freud,* 34.

75. Lacan, *Psychoses,* 238.

76. Ibid.

77. Lacan, *Ego in Freud,* 316.

78. Ibid., 304.

79. Ibid., 47.

Chapter 4

1. Chaitin, *Rhetoric and Culture in Lacan,* 4.

2. Ibid.

3. Victoria Kahn, *Rhetoric, Prudence, and Skepticism in the Renaissance* (Ithaca: Cornell University Press, 1985), 147.

4. Jean-Joseph Goux, *Symbolic Economies: After Marx and Freud,* trans. Jennifer Curtiss Gage (Ithaca, NY: Cornell University Press, 1990).

5. Friedrich Nietzsche, "On Truth and Lie in an Extra Moral Sense," in *The Portable Nietzsche,* ed. Walter Kaufmann (Harmondsworth: Penguin, 1954), 46–47.

6. Giambattista Vico, *The New Science of Giambattista Vico,* trans. Thomas Goddard Bergin and Max Harold Fisch (Ithaca: Cornell University Press, 1984).

7. Hayden White, *Metahistory: The Historical Imagination in Nineteenth-Century Europe* (Baltimore: Johns Hopkins University Press: 1975), 31.

8. Kenneth Burke, *A Grammar of Motives* (Berkeley: University of California Press, 1969), 503. There are other candidates that might be included on this list, including Northrop Frye and Jacques Derrida. I have included these four because they represent the most cited and most typical approaches to the trope in rhetorical studies, and though there are important outliers, they are beyond the scope of this project.

9. See Gérard Genette's, *Figures I.* Collection Points, 74. Littérature. (Paris: Editions du Seuil, 1966).

10. Burke, *Grammar of Motives,* 503.

11. Paul de Man, *Allegories of Reading: Figural Language in Rousseau, Nietzsche, Rilke, and Proust* (New Haven: Yale University Press, 1982), 131.

12. Peter de Bolla, *Harold Bloom: Towards Historical Rhetorics* (London: Routledge, 1988), 107.

13. De Bolla, *Harold Bloom* 107.

14. Ibid., 109.

15. Ludwig Wittgenstein, *Culture and Value,* trans. Peter Winch (Chicago: University of Chicago Press, 1980), 9.

16. Zero-degree discourse presumes that signs have a literal, direct, and one-to-one relationship with things, and that as a result, discourse can be simply descriptive. For an attempt to theorize zero-degree discourse, see Group μ, eds. *Collages, Revue d'Esthétique, nos. 3–4.* (Paris: Union Genérale d'Editions, 1978).

17. Hayden White, *Tropics of Discourse: Essays in Cultural Criticism,* (Baltimore: Johns Hopkins University Press, 1985), 2.

18. White, *Tropics of Discourse,* 2.

19. Lacan, *Ego in Freud,* 5.

20. Lacan, *Psychoses,* 252.

21. Ibid., 218.

22. Ibid.

23. Chaitin, *Rhetoric and Culture in Lacan,* 3.

24. Lacan, *Psychoses,* 218.

25. Ibid., 218–19.

26. Ibid., 226.

27. Ibid., 222.

28. Ibid., 220–21.

29. Lacan, "Instance of the Letter," 421.

30. Lacan, *Psychoses,* 224.

31. Lacan, *Psychoses,* 229.

32. All figures are taken from "Instance of the Letter," 428–29.

33. Lacan, *On Femenine Sexuality,* 18.

34. Lacan, "Instance of the Letter," 428.

35. Ibid.

36. Ibid.

37. Lacan, *Four Fundamental Concepts,* 235.

38. Lacan, "Instance of the Letter," 429.

39. Lacan, *Four Fundamental Concepts,* 188.

40. Ibid., 188.

41. Lacan, "Function and Field of Speech," 219.

42. Wilden's essay is included in his translation of Lacan's *The Language of the Self: The Function of Language in Psychoanalysis,* 174.

43. Lacan, *On Feminine Sexuality,* 142.

44. Ibid., 4.

45. Ibid., 5.

46. Ibid., 4.

47. Jacques Lacan, *The Other Side of Psychoanalysis (The Seminar of Jacques Lacan, Book XVII),* ed. Jacques Alain Miller, trans. Russel Grigg (New York: W. W. Norton, 2006), 125.

48. For an elaboration of the distinction between agency and subject as agent, see Christian Lundberg and Joshua Gunn's "'Ouija Board, Are There Any Communications?' Agency, Ontotheology, and the Death of the Humanist Subject, or, Continuing the ARS Conversation," *Rhetoric Society Quarterly* 35, no. 4 (2005): 83–105.

49. Lacan, *Freud's Papers,* 251.

50. Ibid., 284, 6.

51. Lacan, *Ego in Freud,* 255.

52. Lacan, *Ethics of Psychoanalysis,* 33.

53. Ibid., 73.

54. Lacan, *Other Side,* 93; and *On Feminine Sexuality,* 116.

55. Maria Rüegg, "Metaphor and Metonymy: The Logic of Structuralist Rhetoric," *Glyph* 6 (1979): 141–57.

56. Andrew Robinson, "The Political Theory of Constitutive Lack: A Critique," *Theory and Event* 8, no. 1 (2005); Jacques Derrida, *Archive Fever: A Freudian Impression,* trans. Eric Prenowitz (Chicago: University of Chicago Press, 1998); and Jacques Derrida, "Psychoanalysis Searches the States of Its Soul: The Impossible Beyond of a Sovereign Culture," in *Without Alibi,* ed. Peggy Kamuf (Stanford, CA: Meridian, 2002).

57. Jacques Derrida, "Structure, Sign and Play in the Discourse of the Human Sciences," in *Writing and Difference,* trans. Alan Bass (London: Routledge, 1980).

58. Milton Friedman, "The Methodology of Positive Economics," in *Essays in Positive Economics* (Chicago: University of Chicago Press, 1966).

59. Friedman, "Methodology of Positive Economics," 32.

60. Ibid., 43.

61. This is a word coined by Lacan to signify the realm of tuché. Lacan, *Four Fundamental Concepts,* 70–71.

62. Ibid., 53.

63. Ibid., 55.

64. Lacan, "Of Structure as an Inmixing of Otherness," 189.

65. Ibid., 190.

66. Ibid.

67. Lacan, *Other Side,* 190.

68. Ehsan Azari, *Lacan and the Destiny of Literature: Desire, Jouissance, and the Sinthome in Shakespeare, Donne, Joyce, and Ashbery* (New York: Continuum, 2008) 72.

69. Azari, *Lacan and the Destiny of Literature,* 72, 73.

70. See, for example, Shoshana Felman's *Jacques Lacan and the Adventure of Insight* (Boston: Harvard University Press, 1989).

71. Rabate, *Jacques Lacan,* 4.

72. Ibid., 3; quoting Jacques Lacan, "C'est a la lecture de Freud," in Robert Georgin, *Lacan* (Lausanne: L'Age d'Homme-Cistre, 1977), 15.

73. Rabate, *Jacques Lacan,* 4.

74. Ibid., 6.

75. Ibid., 4; quoting Jacques Lacan, "C'est a la lecture," 16.

Chapter 5

1. See, for example, Dana L. Cloud, "The Materiality of Discourse as an Oxymoron: A Challenge to Critical Rhetoric," *Western Journal of Communication* 58, no. 3 (1994).

2. Lacan, *Freud's Papers,* 244.

3. Lacan, *On Feminine Sexuality,* 4, 23.

4. For a representative example of how a Lacanian analytic would theorize this kind of intrusion, see Slavoj Žižek's *Welcome to the Desert of the Real: Five Essays on September 11 and Related Dates* (London: Verso, 2002).

5. I include here concepts like the materiality of the sign, the microanalytics of power, and articulation theory. Exemplars of these positions include rhetoricians who draw theoretical inspiration from Foucault's conception of discourse—for example, Carole Blair, Raymond McKerrow, Maurice Charland, and more recently, Ronald Greene.

6. Michael Calvin McGee, "A Materialist's Conception of Rhetoric," in *Explorations in Rhetoric: Essays in honor of Douglas Ehninger,* ed. R. E. McKerrow (Glenview, IL: Scott, Foresman, 1982), 38.

7. Plato, *Symposium,* 202d13-e1.

8. Lacoue-Labarthe and Nancy, *Retreating the Political,* 28.

9. Ibid., 21, 27.

10. Augusto Boal, *The Rainbow of Desire: The Boal Method of Theatre and Therapy* (New York: Routledge, 1995), 43.

11. Jacques Lacan, *The Seminar of Jacques Lacan VIII: Transference,* trans. Cormac Gallagher (London: Karnac Books, 2002), IX, 6.

12. Lacan, *Transference,* IX, 6.

13. Ibid.

14. Ibid., III, 10.

15. Gunn, "For the Love of Rhetoric," 131–33.

16. Nathan Stormer, "Articulation: A Working Paper on Rhetoric and Taxis" *Quarterly Journal of Speech* 90, no. 3 (2004): 261.

17. Cloud, "Materiality of Discourse as Oxymoron," 142.

18. Lacan, "Function and Field of Speech," 65.

19. See Jennifer Edbauer's "The New 'New': Making a Case for Critical Affect Studies," *Quarterly Journal of Speech* 94, no. 2 (2008): 200–212.

20. Gilles Deleuze, "Lecture Transcripts on Spinoza's Concept of Affect," http://www.goldsmiths.ac.uk/csisp/papers/deleuze_spinoza_affect.pdf (accessed 2 April 2006).

21. For an explanation of this linkage, see, for example, Brian Massumi's "Sensing the Virtual, Building the Insensible," in "Hypersurface Architecture," ed. Stephen Perrella, special issue, *Architectural Design* (Profile no. 133) 68, nos. 5/6 (May–June 1998): 16–24.

22. Lawrence Grossberg, *We Gotta Get Out of This Place* (New York: Routledge, 1992), 79.

23. See Freud's *On the Interpretation of Dreams,* trans. James Strachey, (New York: Avon Books, 1965), esp. chapter 6.

24. Jacques Lacan, *The Seminar of Jacques Lacan X: Anxiety,* trans. Cormac Gallagher (London: Karnac Books, 2002), 11.

25. Lacan, *Anxiety,* 11.

26. Lacan, *Freud's Papers,* 14.

27. Lacan, *Ethics,* 102.

28. Ibid., 103.

29. See, Gilles Deleuze and Felix Guattari's *A Thousand Plateaus: Capitalism and Schizophrenia,* trans. Brian Massumi (Minneapolis: University of Minnesota Press, 1987), esp. chapter 4, "The Postulates of Linguistics," and chapter 5, "Several Regimes of Signs."

30. Lacan, *Other Side,* 151.

31. Lacan writes that there is a gap "between this One (of phallic jouissance) and something that is related to being, and behind being, to jouissance" (*On Feminine Sexuality,* 6).

32. Ibid.

33. Lacan, "Agency of the Letter," 147.

34. Ibid.

35. Ibid., 149.

36. Greene, "Another Materialist Rhetoric," 29.

37. Lacan, *On Feminine Sexuality,* 23.

38. Lacan's affinity with the performatively flavored account of materiality as a (dis)embodied habitus constituted by enjoyment is demonstrated in the following passage: "the signifier is situated at the level of enjoying substance (*substance*

jouissante).... The signifier is the cause of jouissance. Without the signifier how could we even approach . . . the body? Without the signifier, how could we center something that is the material cause of jouissance? However fuzzy or confused it may be, it is a part of the body that is signified in this contribution" (*On Feminine Sexuality,* 224).

39. As Lacan argues, "the kind of exchange involved here is the exchange . . . of those social supports, which in a different context, are known as subjects" (*Four Fundamental Concepts,* 5).

40. Lacan, "Agency of the Letter," 147.

41. Lacan, *Ego in Freud,* 82.

42. Lacan, *Other Side,* 124.

43. Lacan, *On Feminine Sexuality,* 22.

44. McGee, "Materialist's Conception," 45.

45. As McGee defines it: "Rhetoric is a natural social phenomenon in the context of which symbolic claims are made on the action and/or belief of one or more persons, allegedly in the interest of such individuals, and with the strong presumption that such claims will cause meaningful change" ("Materialist's Conception," 59).

46. Lacan, *On Feminine Sexuality,* 2.

47. Ibid., 12.

48. Ibid., 3.

49. Greene, "Another Materialist Rhetoric," 38.

50. Of course, a theory of articulation can solve this problem by including the subject that engages the field of articulations as a part of that same field. This is, for example, the thrust of Grossberg's work in arguing for cultural studies as a practice of radical contextualism (see Grossberg, *Cultural Studies in the Future Tense*). Though this solution addresses the problem of an implicit observational hermeneutic in part, it also forces the question of what relationship inheres between the subject of articulation's representations of the world and the Real that is external to it.

51. Greene's treatment of interpellation is his most lawyerly moment: "As an alternative conceptualization for a materialist rhetoric I am suggesting that critics focus on how rhetorical practices create conditions of possibility of a governing apparatus to judge and *program* reality" ("Another Materialist Rhetoric," 41).

52. Lacan, "Agency of the Letter," 148.

53. Ekaterina Haskins, "Embracing the Superficial: Michael Calvin McGee, Rhetoric, and the Postmodern Condition," *American Journal of Communication* 6, no. 4 (2003): 3.

54. It is of course possible to argue that McGee's later works address this problem. For instance in his famous essay "Text Context and Fragmentation," he argues that criticism is a kind of intentional reconstruction of the rhetorical object by the critic. This move does, in some way, concede that interpretive protocols are not naturally derivable from the fragmented conditions of "postmodern" discourse. Yet this version of the critical act does not vindicate McGee from the problems of reference and may be an insufficient account of the relationship between interpretation and en-

joyment. McGee is only able to sustain his claim, as Greene notes, by presuming that the material processes of rhetoric seamlessly match the changing social context of mediation, which is a kind of employment of the politics of reference that does not significantly revise the earlier claims to the materiality of rhetoric, as much as it provides a caveat that creates a kind of interpretive humility.

55. McGee, "Materialist's Conception," 23.

56. Ibid., 24.

57. The term "jouissance" is related to the French slang word for orgasm: *jouir.* Lacan intends the term, as opposed to a concept like pleasure, to capture a kind of enjoyment that is, in some ways, unbearable or insufferable, as if the moment before climax were extended forever without release.

Chapter 6

1. Arthur Strum, "Bibliography of the Concept of Offentlichkeit," *New German Critique* 61 (1994): 161–202, 163.

2. See Jurgen Habermas, *The Structural Transformation of the Public Sphere: An Inquiry into a Category of Bourgeois Society* (Cambridge: Polity Press, 1989); and Michael Warner's essay "Publics and Counterpublics" in *Publics and Counterpublics* (Brooklyn: Zone Books, 2002), esp. 67–70 for the idea that publics are self-organized and autotelic.

3. Frederic Jameson, "Imaginary and Symbolic in Lacan: Marxism, Psychoanalytic Criticism, and the Problem of the Subject," in *Literature and Psychoanalysis: The Quesiton of Reading Otherwise,* ed. Shoshana Feldman (Baltimore: Johns Hopkins University Press, 1980), 339.

4. Perhaps the work that comes closest to a Lacanian inspired reading of publics is Jodi Dean's *Publicity's Secret* (Ithaca: Cornell University Press, 2002). In it, Dean treats the public as a fantasy constituted by secrets.

5. Frederick Dolan, "Political Action and the Unconscious: Arendt and Lacan on Decentring the Subject," *Political Theory* 23, no. 2 (1995): 330–52.

6. Hannah Arendt, *The Human Condition* (Chicago: University of Chicago Press, 1998), 50, 51, 52, 55, respectively.

7. Lacan, *Ego in Freud,* 20.

8. Jean-Paul Sartre, *No Exit* (New York: Vantage Books, 1947), 47.

9. Lacan, *Four Fundamental Concepts,* 72.

10. Ibid., 75.

11. Ibid., 73.

12. Malcolm Bowie, *Lacan* (Boston: Harvard Univeristy Press, 1993), 68.

13. Lacan, *Psychoses,* 59.

14. Ibid.

15. See Michael Warner's "The Mass Public and the Mass Subject," in *Publics and Counterpublics,* 159–86.

16. Lacan, *Psychoses,* 60.

17. Lacan, *On Feminine Sexuality,* 20.

18. Lacan, *Four Fundamental Concepts,* 23.

19. Robert J. C. Young, "Freud's Secret: *The Interpretation of Dreams* Was a Gothic Novel," in *Sigmund Freud's* The Interpretation of Dreams*: New Interdisciplinary Essays,* ed. Laura Marcus (Manchester: Manchester University Press, 1999), 222.

20. On image, see Joan Copjec, *Imagine There's No Woman: Ethics and Sublimation* (Boston: MIT Press, 2004), 62–67; on narcissism, see Philippe Lacoue-Labarthe and Jean-Luc Nancy, *Retreating the Political* (London: Routledge, 1997), 11, 15, 26.

21. De Man, *Allegories of Reading,* 15–16.

22. Lacan, *On Feminine Sexuality,* 2.

23. Lacan, *Ethics,* 112.

24. Ibid., 94.

25. Ibid., 99.

26. Ibid., 118.

27. Jameson, "Imaginary and Symbolic in Lacan," 339.

28. Immanuel Kant, "Appendix A: Immanuel Kant, 'An Answer to the Question: What is Enlightnment,'" in *Groundwork for the Metaphysics of Morals,* ed. Lara Denis (Orchard Park, NY: Broadview Press, 2005).

29. John Dewey, "Renascent Liberalism," in *The Later Works of John Dewey, 1925–1953: Volume 11, 1935–1937; Essays: Liberalism and Social Action,* ed. Jo Ann Boydston (Carbondale: Southern Illinois University Press, 1988), 41.

30. Jurgen Habermas, *Between Facts and Norms* (Boston: MIT Press, 1998), 148.

31. Lacan, "Aggressiveness in Psychoanalysis," 88.

32. Ibid., 89.

33. John T. Kirby, "The 'Great Triangle' in Early Greek Rhetoric and Poetics," in *Landmark Essays on Classical Greek Rhetoric,* ed. Ed Schiappa (Davis, CA: Hermagoras Press), 5.

34. Vincent Farenga, "Periphrasis on the Origin of Rhetoric," *MLN* 94, no. 5 (1979): 1033–55.

35. Lacan, "Mirror Stage," 79.

36. Ibid., 80.

37. This debate spanned volumes 2 and 3 of the journal *Dissent.* The central essays in this debate are available from Fromm's collected papers at http://www.erich-fromm.de/data/pdf/1956b-e.pdf.

38. Harvey Yunis, "Eros in Plato's Phaedrus and the Shape of Greek Rhetoric," *Arion* 13, no. 1 (2005): 113.

39. Herbert Marcuse, "A Reply to Erich Fromm," *Dissent* 3 (1956): 81–83.

40. Lacan, *On Feminine Sexuality,* 4.

41. Ibid., 6.

42. Ibid., 69–70.

43. Bruce Fink, in Lacan, *On Feminine Sexuality,* 69, footnote 13.

44. Lacan, *On Feminine Sexuality,* 69.

45. Ibid., esp. "God and the Jouissance of the Woman."

46. Copjec, *Imagine,* 61.

47. Copjec, *Imagine,* 61.

48. Ibid.

49. See, for example, chapter 8, "Sex and the Euthanasia of Reason" in Copjec's *Read My Desire: Lacan Against the Historicists* (Boston: MIT Press, 1996).

50. Copjec, *Read My Desire,* 207.

Chapter 7

1. These cases are exemplary, but they are also only exemplary. In large part, I have selected them because of their value as examples, and because they represent questions that cannot be answered as easily by existing rhetorical theories. The wager of this volume is that similar readings might be made of any specific economy of discursive exchange.

2. Michael Warner, "Publics and Counterpublics," *Public Culture* 14, no. 1 (2000): 50, 55, 60.

3. "No single text can create a public," argues Warner, because "a public is . . . an ongoing space of encounter for discourse. . . . [O]nly when a previously existing discourse can be supposed, and a responding discourse be postulated, can a text address a public" ("Publics and Counterpublics," 61).

4. Evangelicalism is a notoriously difficult concept to define, though here I define it operationally as an economy of tropes entailing an intense commitment to a literal conception of the Bible, a concern for spreading the gospel message, and a specific relation to mass culture premised on marginality.

5. Of course, *The Passion* was viewed by non-evangelicals, and my goal is not the impossible task of defining "the" public of *The Passion*; rather I would like to define the logics of affinity through which a specific public, the evangelical public paying attention to Gibson's film, comes into being around the trope of marginality. For a fuller accounting of evangelical marginality, see Christian Smith's *American Evangelicalism: Embattled and Thriving* (Chicago: University of Chicago Press, 1998); and *Revive Us Again: The Reawakening of American Fundamentalism* (New York: Oxford University Press, 1999).

6. Thomas Hibbs's "Unparalleled *Passion,*" *National Review Online,* http://www.nationalreview.com/comment/hibbs200402250836.asp (last modified 25 February 2004; accessed 25 February 2007). Mark Douglas has argued that revulsion is intended effect of *The Passion,* arguing that the film "asks its audience to feel revulsion" ("Mel Gibson's Bible: Religion, Popular Culture, and 'The Passion of the Christ,'" in *The Passion of the Christ: Biblical and Theological Perspectives,* ed. Timothy Beale and Tod Linafelt [Chicago: University of Chicago Press, 2005]).

7. Christian Film News, "October Update," *Christian Film News* 5 (October 2003), http://www.christiananswers.net/spotlight/news/cen-03v05.html (accessed 10 October 2004).

8. Peter Maresco, "Mel Gibson's *The Passion of The Christ:* Market Segmenta-

tion, Mass Marketing and Promotion, and the Internet," *Journal of Religion and Popular Culture* 8 (2004).

9. The Barna Group, "New Survey Examines the Impact of Gibson's 'Passion' Movie," 10 July 2004, http://www.barna.org/FlexPage.aspx?Page=BarnaUpdateNarrow & BarnaUpdateID=167 (accessed 17 February 2005).

10. Barna, "New Survey."

11. Robert Wyatt, Ken Blake, John Bodle, and Zeny Panol, "Mel Gibson's '*Passion*' May be 'Preaching to the Choir,'" The Survey Group at Middle Tennessee State University, www.mtsusurveygroup.org/mtpoll/s2004/MTSUPollS04_melpassion_release_0307.pdf, 2004 (accessed 2 April 2006).

12. For a fuller treatment of this dynamic in the case of evangelical belief, see Michael Lindsay's "Mind the Gap: Religion and the Crucible of Marginality," *Sociological Quarterly* 49, no. 4 (Fall 2008): 653–88.

13. Mel Gibson, interview with Raymond Arroyo, "The World Over," http://www.ewtn.com/vondemand/audio/seriessearchprog.asp?seriesID=-6892288 (last modified 14 March 2003; accessed 5 January 2004).

14. John 19:1.

15. Mark 15:15.

16. Gibson, interview, "The World Over."

17. Romans 12:5.

18. Gibson, interview, "The World Over."

19. Gibson, interview, "The World Over."

20. John 15:20.

21. Lacan, *Four Fundamental Concepts,* 119.

22. Albert Winseman of the Gallup Organization estimates that there are roughly 65 million evangelical Americans comprising 22 percent of the total American population. Arthur Winseman, "U.S. Evangelicals: How Many Walk the Walk," *Gallup Poll News Service Commentary,* The Gallup Organization (2005), www.gallup.com (accessed 10 December 2005).

23. Richard B. Gregg, "The Ego-Function of the Rhetoric of Protest," *Philosophy & Rhetoric* 4, no. 2 (Spring 1971): 71–91.

24. Josef Schneider, "Portlanders Shut-Out of Mexican Government's 'Watch List,'" newswire article, Portland Independent Media Center, http://portland.indymedia.org/en/2003/09/271482.shtml (accessed 3 January 2007).

25. Schneider, "Portlanders Shut-Out."

26. The petition is available at http://www.mexicosolidarity.org/cancun_list.htm (accessed 3 March 2004).

27. Slavoj Žižek, *The Ticklish Subject: The Absent Center of Political Ontology* (London: Verso, 2000).

28. Jason Glynos and Yannis Stavrakakis, "Encounters of the Real Kind: Sussing Out the Limits of Laclau's Embrace of Lacan," in *Laclau: A Critical Reader,* ed. Simon Critchely and Oliver Marchart (New York: Routledge, 2006), 202.

29. Glynos and Stavrakakis, "Encounters of the Real," 209.

30. Laclau, *On Populist Reason,* 116.

31. Sigmund Freud, "The Question of Lay Analysis," *The Essentials of Psychoanalysis,* ed. Anna Freud (London: Hogarth Press, 1986), 22.

32. Freud, *Civilization and Its Discontents,* 68, 76, 103.

33. Lacan, *On Feminine Sexuality,* 142.

34. Lacan, "Mirror Stage," 4.

35. Alan Sheridan, "Introduction," in *Écrits,* viii.

36. Jacques Lacan, "Signification of the Phallus," in *Écrits: A Selection,* trans. Alan Sheridan (London: Tavistock Publications, 1977), 286.

37. Lacan, "Signification of the Phallus," 287.

38. Lacan, "Subversion of the Subject and the Dialectic of Desire," in *Écrits: A Selection,* trans. Alan Sheridan (London: Tavistock Publications, 1977), 311.

39. Lacan, "Signification of the Phallus," 289.

40. Antony Easthope, *The Unconscious* (New York: Routledge, 2000), 94–95.

41. Lacan, *Ego in Freud,* 228–29.

42. Bruce Fink, *The Lacanian Subject: Between Language and Jouissance* (Princeton: Princeton Universtiy Press, 1996), 90.

43. Lacan, *Ethics,* 53.

44. Gerard Wajcman, "The Hysteric's Discourse," *Symptom* 4 (2003), http://www.lacan.com/hystericdiscf.htm (accessed 5 March 2004).

45. Lawrence Grossberg, *Bringing It All Back Home* (Durham, NC: Duke University Press, 1997), 4.

46. Lacan, "Signification of the Phallus," 286.

Postscript

1. Nancy Streuver, *Rhetoric, Modality, Modernity* (Chicago: University of Chicago Press, 2009), 2.

2. Ernesto Grassi, *Rhetoric as Philosophy: The Humanist Tradition,* trans. John Michael Krois and Azizeh Azodi (Carbondale: Southern Illinois University Press, 2001), 69.

3. Grassi, *Rhetoric as Philosophy,* 91.

4. Ibid.

5. Ibid., 7.

6. Ibid.

7. Ibid., 20.

8. Ibid.

9. Ibid., 9.

10. Diane Davis, "Identification: Burke and Freud on Who You Are," *RSQ* 38, no. 2 (2008): 123–47; Joshua Gunn, "For the Love of Rhetoric, with Continual Reference to Kenny and Dolly," *Quarterly Journal of Speech* 94, no. 2 (2008): 131–55.

11. Streuver, *Rhetoric, Modality, Modernity,* 6.

12. Their original findings were published in "Authenticating Aristotle's Protrepticus," *Oxford Studies in Ancient Philosophy* 29 (Winter 2005), ed. David Shedley, which both reproduces the text and defines their methodology.

13. D. S. Hutchinson and Monte Ransome Johnson, *Aristotle, Protrepticus* (2010) viii, 31; http://www.protreptic.info/ (accessed 12 September 2011).

14. Hutchinson and Johnson, *Aristotle, Protrepticus,* 4.

15. Ibid., 3.

16. Ibid., 7.

17. Ibid., 12.

18. Aristotle, *Nicomachean Ethics,* trans. W. D. Ross (Internet Classics Archive, 1994–2000), http://classics.mit.edu/Aristotle/nicomachaen.mb.txt, (accessed 19 July 2011), I.3.

19. Hutchinson and Johnson, *Aristotle, Protrepticus,* 16.

20. Ibid., 18.

21. Ibid., 25.

22. Ibid., 25–26.

23. Ibid., 27.

24. Ibid., 28.

25. Metzger, *Lost Cause of Rhetoric,* 81–82.

26. Mark D. Jordan, "Ancient Philosophic Protreptic and the Problem of Persuasive Genres," *Rhetorica: A Journal of the History of Rhetoric* 4, no. 4 (Autumn 1986): 309–33.

27. Grassi, *Rhetoric as Philosophy,* 114.

Bibliography

Arendt, Hannah. *The Human Condition*. Chicago: University of Chicago Press, 1998.

Aristotle. *De Anima*. Translated by R. D. Hicks. New York: Cosimo Books, 2008.

———. *On Rhetoric: A Theory of Civic Discourse*. Translated by George Kennedy. New York: Oxford University Press, 1991.

———. *On Rhetoric: A Theory of Civil Discourse*, 2nd edition. Translated by George Kennedy. New York: Oxford University Press, 2007.

Azari, Ehsan. *Lacan and the Destiny of Literature: Desire, Jouissance, and the Sinthome in Shakespeare, Donne, Joyce, and Ashbery*. New York: Continuum, 2008.

Badiou, Alain. *Being and Event*. New York: Continuum, 2007.

Bercovitch, Sacvan, and Cyrus R. K. Patell. *The Cambridge History of American Literature: Poetry and Criticism, 1940–1955*. London: Cambridge University Press, 1996.

Biesecker, Barbara. "No Time for Mourning: The Rhetorical Production of the Melancholic Citizen-Subject in the War on Terror." *Philosophy and Rhetoric* 40, no. 1 (2007): 147–69.

———. "Rethinking the Rhetorical Situation from Within the Thematic of *Différance*." *Philosophy and Rhetoric* 22, no. 2 (1989): 110–30.

———. "Rhetorical Studies and the 'New' Psychoanalysis: What's the Real Problem? or Framing the Problem of the Real." *Quarterly Journal of Speech* 84 (1998): 222–39.

———. "Whither Ideology? Toward a Different Take on Enjoyment as a Political Factor." *Western Journal of Communication* 75, no. 4 (2011): 445–50.

Bitzer, Lloyd. "The Rhetorical Situation." *Philosophy and Rhetoric* 1, no. 1 (1968): 1–11.

Black, Edwin. "The Second Persona." *Quarterly Journal of Speech* 56, no. 2 (1970): 101–19.

Boal, Augusto. *The Rainbow of Desire: The Boal Method of Theatre and Therapy*. New York: Routledge, 1995.

Bowie, Malcolm. *Lacan*. Boston: Harvard University Press, 1993.

Brooks, Peter. "The Idea of a Psychoanalytic Literary Criticism." *Critical Inquiry* 13, no. 2 (1987): 334–48.

Burke, Kenneth. *A Grammar of Motives*. Berkeley: University of California Press, 1969.

Ceccarelli, Leah. "Polysemy: Multiple Meanings in Rhetorical Criticism." *Quarterly Journal of Speech* 84 (1998): 395–415.

Chaitin, Gilbert. *Rhetoric and Culture in Lacan.* London: Cambridge University Press, 1996.

Charland, Maurice. "Constitutive Rhetoric: The Case of the Peuple Quebecois." *Quarterly Journal of Speech* 73, no. 2 (1987): 133–50.

Cloud, Dana L. "The Materiality of Discourse as an Oxymoron: A Challenge to Critical Rhetoric." *Western Journal of Communication* 58, no. 3 (1994): 141–63.

Copjec, Joan. *Imagine There's No Woman: Ethics and Sublimation.* Boston: MIT Press, 2004.

———. *Read My Desire: Lacan Against the Historicists.* Boston: MIT Press, 1996.

Crowley, Sharon. "Rhetoric, Literature, and the Dissociation of Invention." *Journal of Advanced Composition* 6, no. 1 (1985–86): 17–32.

Davis, Diane. "Addressing Alterity: Rhetoric, Hermeneutics, and the Nonappropriative Relation." *Philosophy and Rhetoric* 38, no. 3 (2005): 191–212.

———. "Identification: Burke and Freud on Who You Are." *Rhetoric Society Quarterly* 38, no. 2 (2008): 123–47.

Dean, Jodi. *Publicity's Secret.* Ithaca: Cornell University Press, 2002.

De Bolla, Peter. *Harold Bloom: Towards Historical Rhetorics.* London: Routledge, 1988.

Deleuze, Gilles. "Gilles Deleuze, Lecture Transcripts on Spinoza's Concept of Affect." http://www.goldsmiths.ac.uk/csisp/papers/deleuze_spinoza_affect.pdf (accessed 3 April 2006).

Deleuze, Gilles, and Felix Guattari. *A Thousand Plateaus: Capitalism and Schizophrenia.* Translated by Brian Massumi. Minneapolis: University of Minnesota Press, 1987.

de Man, Paul. *Allegories of Reading: Figural Language in Rousseau, Nietzsche, Rilke, and Proust.* New Haven: Yale University Press, 1982.

Derrida, Jacques. *Archive Fever: A Freudian Impression.* Translated by Eric Prenowitz. Chicago: University of Chicago Press, 1998.

———. "Psychoanalysis Searches the States of Its Soul: The Impossible Beyond of a Sovereign Culture." In *Without Alibi,* edited by Peggy Kamuf, 238–80. Stanford, CA: Meridian, 2002.

———. "Structure, Sign and Play in the Discourse of the Human Sciences." In *Writing and Difference,* translated by Alan Bass. London: Routledge, 1980.

Dewey, John. "Renascent Liberalism." In *The Later Works of John Dewey, 1925–1953: Volume 11, 1935–1937; Essays: Liberalism and Social Action,* edited by Jo Ann Boydston. Carbondale: Southern Illinois University Press, 1988.

Douglas, Mark. "Mel Gibson's Bible: Religion, Popular Culture, and 'The Passion of the Christ.'" In *The Passion of the Christ: Biblical and Theological Perspectives,* edited by Timothy Beale and Tod Linafelt, 129–38. Chicago: University of Chicago Press, 2005.

Easthope, Antony. *The Unconscious.* New York: Routledge, 2000.

Edbauer, Jennifer. "The New 'New': Making a Case for Critical Affect Studies." *Quarterly Journal of Speech* 94, no. 2 (2008): 200–212.

Evans, Dylan. *An Introductory Dictionary of Lacanian Psychoanalysis.* London: Routledge, 1996.

Felman, Shoshana. *Jacques Lacan and the Adventure of Insight.* Boston: Harvard University Press, 1989.

Fink, Bruce. *Lacan to the Letter: Reading Écrits Closely.* Minneapolis: University of Minnesota Press, 2004.

———. *The Lacanian Subject: Between Language and Jouissance.* Princeton: Princeton University Press, 1996.

Freud, Sigmund *Civilization and Its Discontents.* trans. James Strachey. London: Norton, 1989.

———. *The Interpretation of Dreams.* Translated by James Strachey. New York: Avon Books, 1998.

———. "Notes Upon a Case of Obsessional Neurosis" [1909]. In *Three Case Histories,* edited by Philip Rieff. New York: Scribner Paper Fiction, 1963.

———. "The Question of Lay Analysis." In *The Essentials of Psychoanalysis,* edited by Anna Freud. London: Hogarth Press, 1986.

Friedman, Milton. "The Methodology of Positive Economics." In *Essays in Positive Economics.* Chicago: University of Chicago Press, 1966.

Gadamer, Hans Georg. *Truth and Method.* Translated by Joel Weinsheimer and Donald Marshall. New York: Continuum, 2006.

Gallop, Jane. "Lacan and Literature: A Case for Transference." *Poetics* 13 (1989): 307.

———. *Reading Lacan.* Ithaca: Cornell University Press, 1985.

Gaonkar, Dilip Parameshwar. "Object and Method in Rhetorical Criticism: From Wichelns to Leff and McGee." *Western Journal of Speech Communication* 54, no. 2 (1990): 290–316.

Genette, Gérard. *Figures I.* Collection Points, 74. Littérature. Paris: Editions du Seuil, 1966.

Gibson, Mel. Interview with Raymond Arroyo, "The World Over," 14 March 2003. http://www.ewtn.com/vondemand/audio/seriessearchprog.asp?seriesID=-6892288 (accessed 5 January 2004).

Glynos, Jason, and Yannis Stavrakakis. "Encounters of the Real Kind: Sussing Out the Limits of Laclau's Embrace of Lacan." In *Laclau: A Critical Reader,* edited by Simon Critchely and Oliver Marchart, 201–16. New York: Routledge, 2006.

Goux, Jean-Joseph. *Symbolic Economies: After Marx and Freud.* Translated by Jennifer Curtiss Gage. Ithaca: Cornell University Press, 1990.

Greene, Ronald Walter. "Another Materialist Rhetoric." *Critical Studies in Mass Communication* 15, no. 1 (1998): 21–41.

Grossberg, Lawrence. *Bringing It All Back Home.* Durham, NC: Duke University Press, 1997.

———. *Cultural Studies in the Future Tense.* Durham, NC: Duke University Press, 2010.

———. *We Gotta Get Out of This Place.* New York: Routledge, 1992.

Group μ. *A General Rhetoric.* Translated by Paul B. Burrell and Edgar M. Slotkin. Baltimore: Johns Hopkins University Press, 1981.

Gunn, Joshua. "For the Love of Rhetoric, with Continual Reference to Kenny and Dolly." *Quarterly Journal of Speech* 94, no. 2 (2008): 131–55.

———. "Mourning Speech: Haunting and the Spectral Voices of Nine-Eleven." *Text and Performance Quarterly* 24, no. 2 (2004): 91–114.

———. "Refitting Fantasy: Psychoanalysis, Subjectivity, and Talking to the Dead." *Quarterly Journal of Speech* 90, no. 1 (2004): 1–23.

Habermas, Jürgen. *Between Facts and Norms.* Boston: MIT Press, 1998.

———. *The Structural Transformation of the Public Sphere: An Inquiry into a Category of Bourgeois Society.* Cambridge: Polity Press, 1989.

Haskins, Ekaterina. "Embracing the Superficial: Michael Calvin McGee, Rhetoric, and the Postmodern Condition." *American Journal of Communication* 6, no. 4 (2003).

Heidegger, Martin. "On the Essence of Truth." In *Basic Writings,* 2nd ed., revised and expanded, edited by David Farrell Krell. San Francisco: Harper Books, 1993.

———. *What is Philosophy?* Translated by Jean T. Wilde and William Kluback. New York: Rowman and Littlefield, 1956.

Hibbs, Thomas. "Unparalleled *Passion.*" National Review Online, 25 February 2004. http://www.nationalreview.com/comment/hibbs200402250836.asp (accessed 25 February 2007).

Homer, Sean. *Jacques Lacan.* New York: Routledge, 2005.

Hyde, Michael. "Jacques Lacan's Psychoanalytic Theory of Speech and Language." *Quarterly Journal of Speech* 66, no. 1 (1980): 96–118.

Jakobson, Roman. "The Metaphoric and Metonymic Poles." In *Metaphor and Metonymy in Comparison and Contrast,* edited and translated by Rene Dirven and Ralf Porings, 41–48. Berlin: Mouton de Gruyter, 2002.

Jameson, Frederic. "Imaginary and Symbolic in Lacan: Marxism, Psychoanalytic Criticism, and the Problem of the Subject." In *Literature and Psychoanalysis: The Question of Reading Otherwise,* edited by Shoshana Felman, 338–95. Baltimore: Johns Hopkins University Press, 1980.

Kahn, Victoria. *Rhetoric, Prudence, and Skepticism in the Renaissance.* Ithaca: Cornell University Press, 1985.

Kant, Immanuel. "Appendix A: Immanuel Kant, 'An Answer to the Question: What is Enlightenment.'" In *Groundwork for the Metaphysics of Morals,* edited by Lara Denis. Orchard Park, NY: Broadview Press, 2005.

———. *The Critique of Pure Reason.* Translated by J. M. D. Mieklejohn. London: Henry G. Bohn Publishers, 1855.

Kaplan, Michael. "The Rhetoric of Hegemony: Laclau, Radical Democracy, and the Rule of Tropes." *Philosophy and Rhetoric* 43, no. 3 (2010): 253–83.

Kinneavy, James. *A Theory of Discourse: The Aims of Discourse.* New York: Norton Publishers, 1980.

Kirby, John T. "The 'Great Triangle' in Early Greek Rhetoric and Poetics." In *Landmark Essays on Classical Greek Rhetoric,* edited by Ed Schiappa, 3–16. Davis, CA: Hermagoras Press.

Kittler, Friedrich. "There is No Software." 18 October 1995. http://www.ctheory.net/articles.aspx?id=74 (accessed 12 January 2011).

Krips, Henry. *Fetish: An Erotics of Culture.* Ithaca: Cornell University Press, 1999.

Lacan, Jacques. "The Agency of the Letter in the Unconscious or Reason since Freud." In *Écrits,* translated by Alan Sheridan, 146–78. New York: W. W. Norton 1977.

———. "Aggressiveness in Psychoanalysis." In *Écrits,* translated by Bruce Fink, 82–101. New York: W. W. Norton, 2006.

———. "Appendix II: Metaphor of the Subject." In *Écrits,* translated by Bruce Fink, 755–58. New York: W. W. Norton, 2006.

———. *The Ego in Freud's Theory and in the Technique of Psychoanalysis (The Seminar of Jacques Lacan, Book II).* Edited by Jacques-Alain Miller. Translated by Sylvana Thomaselli. New York: W. W. Norton, 1988.

———. *The Ethics of Psychoanalysis (The Seminar of Jacques Lacan, Book VII).* Edited by Jacques-Alain Miller. Translated by Dennis Porter. New York, W. W. Norton, 1997.

———. *On Feminine Sexuality: The Limits of Love and Knowledge; Encore (The Seminar of Jacques Lacan, Book XX).* Edited by Jacques-Alain Miller. Translated by Bruce Fink. New York: W. W. Norton, 1999.

———. *Freud's Papers on Technique (The Seminar of Jacques Lacan, Book I).* Edited by Jacques-Alain Miller. Translated by John Forrester. New York: W. W. Norton, 1988.

———. *The Four Fundamental Concepts of Psychoanalysis (The Seminar of Jacques Lacan, Book XI).* Edited by Jacques-Alain Miller. Translated by Alan Sheridan. New York: W. W. Norton, 1998.

———. "The Function and Field of Speech and Language in Psychoanalysis." In *Écrits: A Selection,* translated by Alan Sheridan, 30–113. New York: W. W. Norton, 1977.

———. "The Function and Field of Speech and Language in Psychoanalysis." In *Écrits,* translated by Bruce Fink, 197–265. New York: W. W. Norton, 2006.

———. "The Instance of the Letter in the Unconscious, or Reason since Freud." In *Écrits,* translated by Bruce Fink,412–44. New York: W. W. Norton, 2006.

———. "The Mirror Stage as Formative of the *I* Function as Revealed in Psychoanalytic Experience." In *Écrits,* translated by Bruce Fink, 75–81. New York: W. W. Norton, 2006.

———. "Of Structure as an Inmixing of Otherness Prerequisite to Any Subject Whatsoever," in *The Languages of Criticism and the Sciences of Man: The Structuralist Controversy,* ed. R. Macksey and E. Donato, 186–94. Baltimore, MD: The Johns Hopkins University Press, 1970.

———. "On a Question Preliminary to any Possible Treatment of Psychosis." In *Écrits: A Selection,* translated by Alan Sheridan, 178–225. New York: W. W. Norton, 1977.

———. *The Other Side of Psychoanalysis (The Seminar of Jacques Lacan, Book XVII).* Edited by Jacques-Alain Miller. Translated by Russell Grigg. New York: W. W. Norton, 2006.

———. "Psychoanalysis and Its Teaching." In *Écrits,* translated by Bruce Fink, 364–83. New York: W. W. Norton, 2006.

———. *The Psychoses (The Seminar of Jacques Lacan, Book III).* Edited by Jacques-Alain Miller. Translated by Russell Grigg. New York: W. W. Norton, 1999.

———. "Response to Jean Hyppolite's Commentary on Freud's *Verneinung.*" In *Écrits,* translated by Bruce Fink, 318–33. New York: W. W. Norton, 2006.

———. *The Seminar of Jacques Lacan VIII: Transference.* Translated by Cormac Gallagher. London: Karnac Books, 2002.

———. "The Seminar on the Purloined Letter." In *Écrits,* translated by Bruce Fink, 6–50. New York: W. W. Norton, 2006

———. "Signification of the Phallus." In *Écrits: A Selection,* translated by Alan Sheridan, 281–91. London: Tavistock Publications, 1977.

———. "The Subversion of the Subject and the Dialectic of Desire." In *Écrits: A Selection,* translated by Alan Sheridan, 178–225. London: Tavistock Publications, 1977.

———. "The Subversion of the Subject and the Dialectic of Desire." In *Écrits,* translated by Bruce Fink, 671–702. New York: W. W. Norton, 2006.

———. "A Theoretical Introduction to the Functions of Psychoanalysis in Criminology." In *Écrits,* translated by Bruce Fink, 102-122. New York: W. W. Norton, 2006.

———. "Une Pratique de Bavardage." *Ornicar? Bulletin Périodique du Champ Freudien* 19 (1977): 7–14.

———. "Variations on the Standard Treatment." In *Écrits,* translated by Bruce Fink, 269–302. New York: W. W. Norton, 2006.

Laclau, Ernesto. *On Populist Reason.* London: Verso, 2005.

Laclau, Ernesto, and Chantal Mouffe. *Hegemony and Socialist Strategy.* London: Verso, 1985.

Lacoue-Labarthe, Philippe, and Jean-Luc Nancy. *Retreating the Political.* London: Routledge, 1997.

Leff, Michael C. "Lincoln at Cooper Union: Neo-Classical Criticism Revisited." *Western Journal of Communication* 65, no. 3 (2001): 232–48.

Leff, Michael C., and Gerald P. Mohrmann. "Lincoln at Cooper Union: A Rhetorical Analysis of the Text." *Quarterly Journal of Speech* 60, no. 3 (1974): 346–58.

Lewis, David. "General Semantics." *Synthese* 22 (1970): 18–67.

Lindsay, Michael. "Mind the Gap: Religion and the Crucible of Marginality." *Sociological Quarterly,* 49, no. 4 (2008): 653–88.

Lundberg, Christian, and Joshua Gunn "'Ouija Board, Are There Any Communications?' Agency, Ontotheology, and the Death of the Humanist Subject, or, Continuing the ARS Conversation." *Rhetoric Society Quarterly* 35, no. 4 (2005): 83–105.

MacCannell, Juliet Flower. *Figuring Lacan: Criticism and the Cultural Unconscious.* Lincoln: University of Nebraska Press, 1986.

Marcuse, Herbert. "A Reply to Erich Fromm." *Dissent* 3 (1956): 81–83.

Maresco, Peter. "Mel Gibson's *The Passion of The Christ:* Market Segmentation, Mass Marketing and Promotion, and the Internet." *Journal of Religion and Popular Culture* 8 (2004).

Marini, Marcelle. *Jacques Lacan: The French Tradition.* Translated by Anne Tomiche. New Brunswick, NJ: Rutgers University Press, 1992.

McDaniel, James P. "Fantasm: The Triumph of Form (an Essay on the Democratic Sublime)." *Quarterly Journal of Speech* 86, no. 1 (2000): 48–66.

———. "Figures of Evil: A Triad of Rhetorical Strategies for Theo-Politics." *Rhetoric & Public Affairs* 6, no. 3 (2003): 539–50.

———. "Speaking Like a State: Listening to Benjamin Franklin in Times of Terror." *Communication and Critical/Cultural Studies* 2, no. 4 (2005): 324–50.

McGee, Michael Calvin. "A Materialist's Conception of Rhetoric." In *Explorations in Rhetoric: Essays in Honor of Douglas Ehninger,* edited by R. E. McKerrow, 23–48. Glenview, IL: Scott, Foresman, 1982.

McKerrow, Raymie. "Critical Rhetoric: Theory and Praxis." *Communication Monographs* 56, no. 2 (1989): 91–111.

Meillassoux, Quentin. *After Finitude: An Essay on the Necessity of Contingency.* New York: Continuum, 2010.

Metzger, David. *The Lost Cause of Rhetoric: The Relation of Rhetoric and Geometry in Aristotle and Lacan.* Carbondale: Southern Illinois University Press, 1995.

Miller, Jacques-Alain. "Extimacy." *Symptom* 9 (2008). http://www.lacan.com/symptom/?p=36 (accessed 7 February 2010).

Nancy, Jean-Luc, and Philippe Lacoue-Labarthe. *The Title of the Letter: A Reading of Lacan.* Translated by Francois Raffant and David Pettigrew. Albany: State University of New York Press.

Nealon, Jeffery T. "The Cash Value of Paradox: Žižek's Rhetoric." *JAC* 21, no. 3 (2001): 599–605.

Nietzsche, Friedrich. "On Truth and Lie in an Extra Moral sense." In *The Portable Nietzsche,* edited by Walter Kaufmann. Harmondsworth: Penguin, 1954.

Pettegrew, Lloyd S. "Psychoanalytic Theory: A Neglected Rhetorical Dimension." *Philosophy and Rhetoric* 10 (1977): 46–59.

Plato. *Symposium.* Translated by W. R. M. Lamb. In *Plato: Lysis, Symposium, Gorgias,* Loeb Classical Library, vol. 166. Boston: Harvard University Press, 2001.

Rabate, Jean-Michel. *Jacques Lacan: Psychoanalysis and the Subject of Literature.* New York: Palgrave Press, 2001.

Ragland-Sullivan, Ellie. *Jacques Lacan and the Philosophy of Psychoanalysis.* Champaign-Urbana: University of Illinois Press, 1986.

———. "Stealing Material: The Materiality of Language According to Freud and Lacan." In *Lacan and the Human Sciences,* edited by Alexandre Leupin, 59–105. Omaha: University of Nebraska Press, 1991.

Robinson, Andrew. "The Political Theory of Constitutive Lack: A Critique." *Theory and Event* 8, no. 1 (2005).

Rüegg, Maria. "Metaphor and Metonymy: The Logic of Structuralist Rhetoric." *Glyph* 6 (1979): 141–57.

Sartre, Jean-Paul. *No Exit.* New York: Vantage Books, 1947.

Schneider, Josef. "Portlanders Shut-Out of Mexican Government's 'Watch List,'" newswire article, Portland Independent Media Center. http://portland.indymedia.org/en/2003/09/271482.shtml (accessed 3 January 2007).

Schneiderman, Stuart. *Jacques Lacan: The Death of an Intellectual Hero.* Boston: Harvard University Press, 1983.

Scott, Robert. "On *Not* Defining 'Rhetoric.'" *Philosophy and Rhetoric* 6, no. 2 (1973): 81–96.

Shepherdson, Charles. *Lacan and the Limits of Language.* Philadelphia: Fordham University Press, 2008.

Smith, Christian. *American Evangelicalism: Embattled and Thriving.* Chicago, IL: University of Chicago Press, 1998.

———. *Revive Us Again: The Reawakening of American Fundamentalism.* New York: Oxford University Press, 1999.

Stavrakakis, Yannis. *Lacan and the Political.* New York: Routledge, 2000.

Stoltzfus, Ben. *Lacan and Literature: Purloined Pretexts.* New York: State University of New York Press, 1996.

Stormer, Nathan. "Articulation: A Working Paper on Rhetoric and Taxis." *Quarterly Journal of Speech* 90, no. 3 (2004): 257–84.

Streuver, Nancy. *Rhetoric, Modality, Modernity.* Chicago: University of Chicago Press, 2009.

Strum, Arthur. "Bibliography of the Concept of Offentlichkeit." *New German Critique* 61 (1994): 161–202.

Taylor, Charles. *Modern Social Imaginaries.* Durham, NC: Duke University Press, 2005.

Thomas, Douglas. "Burke, Nietzsche, and Lacan: Three Perspectives on the Rhetoric of Order." *Quarterly Journal of Speech* 79, no. 3 (1993): 336–56.

Vanier, Alain. *Lacan.* New York: Other Press, 2000,

Vico, Giambattista. *The New Science of Giambattista Vico.* Translated by Thomas Goddard Bergin and Max Harold Fisch. Ithaca: Cornell University Press, 1984.

Vitanza, Victor J. "Critical Sub/Versions of the History of Philosophical Rhetoric." *Rhetoric Review* 6, no. 1 (1987): 41–66.

Wajcman, Gerard. "The Hysteric's Discourse." *Symptom* 4 (2003). http://www.lacan.com/hystericdiscf.htm (accessed 5 March 2004).

Warner, Michael. *Publics and Counterpublics.* Brooklyn: Zone Books, 2002.

———. "Publics and Counterpublics." *Public Culture* 14, no. 1 (2000).

Weiss, Steven M. "Rhetoric and Poetics: A Re-Evaluation of the Aristotelian Distinction." *Rhetoric Society Quarterly* 12, no. 1 (1982): 21–29.

Wells, Susan. *Sweet Reason: Rhetoric and the Discourses of Modernity.* Chicago: University of Chicago Press, 1996.

White, Hayden. *Metahistory: The Historical Imagination in Nineteenth-Century Europe.* Baltimore: Johns Hopkins University Press, 1975.

———. *Tropics of Discourse; Essays in Cultural Criticism.* Baltimore: Johns Hopkins University Press, 1985.

Wichelns, Herbert. "The Literary Criticism of Oratory." In *Landmark Essays on Rhetorical Criticism,* edited by Thomas Benson, 1–32. Davis, CA: Hermagoras Press, 1993.

Wilden, Anthony. *Speech and Language in Psychoanalysis.* Baltimore: Johns Hopkins University Press, 1968.

Winseman, Arthur. "U.S. Evangelicals: How Many Walk the Walk." *Gallup Poll News Service Commentary,* The Gallup Organization (2005), www.gallup.com (accessed 10 December 2005).

Wyatt, Robert, Ken Blake, John Bodle, and Zeny Panol. "Mel Gibson's '*Passion*' May Be 'Preaching to the Choir.'" The Survey Group at Middle Tennessee State University, 2004. www.mtsusurveygroup.org/mtpoll/s2004/MTSUPollS04_melpassion_release_0307.pdf (accessed 2 April 2006).

Yunis, Harvey. "Eros in Plato's Phaedrus and the Shape of Greek Rhetoric." *Arion* 13, no. 1 (2005): 101–25.

Žižek, Slavoj. "The Limits of the Semiotic Approach to Psychoanalysis." *Interrogating the Real.* New York: Continuum, 2005.

———. "Our Daily Fantasies and Fetishes." *JAC* 21, no. 3 (2001): 648.

———. *The Ticklish Subject: The Absent Center of Political Ontology.* London: Verso, 2000.

———. *Welcome to the Desert of the Real: Five Essays on September 11 and Related Dates.* London: Verso, 2002.

Index